PARENTHOOD

WHO'S RAISING

Strategies for Saving Your Sanity.

Michael M. Thomson, Ph.D.

Mclean Publishing Group

Post Office Box 751 • Dublin, OH 43017-0851

$14.95

Editors:
John Lauritson Ph.D.
Kathy Woodard
Mikalle Speaks

Design and Production:
JD&A Communication, Inc., Columbus, OH
Cover Design: Jim Dildine
Illustration: John Uhrich

ISBN 1-883980-00-3

Although the author has exhaustively researched all
sources to ensure accuracy and completeness of the information contained in this book, we assume no responsibility for errors, inaccuracies, omissions or any other
inconsistency herein. Any slight against people or or-
ganizations is unintentional. This book is not meant to
replace the advice of a professional working with children and families. Readers should consult a professional
for specific application to their individual problems.

For

Carol, my wife; Christopher, my son; and Holly, my daughter

It's not by chance God gave me two ears and one mouth.
Thanks for allowing me to listen in on your lives over these precious years.
You have taught me so much about who I am as a person
and the world of parenthood. I love you all.

Dad

TABLE OF CONTENTS

ACKNOWLEDGEMENT VII

AUTHOR'S NOTE VIII

FORWARD IX

CHAPTER 1
Nobody Gave Us A Manual 2

CHAPTER 2
So You Want To Be A Parent...
How We Lost Our Sanity 8
Honey ... I think I'm pregnant 8
It's time, it's time 9

CHAPTER 3
Early childhood:
Learning How To Fish 12
Those terrible two's 13
The crib—a baby jail 14
Entering the school daze 15

CHAPTER 4
Adolescence: The Wonder Years
or Thunder Years? 18
A new style of walk 18
A new style of dress 18
Who's under all that makeup? 19
Hair, hair, hair 19
Earrings on boys! 19
Physical and psychological changes 19
What do they want from us? 20
The good old days 21
The "know-it-all" syndrome 23

CHAPTER 5
All Behaviors Are Purposeful 24
Efficient behaviors 25
Inefficient behaviors 25
Purposeful behaviors 26
What parents want 28
What parents have 29

Parents as need-fulfilling or
need-reducing 30

CHAPTER 6
Where Most Parents Are (WhMPA) 32
Stopping a bad habit 32
Starting with actions 34
Just think positively 34
Working to be comfortable 35
If only my kids would change,
my life would be better 35
How does that make you feel? 36
I know that I can help you 37
Using the best choice at the time 38

CHAPTER 7
Regaining Our Sanity Through
Productive Thinking Skills—Going
Beyond WhMPA 40

CHAPTER 8
Productive Thinking Skill 1—
Our Thinking Directs Our Actions And
Our Feelings 42
Feelings 44
Actions 44
Thinking 45
We set the tone of our
children's environment 47
How we interpret events around us 49
Evaluating our present thoughts,
actions and feelings 49
The A-B-C's of problems 50
Productive thinking 51
WhMPA thinking 51
Understanding our self-talk 53
Choosing to think the way we want 54
Ninety-eight percent of all problems
in life will not result in death 57
Key points to remember 59
Helpful hints 60

CHAPTER 9
Productive Thinking Skill 2—
Problems Are Differences Between What
We Want And What We Have **62**
Pure thoughts, pure actions, pure feelings **64**
Frustration levels are like shirt sizes **65**
How WhMPA's react when frustrated **66**
The choices people make when frustrated **67**
Unhappiness is a choice **67**
The reasons for choosing unhappiness **70**
Self-awareness exercise **72**
Key points to remember **73**
Helpful hints **73**

CHAPTER 10
Productive Thinking Skill 3—
Increasing Your Control Over Feeling
Good By Thinking From Out-Of-Control
To In-Control **74**
What do parents want? **74**
Parental-self awareness exercise **76**
    What I can control **77**
    What I can influence **77**
    What I cannot control **77**
    What your kids have control over **78**
    What your kids have influence over **78**
    What your kids have no control over **78**
Self-awareness exercise in roles other
than parenthood **78**
Acknowledging, accepting,
allowing and adjusting **81**
Acknowledging **81**
Accepting **81**
Allowing **81**
Adjusting **81**
Productive thinking gives you control **81**
Increasing our influence over kids **83**
Demonstrating caring **83**

Asking questions **84**
    Open-ended questions **84**
    Closed-ended questions **85**
    Comparison questions **85**
Making statements **87**
Providing alternative choices **87**
Key points to remember **89**
Helpful hints **90**

CHAPTER 11
Productive Thinking Skill 4—
Thinking From
No-Choice To Choice **92**
Changes in time **92**
Out-of-control parents **92**
Out-of-control kids **93**
Gaining control through punishment **94**
You're not the boss of me **94**
Leading the horse to water **95**
Letting go **97**
Problem, problem, who owns the problem? **98**
The stubborn child **100**
Turning over responsibility for life **101**
Choices, choices, whose choice is it? **103**
Setting the structure **104**
Independence **105**
The willingness to wear a helmet
and a flak jacket **105**
Accountability **108**
You can't take these things
away from kids—can you? **109**
Natural consequences **112**
Logical consequences **113**
Home versus house—is there a difference? **114**
    The art of communication **114**
    The element of trust **115**
    The sharing of feelings **116**
    Loyalty to the family **117**

Key points to remember **118**
Helpful hints **118**

CHAPTER 12
Productive Thinking Skill 5—
Thinking From Wants And Behaviors To
Psychological Needs 120
Security **121**
    Productive thinking model **122**
    What you can do to create a sense of
    Security **123**
Faith **123**
    What you can do to create an
    environment of Faith **125**
Worth **125**
    What you can do to create an
    environment of Worth **129**
Freedom **129**
    What you can do to create an
    environment of Freedom **131**
Belonging **131**
    What you can do to create an environment
    of Belonging **134**
Fun/Pleasure **135**
    What you can do to create
    a Fun environment **136**
Knowledge **136**
    What you can do to create an
    environment for Knowledge **138**
Health **138**
    What you can do to create an environment
    that models healthy choices **139**
Key points to remember **139**
Helpful hints **139**

CHAPTER 13
Productive Thinking Skill 6—
Thinking From Outcome To Process 142
Carpe Diem **144**
Key points to remember **146**
Helpful hints **146**

CHAPTER 14
Productive Thinking Skill 7—
Thinking From Problems
To Opportunities 148
Choosing to view problems differently **151**
WhMPA's responses to frustration **151**
Productive thinkers responses to frustration **151**
Winners and losers **152**
Traits of winners and losers **153**
Creating controllable stress **153**
Applying the productive
thinking strategy **154**
Key points to remember **156**
Helpful hints **156**

CHAPTER 15
What's This
Personality Stuff Anyway? 158
Orientation of energy **159**
    Extrovert **159**
    Introvert **160**
Perceptive functions **162**
    Sensing **162**
    Intuition **163**
Judging functions **164**
    Thinking **164**
    Feeling **165**
Orientation to outer life **166**
    Judging **166**
    Perceiving **166**
Verifying your type and your child's type **167**

CHAPTER 16
YATS ESOOL! 170
Suggested Purchase List **172**
Did You Borrow This Copy? **173**
About The Author—You Can Always
Write To Dr. Thomson **174**
Index **175**

Acknowledgments

The views on Parenthood used in this book have been influenced by the writings and training of many influential people in my life: William Glasser, M.D., founder of Reality Therapy, in which I am a certified therapist; Gary Applegate, Ph.D., author of Happiness: It's Your Choice, and founder of the Skill Development Theory for Successful Change in which I became certified and subsequently a senior faculty member with The Center For Skill Development in Los Angeles; Edward Ford, author of several books, including For The Love Of Children, with whom I have shared many years of close friendship; the writings of Albert Ellis, Ph.D., founder of Rational Emotive Therapy; Aaron T. Beck, the father of cognitive therapy; and David Burns, M.D.

All of these people have cleared the path, as the early settlers did in this country, for many like myself to follow and expand upon ideas and strategies to help people. I owe all of them gratitude for their wisdom and teachings that widen my lenses as I continue to view the world of children, parents and the people with whom I come in contact daily.

My long-term exposure to the creative mind and talents of Dr. Applegate is reflected in many of the ideas found in this book. My initial exposure to Dr. Applegate was through my training in Reality Therapy. It launched a personal and professional friendship that continues to this day. Expanding on the basic concepts of Reality Therapy brought us together over the years to our present day work on many projects presenting these productive thinking skills to others around the world.

To my parents, Robert and Eileen, I owe everything. They were and are the best of the best when it comes to parents. Because of this, they have not only taught me the necessary skills in life, but modeled to me the skills that I now teach and model to other parents and kids around the world. For these attributes, I thank them so very much. Mark Twain understood me when he said, *"When I was fourteen it seemed to me that my parents did not know anything. I could hardly stand to have them around. By the time I was twenty-one, I was impressed at how much they had learned."* They did good.

To my brother Brent, all of my memories of childhood are filled with the days of hockey, camping, movies together, fighting as cub bears and the friendship that continues to this day. Brent had the good fortune of doing his doctoral work at The Ohio State University in conjunction with a Drug Free Schools project I was on. Throughout his stay we had many discussions concerning this manuscript input and support. I am grateful for this. He models naturally what many people search a lifetime for. Thanks.

Others I wish to acknowledge include the professors in my life who carried me through my educational travels. Dr. Rhea Das and Dr. Janice Kuldau from the University of Wisconsin-Superior welcomed me into the university world with open and supportive arms of encouragement to gather as much academic exposure as possible in the pursuit of my bachelor's degree in psychology. Dr. Tim Hatfield from Winona State University in Minnesota provided me with the opportunity to expand my thinking skills and to incorporate my beliefs into the alcohol and drug treatment fields. His wit and ever-present assistance was greatly appreciated in my Masters of Science training.

Dr. Joseph Quaranta, Jr. opened the door for my doctoral work in the Department of Education Theory and Practice at The Ohio State University. Dr. Quaranta was not only my advisor, but a terrific mentor who supervised my internship toward licensure as a psychologist. He is special, filled with a tremendous intelligence, wit and humor that makes my association with him a delight. Also with The Ohio State University was Dr. Bruce Walsh of the Department of Psychology who supervised my coursework towards a license in psychology with his "the-door-is-always-open" attitude. What a great guy.

One last person to acknowledge: Dr. Robert Niven. My experience at The Mayo Clinic in the Department of Psychology and Psychiatry virtually widened my lenses to the multitude of behaviors people exhibit and the treatment techniques to help them. Dr. Niven not only allowed me, but encouraged me to continually increase my education and understanding while refining my skills and, as a result, became an important role model of professional techniques and strategies in working with people.

Author's Note

I appreciate the lack of a universally acceptable, unigender personal pronoun. In hope of preserving a readable text, I have chosen to use "she" in some instances of universal statements and "he" in others. My intent is not to favor or discount either sex.

The case histories presented in this book are for instructional purposes. Names have been changed and some cases represent a composite of several individuals or families. For the most part, much of the clinical material presented represents a composite picture associated with the problem areas experienced by the many children and parents with whom I have worked and had contact with over the years.

I wish to extend my sincere appreciation to those who have granted me permission to tell their stories.

This could have been a book about the positives of being a child—the tremendous zest for life, the great friendships, the learning experiences and so on. I chose to write about the tough times, the struggles that not only parents face in raising a child, but the kids face in being raised by parents.

Fasten your seat belts and prepare yourself for a ride through life as a parent—the good times, as well as the rough times. Be prepared to challenge your present thoughts regarding parenting and your present actions in parenting, as well as how you view the behaviors of your children. Understand and accept that as parents we need all the suggestions we can get when dealing with today's children. Today many of us feel as if we have been shot to a different planet when compared to the "planet" we grew up on. Read this book until the pages curl right up. I know that you will find it tremendously helpful in your role as a parent. Good luck, and keep on learning and growing.

For those of you in the helping professions, a final thought before you begin to digest this material: as you read, think of how this material applies within the context of your own life first, rather than how it might apply to the lives of the people you work or live with.

There are four reasons for this suggestion. First, we each know ourselves better than anyone else and because of this, we can effectively learn and apply this material in our own lives.

Second, an important component of this book is learning to teach our thinking and process skills to others. Although most teaching is what we call "rote" teaching, that is giving new information to others and then testing their abilities to recall the information, a better method of teaching is modeling ideas, values and so on. Not practicing what we preach can be quite confusing. Becoming an effective role model and teacher of skills for your children should be your goal.

Third, there is, in my opinion, a serious ethical question raised when we "practice" new ideas and skills on those we work with. Although we can't realistically prevent such practicing totally because we are constantly learning and changing, we can do better by first practicing with ourselves.

Finally, we have all read books, attended classes, workshops and conferences that leave us optimistic, highly motivated and eager to "run" back to our professional settings and try out these new ideas. We then fully expect the people we work with to become healthy, functioning members of our society by noon the following day, at the latest. Of course this doesn't occur and most likely the newly acquired information loses its luster, and is quietly filed and forgotten.

A better plan is to move with greater caution, to challenge, criticize, and try out the ideas and skills ourselves, to observe our own life, observe others, begin to apply the skills slowly in small increments in our own lives, then begin to decide if the ideas and skills contained in this book are beginning to give you more control over your life. Take your time.

Whatever your chronological age today, it has taken you that long to develop into who you are, with your knowledge, values, thoughts, feelings and how you as a unique individual look at your world.

FORWARD

For years people like Dr. Michael Thomson, who have been involved closely with the Center For Skill Development and Productive Thinking, have searched for better ways to teach people how to think productively and achieve better results. In writing Parenthood: Who's Raising Whom?, Dr. Thomson has created a significant contribution that elegantly fills the gap that often exists between theory and practice. He has applied Skill Development theory to his many years of personal and professional experiences to give, you, the reader a fun-filled practical step-by-step guide to successful parenting.

Dr. Thomson knows that parenting can be a difficult and often confusing task. It is also a role we choose for a very long time—in some cases, our entire lives. As you already know, relying only on what our parents did to raise us or doing what others expect of us can lead to some very frustrating results.

As you read the first few chapters you'll soon discover that the application of Productive Think-ing is different than most other approaches. You'll discover that it's not just a technique but an ongoing style of thinking and doing. Your change will be sudden at first, then gradual and then almost effortless as each day you achieve more strength and happiness.

Initially the most difficult part of your learning transition will be from a life style of wanting others to meet your needs to you meeting your needs in spite of what others are doing. These changes will require a maximum amount of focusing and re-thinking each day. The outcome will be a new you. You'll change from having to be a controlling and manipulating parent to wanting to be a teacher, guide and coach. The burden of the responsibility will shift from your shoulders to your child's. Isn't that a pleasant thought?

With these few insights in mind I offer my congratulations and my sincere appreciation to Michael for this wonderful application of Productive Thinking to the real world of parenthood. I am sure you will feel the same after your journey.

Gary Applegate, Ph.D.
President, Center For Productive Thinking
Author of Happiness It's Your Choice

CHAPTER 1

NOBODY GAVE US A MANUAL!

"I talk and talk and none of the kids listen to me. I feel like I'm losing my mind. They look at me and just shrug their shoulders when I ask them to listen. I can't stand it anymore."
—Parent of four, seven and nine year-olds

"Every time I think I'm going to get a break, he cries again. Doesn't this kid know when to sleep and when to stay awake? If I make it through this it will be a miracle. This is so frustrating!"
—Parent of a two year-old

"You take a privilege away and they say 'so,' or 'doesn't bother me,' or the classic 'whatever.' My kids tell me 'you're not the boss of me' on a regular basis. This is nuts! I'm counting the days until they are 18!"
—Parent of ten, twelve and sixteen year-olds

"My kids don't see school as that important. They bring home very little, if any, homework. Getting them to do it is another thing. Some days it's an-all out war to get them up for school. Coming home on time is another thing. They say they can't wait until they are 18—neither can I!"
—Parent of thirteen and seventeen year-olds

"I fight with my kids to get them to bed. I fight with my kids to get them up in the morning. They are impossible. They blame everything on others, including me. They never take responsibility for anything. How do you teach them responsibility and good decisions?"
—Parent of ten, twelve and fourteen year-olds

First question ... **Would you be interested in learning a strategy to save your sanity?** Second question ... **Have you already lost your sanity?** In this book I will tell you how and when you lost your sanity and better yet, I will teach you how to get your sanity back!

It didn't happen overnight—the world gradually changed around us. The world of parenthood is trying at best! You need a license to fish, a license to hunt, a license to drive a car, a license to get married—but when it comes to parenthood, no license is required. There are no classes to take, and no surefire tricks to learn. Advice from everyone—from our parents, to grandparents to friends and even strangers—varies from the reasonably sane to the ridiculous. **Nobody gave us a manual with our children. In fact, you get more instructions with a new microwave than you do with a child!** Everybody seems to have "the" answer that works with every situation. *"This is what I would do when that happened."* Oh sure! Well, it doesn't work that well for me when I try it. Maybe I'm deformed in some way. Maybe I wasn't meant to parent. Maybe I need some new skills to help me through this trying time. What parents want are practical and easily understood ideas to help their kids become healthy, responsible and capable children and adults.

At the same time, parents want a strategy they can put into their own lives to save what's left of their own sanity. This strategy should be practical. Parents don't want some theory that works well in the lab and not in the home. They have watched every rerun of "Leave it To Beaver," "Father Knows Best," and "The Brady Bunch" and are still frustrated. Parents want something simple that will be applicable to all situations. Once parents learn a strategy for themselves, they want to then be able to teach and model it to their children so that they too can take more effective control of their own lives.

Such a strategy will provide kids with the practical skills to deal with the daily problems of living. Of course, we want to prepare our kids for life after they leave home as well. Each of us can use all the help we can get to develop more efficient skills as parents for handling the frustrations that accompany raising children. Or, at least to better understand **who's raising whom?**

If I've met one, I've met a thousand parents who want to teach their children how to **be responsible, how to make better decisions**, and how **to take care of themselves** in a world that does not and will not always give them what they want. If I've met one, I've met a thousand kids who have said the same thing. They want to be responsible for their own lives: *"Quit running my life; get off my back." "I want to make the decisions about where and how I am going to live my life."* We, as parents, need to find the balance so that we allow our children to reach these mutually agreed upon goals. How do we do that? What are the skills we need to know? Finding the answers to these questions is one of the reasons you purchased this book. Read on.

Because you have children, you will have problems. **We need to begin thinking that the only people without problems are dead!** That's right, dead! Since you are reading this book, you are obviously not dead. Welcome to parenthood and to a life filled with problems. Problems that can be looked at in a whole new way. Welcome to a strategy called productive thinking that allows problems to be viewed as opportunities for growth, a strategy that will virtually save your sanity, a strategy that will do the same for your kids and their kids to come. Knowing that all people have problems should relieve some of your stress. Notice I said some. As with all problems, you can reduce the degree of stress and frustration you experience, but you cannot totally eliminate it. I worry about all of those seminars that teach people that they can eliminate stress. Get the guns, the pills, the ropes and other means available, and you know the rest. Not me. I want a better way. A more efficient way. A way that gives me control over my own life. A way that does not rely totally on other people or a power greater than myself. I want not only to relieve your stress and frustration with parenthood and other life hassles, but to **EMPOWER you with a whole new set of thinking skills and more efficient action skills** to deal with the daily problems of living. These new skills will provide you with more alternatives for future problems that arise which are similar in nature. The more efficient skills you have in dealing with problems, the more secure you will feel when problems arise. Feeling secure and in control is what all of us want.

Let me ask you a few questions. Would you be interested in learning how to teach your children to be responsible for what they do, what they think and how they ultimately feel? I mean really being responsible for their good choices and their poor choices? Would you be interested in learning a strategy to teach your children how to make good decisions, so they are less at risk for making the poor choices that lead to drinking, drugging, inappropriate sexual promiscuity, delinquent behavior, along with generally disruptive behavior? How about a strategy for getting them to do their homework, clean up their messes, use good manners, earn trust, to do their chores, clean their rooms, make their beds, throw down the dirty laundry, go to bed on time, or get up in the morning without being screamed at? Would it be less stressful if they just did one of these? What if they did all of them? I can see it now, your kids would be dialing 911 because you dropped to the floor in shock! What about learning how to teach your children to take effective control of their own lives so they have that internal power to resist influences from their peers and others? I am continually asked by audiences for the answers to these very questions in the ever frustrating quest for the key to parenthood. In this book, you will receive the answers to these questions as well as answers to other frequent and frustrating problems.

The philosophy on which this book is based upon can be best exemplified by the familiar concept:

You can give a man a fish and feed him for the evening; Or you can teach him how to fish so he can feed himself for the rest of his life.

As a parent, you are hungry for answers. I can give you the "pat" answers to many frequently asked questions, but that would be giving you a fish and only solve the problem temporarily. It's like putting mud in a crack in the dam. It will hold for a while, but how long? I believe that if I teach you productive thinking skills to put into your life to help you in parenthood and in all areas of your life (both personal and professional) you will be able to feed yourself for the rest of your life.

Our kids come into the world like the hungry man looking for food. It seems that our primary goal as parents is to prepare our children for the world they will enter. That preparation occurs while they are living with us and represents our best attempt to enable them to live successfully when they eventually leave home. It should ready them for all of the stresses of daily living, and all the ups and downs they will experience. In a sense, we are better off teaching our children "how to fish," so they can feed themselves for the rest of their lives. Many times, however, our kids come wanting us to solve **"their problems"** and make **"their decisions,"** and as a result, accept **"their responsibility"** for **"their choices"** and **"their feelings."** In doing so we are only giving them a fish, or problem solving **"for them"** every time they run into difficulty. We will be there to help when they need help. But in the long run does this really help? Does it become a problem for us and for them when we are always stepping in to help? When does it get to this point? Does it become a pattern where every time they have a problem or a decision to be made, they run to someone "out there" for the solution? You know and I know people right now as adults who can't make decisions on their own. The problem is not theirs alone. The problem is that nobody taught them the productive thinking skills they needed to learn in order to take effective control of their own lives. Who do you think are the teachers of problem solving and decision making skills? Yeah, you're right—us. But wait a minute, who taught us and was what we were taught the right method?

With this philosophy and base as our inspiration, I can take you beyond the traditional approaches to parenthood that I believe are problem-solving and crisis-driven in nature, and **begin to teach you the success-oriented skills required so that control over one's own life is where it belongs—in the hands of the person with the problem.**

Mark Twain once said, *"Everybody talks about the weather, but nobody does anything about it."* A similar observation might be made about parenthood. Have you ever heard people say;

"Kids nowadays are going nowhere in life."

"I can't even begin to imagine what it must be like to grow up in today's society."

"There is nothing you can do with these kids nowadays, just let them do what they want. The heck with them."

Everybody talks about the problems we're having, but too many people do little or nothing to increase their present skills to resolve them. Everybody has an opinion and expresses feelings about the problems we have in today's society and with today's children, but few people are practicing a new strategy to effectively deal with daily problems because a new strategy requires hard work and determination. A new strategy requires you to go beyond where you presently are and begin to increase your own skills. It requires thinking differently about yourself in the sense of not only who you are, but what you want in life. It requires thinking about the world around you, including those who are significant to you. It requires an evaluation of your present skills as a parent. It also requires an evaluation of where you want to be as a parent with your children from this point forward. Because you have chosen to read this book, you have decided, *"I want to put information into my life, information that will increase my present skill level as a parent. The more information I have, the more choices I have and the more skills I have. The more skills I have as a parent, the more secure I will feel."* Your new attitude will take you to a different level than most parents.

Some people get scared off reading such a book as this. The reason, I believe, is that the book and topic require you to make a judgment that what you're presently thinking or doing regarding your children is not working well enough. You are taking the first step and admitting that you do not presently have all the skills necessary to deal effectively with your parenting problems. These problems are frustrating you to various degrees and, in turn, motivate you to get the information you need to reduce the differences between what you want and what you have.

The key words we need to focus on are "efficient skills." If you have efficient skills to deal with problems, your feeling of power will increase. At present you may be making certain choices that are working to "correct" your child. You may also be aware that those choices carry with them consequences—consequences like the child doing what you say "only" when you force him or his hating you for controlling or overpowering him. Or consequences like your child being afraid of you. Consequences such as the loss of relationship these attempts carry with them. Consequences such as thinking that your child is a "bad child." Or consequences such as a child who continues to disobey despite and perhaps because of what you choose to do "to them." Remember, the poor choices many of us have made do not make us bad parents. They only make us parents making poor choices.

If you have followed me so far, you understand that it is not the end of the world if you made poor choices. The consequences may be significant, but you do have control over changing your thoughts and actions. It is developing the *"I have control over me"* and *"I have control over changing myself"* attitude that will make a significant difference in your life. If you feel guilty about choices you made in the past, remember that you were using your best skills at the time. Before you blame yourself, think about who taught you how to parent. Where did you learn how to deal with kids? From your parents? On your own? Through trial and error? From television? The advice others gave you might have been good choices for them and worked in their time and in their situation, but are they working for you? Can you relate to this? Have you ever told your parents or your grandparents about the poor choices that your kids or other kids are making today? Have you been in discussions about the attitude of kids today versus when you were growing up? They will look you straight in the eye and say something like, *"Well I wouldn't put up with that! You mean to tell me that you allow them to do that?,"* leaving you feeling like puppy poop! *"What's wrong with me?"* *"Why can't I get my kids to act the way those other kids do?"* *"Why can't I control them like my parents controlled me?"* *"Maybe the 'good old days' really were the 'good old days' after all?"*

Let's look at some choices concerning thoughts and actions you might relate to. Thoughts like, *"I can't stand it anymore."* *"He's such a jerk."* *"He's so lazy."* *"She's never going to learn."* *"They will never learn to be responsible."* And actions like *excessive yelling, screaming, threatening, spanking and lecturing.* These are examples of thoughts and actions you may already be using. Can you relate to them? Have you ever considered that these thoughts get you nowhere but depressed? Have you ever acted in any of the ways listed? Have you found they have not worked? Do your kids just look at you and say something like *"So."* *"Whatever."* *"Oh—that's cool."* *"Fine, just fine."* *"You can ground me for the rest of my life because I'm not going to change!"* Have you ever heard any of these? Are they driving you crazy? Are you ready to scream? Are you looking for the receipt for the kids so you can return them? Are you looking for the answer? You are not alone ...

This book is a collection of many years of personal and professional experiences working with thousands of parents and kids, presenting seminars, and being raised by my own children, Christopher and Holly. I am really fortunate to have had the experiences with all the people I have worked and lectured to over the past years. They have given me the information this book is based upon. The kids have taught me what they like and hate in parents. The parents have taught me how to parent as well as how not to parent. It's not by chance that God gave me two ears and one mouth; as a result, this book becomes the mouthpiece for my many years of experiences.

The frustration that accompanies raising children has been increasing steadily over the years, and has now brought many a parent to their knees begging for help. Kids show widespread lack of respect towards parents and other adults, and even to their own peers. Many kids are treating their parents like dirt. They verbally abuse them, swear at them, threaten them, and sometimes physically fight with them. Their "demandingness" in the form of a "me" attitude or the *"I-don't-care-about-anyone-but-myself"* attitude is sometimes overshadowed by the ever popular, *"I-can't-wait-until-I'm-eighteen-then-I-can-do-what-I-want"* attitude. Other parents are wondering whether their child's middle name is **"get me, buy me, take me, give me!"** They are so ungrateful. So disrespectful. So demanding. It is no wonder that many a parent has told me at seminars or in my office that the promised joys of parenthood are turning into the real nightmares of parenthood! Parent burnout is on the rise, and the white flag or the *"I-give-up"* attitude seems to be quite fashionably waved around nowadays by many parents. Kids may be saying they can't wait until they are eighteen, but many a parent has expressed to me that they, too, can't wait until the kid is eighteen! The feelings, they say, are mutual. Now I understand why parents buy their kids luggage as a graduation gift! And now they have graduation at the middle school level. I wonder if that says anything about the changing attitude in this country?

I have lectured to nearly one million people throughout the United States and Europe, and keep hearing the same comments over and over from parents:

"Kids don't listen today."
"I want them to shut up when I say shut up!"
"Kids are so irresponsible."

"Let them do what they want to."
"Why ground them? They make life miserable for you."
"You can't take away privileges from teenagers."
"Kids do whatever they want to."
"How do you get them to make good decisions?"
"I wouldn't have been able to sit down for weeks if I had talked to my parents that way."
"How do you get a kid to change when they don't want to?"
"There is nothing we can do!"
"We need to get tougher with them."
"I'll be damned if some kid of mine is going to run my life or this house!"

The comments heard over and over from kids today are:
"Parents don't listen."
"Parents don't give us any responsibility."
"Parents figure that when we turn eighteen we magically develop responsibility—what a joke."
"My parents don't even care about me."
"They do and say what they want, why can't I?"
"Parents just don't understand."
"Do as I say, not as I do—that's a joke."
"They yell and scream at me, and then tell me not to scream at them."
"Everybody thinks we have such a kid problem today; it's not that we have a kid problem, but that we have an adult problem."
"We do as much or as little as our parents allow us to get away with."
"My parents want to trust me, but they never allow me to earn that trust."
"Parents think that it is the end of the world if a kid wears an earring, dresses funky, talks weird or listens to rock music—they are so wrong."
"My parents are really bitchy all the time."
"Parents never let us choose what we want to think, or choose what we want to do—they are so controlling, I can't stand it."
"Parents tell me to listen, but they keep cutting in on me."
"Parents want me to tell them everything about my life, but they always tell me to never mind when I ask about their life."
These comments point to the fact that we are

having problems in our relationship between parents and their kids, and kids and their parents. You can feel the frustration. Much research on the family has focused on what's going wrong in the family, centering in on problems occurring within families rather than on what constitutes a healthy family. By turning on the television set and listening to the nightly news, you can see that peoples' interest is generally directed more toward what's going wrong with the world and catching people in the act of being bad, rather than focusing on "good news" stories. The focus appears to be more on sickness than on health. This book will focus on what we can do to correct the negative aspects of today's families. This book will address each and every one of these statements of concern. Knowing that there are concerns from both sides is one thing; knowing what to do about the concerns is another.

The "fact" that kids today "mature" earlier than they used to was demonstrated by a doctoral study at The Ohio State University which concluded that high school was effectively over by the time a child completed the eleventh grade. Eleventh grade you ask? I thought graduation was in the twelfth grade. According to the attitudinal survey, the eleventh grade graduates consider themselves to be graduated from the "mainstream of high school," and many eleventh grade student behaviors and attitudes reflect this belief. This makes sense if you observe the changes in the behaviors of seniors throughout the country today. Many high school students are now mimicking the behaviors of college age kids. These behaviors include drinking, drugging, sexual promiscuity and acting out behaviors, to name just a few. Many of the behaviors that high school age kids exhibit today were strictly reserved for college age kids, including such events as "spring break." Once upon a time spring break was something that many of us just heard about. Now we have the media airing specials on spring break, focusing their attention on the high school students drinking as well as sexually acting out during a week where no rules exist. There is no adult supervision when you're several states away from home, or should I say states away from a "house." A "home" is where there is structure and supervision and limits to permissible behavior. A house is just a house. The eleventh grade isn't necessarily the lower limit. Many parents have indicated to me that the age is dropping, and kids are requesting more freedom earlier and earlier. When is it going to stop? The little girl who came up to me after my talk at Pepperdine

University on "Who Controls Whom?" For the Youth to Youth National Drug Free Conference said it best: *"We are going around the country teaching and preaching to young people to say no; why aren't we teaching adults to say no to kids?"* Out of the mouths of kids come the answer. So simple, yet so true. As a result of our numerous "houses" around the country, college, I believe, is now becoming five years in length, starting in the senior year of high school. College, as we all know, is a place where absolutely nobody is running the farm!

With these changes in mind and obstacles to overcome, it is my hope you will find the strategies suggested in this book beneficial in "saving your sanity," and at the same time, producing responsible, capable young people.

This book is an attempt to allow the reader to experiment with healthy living strategies that are based both on research and on practical, common sense. I hope that parents and their kids can enjoy it together and also that those working with kids can profit from the information. This book will provide both a theory and a practical strategy to help you in your life not only as a parent, but in all areas of your life, both personal and professional. You will see changes in how you choose to think about yourself and the world around you. It does not offer a set of parenthood rules, but provides a specific **productive thinking strategy** for dealing with a wide range of issues. In other words, I hope to give you the best of what current research has to offer in regard to healthy family living, and to give you some good common sense information. Many who have attended my talks have told me that the title

of the book could easily be **"Forward To The Basics."**

The strategy presented in this book is meant to be preventive, positive and educational. That is, it can be taught and practiced quite easily within your own home. The strategy that will be presented for healthy family living is not presented as the answer to all problems, but rather as a framework on which to build healthy relationships in the family. I promise that if you read this book thoughtfully and practice the suggested skills in your life, you will gain a new set of lenses through which to view the world of parenthood, and have the practical skills to teach and model to your children so they can save their sanity in a world where it is in very short supply. You purchased this book because you are either frustrated with your present life as a parent, frustrated with the actions of your kids, frustrated with the actions of other kids or a combination of these, and you are interested in increasing your present knowledge and skills in order to increase your influence over your children, and to spare them from the myriad of problems kids are running into today. **This book provides parents with the specific skills to rethink their roles as parents, to rethink their kids' choices, and to learn to take more effective control of themselves in their roles and responsibilities as parents.** If you're ready, then welcome to the world of parenthood, and welcome to going beyond general information on parenthood presented up to now and **learning a practical strategy that will virtually save your sanity!**

CHAPTER 2

SO YOU WANT TO BE A PARENT?
How we lost our sanity

Parenthood is the only position in life that requires no special training, no video series, no extra credit workshops, no correspondence course work, or other methods of advanced training. You don't have to rent a video, read a manual or talk to anyone who has had kids in order to be a parent. If everything is working well physically, the act of conception is quite easy, even pleasant.

The plunge into parenthood is either a planned or an unplanned experience, but nevertheless one that thrusts a non-mother and non-father forward into a whole new world, a world where they have never gone before. It's kind of like Captain Kirk and the Starship Enterprise that "boldly goes where no man has gone before." We know plenty of people who have traveled down this path, so how come it's so tough? It's tough because the world around us is always changing. When the world is always changing, people change. Parenthood is one role in life that, even though it may be disliked at times, cannot be easily discarded. Once you're a parent, you're a parent for life. It is not like any job you have ever held before. If you hate a job, you can quit. If you hate parenthood, you can't quit ... that easily.

Honey ... I think I'm pregnant!

The trip to the family doctor to find out what is going on inside sometimes proves positively that the rabbit is dead and the baby is on the way! My wife did one of those *"I think I might be pregnant"* routines. Quick, bring the chariot around, let's get to the clinic to see what's cooking! Sure enough, the doctor with his official lab coat and stethoscope around his neck came out and congratulated us on being pregnant. Us? Hey wait now, she's having this baby, not me. Oh well, I'm just as excited. In fact this is when dad starts yanking up his pants, strutting around the house saying things like,

"Yeah, *I'm going to be a dad, and a good dad at that. This is really easy."*

Then Lamaze classes. What classes? You mean we have to go to class to have a baby? Our doctor suggested that my wife and I go since we were first-time parents and I was to be my wife's coach during birth. I had been a high school hockey coach, so I thought that this shouldn't be much different. He told me that I was needed to teach and coach my wife how to breathe properly during the birthing process. I figured my wife had years of this experience, but we went anyway. There we were huffing and puffing through every class, just like good little students. They informed me that I was to be a part of the delivery process, which made me feel important. My wife rolled her eyes knowing that I virtually was going to be along just for the ride—unless I knew what it was like to pass a bowling ball! With the breathing techniques perfected and class completed we continued the wait. The following months proved that nature has a wonderful way of changing a woman from a woman with a figure that won't quit to a woman with the figure that doesn't quit! My wife had this terrific figure, but I said had. Now she looked as if a tire pump had made its way into her stomach to form a birthing room for the baby. The magical wonder of pregnancy was taking shape, so to speak. I remember the days of *"Honey, can I listen to your stomach?"* Then it was the sight of feet and hands moving around in the womb. These sights and sounds are mystifying. What's going on in there? The gurgling and the various sounds would make Linda Blair of "The Exorcist" envious. The excitement and the anticipation were growing.

My wife, of course, was also growing. Eventually she was humungo! As time passed, she looked more like a sumo wrestler. At first there was no sign of life inside, but then, *"A hand, no it's a foot, it's alive!"* Then there was more gurgling. Placing my head on her stomach was weird to say the least, but wow, what an experience! More changes for the woman. Breast size went from normal to gigantic. The physical and emotional ups and downs made PMS look tranquil. By comparison, Sybil appeared well adjusted! Never fear—I came to the rescue, with Haagen Daz in hand! All was under control.

It's time, it's time!

Then it happened. I came home from work at the high school one day to find my wife at the door with that little glimmer in the eyes, saying softly, "It's time, it's time." "Time for what?" I said? "It's time." "What time?" "It's time." "What time?" "It's time, silly." "Come on, Carol quit being so stubborn, what time is it?" "My water broke." I remember this part from the Lamaze course and those wonderfully educational films. I threw everything in the house into two small bags, ran to the car, strapped my wife to the luggage rack, and flew to the hospital, quick like! Driving like a madman, I yelled out the window, "Look out, move over, my wife's having a baby!" When we arrived at the hospital, they took the mother-to-be from the luggage rack and ever so gently placed her on a gurney, on her back. She looked like the great white whale going down the hall with me running right behind her. I put on my

official hospital booties, pants, shirt, mask and of course the gloves. Looking like someone working at Three Mile Island, I kept saying, "All right the baby is coming, the baby is coming!" I encouraged Carol to keep breathing, using those great techniques we learned in class. She just kept looking at me like "You boob!" I even stopped along the way and called our parents and said, "We're at the hospital, it's time, I will call you back in a few hours, wish us luck."

I will never forget it ... twenty-five hours later the baby still wasn't there! Boy was I getting angry! I had things I needed to do. Just think of the T.V. shows I had given up. The doctor and I grabbed a couple of Pepsi's, slipped into the doctors' lounge, and put our feet up. I remember saying to him, "I can't take much more of this!", while my wife was out there on the table on all fours trying to turn the baby, saying, "Get in here, you're a part of this!" My reply was "just keep breathing, Honey, remember the classes! Loosen up, Honey, it can't be that bad." Carol asked me to come closer to the bed. She put me in a headlock, thrust two fingers in my eyes and said, "Help me out you weenie—you got me in this shape!" Two hours later, after much pushing and pulling, breathing included, (properly of course, due to my instructions) we were blessed with a 9 pound 12 ounce healthy son. Ouch! What a sight to behold. They told us it was a boy. I said, "How can you tell?" Twenty-seven hours in the birth canal, this kid had a cone head that wouldn't quit! We thought about propping him up in the corner and playing ring toss, but thought better of it. Counting the fingers and the toes, and finding out he was healthy, we breathed a sigh of relief. We decided to name him Christopher. According to hospital policy, they had to place him with the other babies in the hospital nursery. Of course they placed him among two five pound kids. He looked like a toddler who got lost in the hospital or a tiny Teamster waiting for a ride to the union meeting! A year and half later we were blessed again with the birth of a healthy, seven pound two ounce daughter. We were not in labor as long for Holly, thank God. Hot dog, a boy and a girl. One of each, one with indoor plumbing and one with outdoor plumbing, plumbing that really worked, and worked well, I might add.

The easy part, at least from the man's point of view, is the delivery process. Before Chris's birth I remember the doctor and friends asking me if I was going into the delivery room when the big moment arrived. Everybody always told me to go into the delivery room. They told me that it would be the most beautiful experience I would ever behold. Liars! It made the movie "Aliens" seem tame. Give me a break! With Holly, it was quite different because she was born when I worked at the Mayo Clinic. Because the Mayo Clinic is a major medical teaching institute, they asked my wife if she would mind having a "few" medical students observe the delivery. A few! I swear there were bleachers set up with ushers checking ticket stubs and popcorn vendors. We did the wave as a warm-up activity!

After Christopher's birth the moment came I had been waiting for—the question that I was waiting to be asked: *"Would you like to hold your son, Mr. Thomson?"* "Heck yes!" Christopher began to squirm and let out a little whimper. *"Shh, you're O.K."* He began to cry. *"Shh, now stop that little one."* He wouldn't stop. The crying continued ... and continued. He squirmed nonstop. It got more and more out of control. The volume of his screaming reached decibel levels I had never heard before. That's when I handed over the blessed child to mother and said, *"Here Carol, he's yours ... Feed him Honey, bottle, breast, nuke 'em if you have to, make it stop!"* Carol fed the baby. Thank God she didn't ask me to! She later asked me if I wanted to hold my son again. Oh yeah! Sure. Fine. I held him up in the air and he peed all over me. Then he burped up that junk on my shoulder. I threw that shirt away; you could never get that smell out. Then, with my hand under his butt, I felt a warm sensation and eventually smelled an odor that was indescribable. You have to be kidding me! Didn't this kid have any standards? Following this initial period of bliss, the baby continued with more crying, more soiled diapers and generally more controlling of the world around him in a variety of ways. Very soon after life began for both of my kids, I found out **who was really raising whom.** There was no question about who really had the control or the power and it wasn't me!

While still in the hospital, I looked for the controller, someone who could get this kid to do what I want him to do. But whom? That great little buzzer in the hospital room was but a mere touch away! We began ringing immediately. In came the nurse, asking, *"What's wrong?"* "Everything! He's pooping, peeing, screaming, whining and generally un-* *controllable! Help me, help me."* She did her nurse duty and whisked the baby away into another room, and returned him fresh and smiling. Now that's the kid I wanted! One who would do what I want him to do. This was really easy. With any problem that occurred, we could ring that buzzer and help arrived. With our first child, Christopher, it was five days in the hospital; with Holly, it was three. Every time they pooped, peed, screamed, cried or made a general nuisance of themselves (didn't do what we wanted) we could rely on the nurse with the **power** to come to the rescue. Because insurance companies are regulating hospital stays, it's not going to be a five-day or even three-day stay. It's going to be like a drive-through at McDonalds! You're going to need to let them know you're there through the speaker at the side of the hospital, deliver at the first window, receive the baby and fries at the second window, and be on your way home!

When you are ready to leave the hospital, the nurse escorts the mother in the wheelchair in accordance with hospital policy, the baby in one arm and an arm load of gifts in the other, down to the business office in order to arrange for payment for the blessed child, while Dad prepares the car, equipped with mandatory car seat, for the journey to Home Sweet Home. The process goes quite smoothly.

Home Sweet Home changes quickly, with every visitor sniffing and saying things like, *"Do you have a baby?"* Diaper smell permeates the house. That plumbing sure works well, and much of it! The first week at home the question is, "Should *we continue with cloth diapers or go to the disposable?"* One rinsing out of the diaper did it for us; we bought Pampers from then on. I would get another job if I had to. Just don't make me rinse or smell any more of those diapers. Once we arrived at home, the 24-hour clock became 36 hours. We wondered *"When does this kid sleep?"* *"Doesn't he know you sleep during the night and stay awake during the day"* or *"Where is the shut-off valve in response to all this pooping and peeing!"* There should be an owners manual with a table of contents you can refer to for these kinds of problems. Where is the manual? Why didn't we get one with the bag of tissues, mouthwash, toothbrushes, baby powder, and bottles the hospital gave us? You get more instructions with a microwave than you do with a baby!

CHAPTER 3

EARLY CHILDHOOD:
Learning how to fish

When we reflect back upon childhood, some of us can recall memories that we want our children to have, those special moments that make us feel warm and that we want to recreate for our children. Others recall sadness, pain and anger about their childhood. They recall fighting between kids and parents, between parents themselves, or between siblings. The beliefs that people create about their own parents range from the holiness of robe and sandals to Freddy Krueger's "Nightmare on Elm Street!"

My father could have been named Ward, my mother, June, my brother, Wally, and me, the Beaver. We were a happy-go-lucky family that would make the Brady Bunch look cold and hard. Saturday was "Brent and Mike day," filled with anything we wanted to do. As a result we overdosed on movies, Ju Ju Fruits and Dots, walks in the woods, drive-in movies, games at the kitchen table, picnics and outdoor activities along with many memorable camping trips, including the making of s'mores over the fire. In the dead of winter, we went ice fishing

and cored apples, filling them with cinnamon and sugar and cooking them over the fire. What great memories.

The challenge of parenthood begins with questions like how to get the child to stop crying and to start eating? Should you breast feed or bottle feed? How do you get them to sleep through the night? To keep food somewhere near their mouth? Or to get them to quit filling that diaper? For you tough guys, do you remember the day you volunteered to change the diaper? You may have played sports, been in the service, or worked hard at labor but as you peeled it back, admit it, you have never seen Doo Doo like that, ever! It was at that moment that selective hearing became a definite option when the words *"Honey would you change the baby?"* rang out. It was time for dad to find that project that always needed fixing, you know the one that never got done. You thought kids' behaviors were the only behaviors that were purposeful.

During the first months a baby learns to control his environment through crying, which is the baby's way to get what he wants and to get others to give him what he wants. When they are hungry, babies cry and they get fed. When they are lonely, they cry and they get hugging and loving. When they are wet, they cry and they get changed. The connection between crying and getting what they want by controlling the environment around them, which includes mom or dad, is very clear. It is hard to determine, at this point in their lives, if their controlling behavior is purposeful and manipulative. Trust me, it is purposeful. But should we let them continue to cry and cry? Will we spoil them? Obviously babies are 100% dependent on us for their need fulfillment in those early days and months. And we would be neglectful if we just stood away from the baby and said something like, *"Grow up, learn to take care of yourself."* With time, we can teach our children alternative choices to get their needs met for themselves. The later chapters of this book will provide you with many typical problems you face as a parent and the suggested alternatives you can provide to your children. When you have the productive thinking skills to view problems in this manner, you will feel secure. When you don't, you will feel insecure.

You will also learn about that wonderful commodity in life called patience. Patience. Now there's a whole new book that could be written just on that topic. Statements such as, *"Wait a minute, shhh, settle down, it's O.K."* will make much more sense to them at a later age. Walking away from them in power struggles, refusing to argue with them, and refusing to accept responsibility for their problems and their choices is patience. Is patience given only to a few? Maybe. But most of us learn it through experience, which can be pretty painful and stressful. For now, grab your kids, hold them, and hug them all you want, whenever you want. You won't be spoiling them or making them excessively dependent on you. You will be providing them the warm, caring and friendly relationship that is so critical to have, not only now but throughout life. The period of time through the first year will be filled with fascination with everything they see and touch—from lights, animals, cars and other material objects to the differences in how people look. They are just beginning to make a connection between themselves and their environment. Sit back, watch and enjoy the wonders of life taking place.

You may, of course, wonder if you are going to make it through that first year. You may take bets. Remember to just grin and bear it. Do what you need to do to take care of yourself. Taking care of yourself during these first years is critical for your psychological health and well being. The word for the day becomes "baby-sitter." If you have that as an option, use it to refuel your own sanity. In order to give you that *"Calgon, take me away"* feeling, work on identifying pleasurable activities for yourself during nap times, bedtimes, etc. Most research confirms the fact that the baby is on cruise control for the first 18 to 24 months and that the age of influence begins around two for the parent.

Those terrible two's

After that, of course, it's getting them through those terrible two's! I told my wife Carol that *"If*

we can get our kids through these terrible two's, it's cruise control from then on out!" The more I listen to parents and kids, the more that I am convinced that all kids come into this world with a tackle box. We don't see it but they are constantly searching for the right "lures" to get what they want. Think of these lures as **choices** people make in an attempt to get what they want. When they find the right lure or behavioral choice, and it works for them, they don't put it back in the tackle box; they put it on their hats like a good fisherman does. It is amazing the number of lures that kids have learned in order to hook or catch their parents and other people's attention. These lures start out as choices, then advance to skills and eventually turn into habits. The problem is that some of the skills and habits used by kids can help them get what they want in the short run but can carry with them some serious prices in the long haul.

To illustrate this, consider the case of the patient in the psychiatric unit who **lacks the necessary skills** to gain attention or form relationships in his life. The patient watches while others in the unit choose a variety of ways to get what they want, from staring at the walls, to catching butterflies that don't exist, to talking to empty chairs. This "lonesome" patient walks down to the end of the hallway and goes through the motions of fishing, using the actions of casting out into the water and watching the bait for bites. As a staff member approaches the patient to ask some questions, he continues with the fishing behavior as if he were avoiding the staff member. As with all staff on a unit such as this, the assistant is trained to get into the world of the patient in order to be effective. He asks the patient whether he is *"Fishing a lake or a stream?"*, to which the patient responds *"Lake."* When asked *"How many are you catching?"* the patient turns to the staff member, winks, and states, *"You're the thirteenth one today!"* Many people call the "crazying" behavioral lure this patient used the patient's **best choice at the time**, and one that worked well for him, as you can see in this story. After all, he did draw the staff member all the way down the hall and engaged him in conversation. It worked for him at the time. It's a lure to be placed on the hat. He will use it again and again as long as it works to control the outside world, to get him what he wants.

The problem is that with a learned "lure" like this, the person has to use a lot of energy in an attempt to control the world around him. In some cases, it may work and in some cases it may not. In fact some people may choose to avoid such a person and as a result the "lure" cannot work; just like a fisherman with no bites, **some people become frustrated and choose other behaviors like pouting, angrying, temper tantrumming or worse yet drunking, depressing or suiciding.** Notice I am putting **"ing"** on the end of these behaviors to show that they are active behaviors that the person chooses as his best attempt to gain control in his life. The use of the "ing" form was pioneered by Buckminster Fuller in his book, <u>I Seem To Be A Verb.</u> **Notice, though, that such people attempt to control the world around them and not themselves.** This is critical if we are to understand the complex world of behavioral choices. To the tiny fishermen we call children, life looks like a series of lakes, streams or oceans. They learn what "lure" to use on the various fishes (we play the role of the fish) and where to use them. If you watch or ask fishermen where they fish, you will notice they'll always return to "their favorite spot." Why? If you're catching fish, why go someplace else? Fishermen also will always tell you about that special lure they use "that always catches the fish."

With this example in mind, what lures can you identify that your kids use on you and others in an attempt to get what they want? Have they used pouting, crying, temper tantrumming, angering, hitting, kicking, biting, suiciding, threatening, depressing? Which "lures" have they caught the most fish with? Are you one of those fish? Is your spouse? How would your kids answer these? Do you feel like the taxidermist should mount your body on your kids' bedroom wall with an inscription such as, "caught off the shores of the family room, with the simple lure of arguing—took three seconds to hook." Do you feel as if your gills have been ripped a few times with those lures? Are your kids grandmasters of "fishing?" Remember that kids will never change a successful "lure" if they are catching or getting what they want, unless they pay heavy prices for using it. Given these examples you can see the critical role that we have in intervening with these behavioral choices and teaching and modeling more effective choices.

The crib—a baby jail

If any problems arise during the first two years of life, you can solve them by just putting your child in the crib. Put some milk in a bottle, nuke it in the microwave and throw it in there to keep him busy and happy. The crib is really a baby jail, you know. It's got little bars. The child stands and shakes the bars just like a prisoner in jail. But when the bottle is empty, look out. You can expect to hear your child late at night singing *"Nobody knows the trouble"* while rapping the bars with his bottle— *"Hey it's feeding time, you're late, get in here!"* he's saying, and it's the rapping and the cry that both spouses argue over in the other room. You wait five, ten, fifteen minutes, the sweat running down your face. Does he want attention? Is he hurt? Is he in trouble? I had training in psychology and kept telling my wife, Carol, *"Don't go in there honey, he's just pulling our chain. No kid has ever died from crying."* But it continues. You wonder if he has his little head stuck between the bars. Then you enter the room and what do you find? Your child standing in the crib, smiling at you. At that moment, you feel like screaming! Doggone it, he is controlling you! This kid is just as slick as the guy who was fishing in the psychiatric unit. Next time you then wait a little longer because you know he's playing with you but again find the child winking at you with that little twinkle in his eye! **What kids learn at an early age is how to control the world around them, which includes you, in order to get what they want.** I'm not suggesting that you leave your child in the crib screaming his lungs out, refusing to check on him, because he may in fact be hurt, or wet or perhaps something else has happened. As you will learn, ninety-eight percent of our choices are not related to life or death situations. Most of the problems we experience will not kill us or our kids. Will they make us or them uncomfortable? Yes, indeed, but crying will not kill a kid nor will temper tantrumming, pouting or certain forms of angering. As you will discover, they are not only getting what they want, but are meeting one or more of their internal psychological needs with these behavioral choices. Unfortunately the methods they learn during these early years sometimes carry negative consequences. Just like the fisherman using the right lure to catch the fish he wants, kids will use the best lure with their parents. Just like the fisherman, they use the lures that catch the most fish. Choices learned at an early age, if uncorrected, may lead to toddler, preadolescent, adolescent and adulthood consequences such as:

❑ Blaming "out there" for their choices.
❑ Trying to change "out there" in an attempt to achieve happiness in their own lives.
❑ Believing that "out there" is responsible for their lives.
❑ Believing that "out there" has total control over their lives and how they think, act and/or feel.

Getting kids through the terrible two's is a challenge in and of itself. This is where many admit that kids are really raising us and we are just along for the ride.

Entering the school daze

Let's not be self-deceived, we are relieved when our children finally enter school! After all, we have been trying to gain control of this little person for the past few years and have been steadily losing ground and sanity in doing so. Many parents wave good-bye to their kids as they walk off to school, close the door, and fall down in relief and exhaustion. We start out believing that my kid is going to think the way I want him to, act the way I want him to and feel the way I want him to feel—because I'm his parent and because that is what I want. But we find out that the little tyke has a brain of his own. He acts on his own and expresses his feelings immediately. We also find out that he has tremendous control over his environment, including us. He has become an excellent fisherman, using every lure he can think of or sees others using. He has found out which lures work and which lures do not. Let's get him in school. Maybe the teachers can get him to think, act, and feel the way we want him to. If they don't, we can blame them or at least not vote for the next school levy. So what if it's blackmail, somebody's got to control them, right?

Of course, we are also eager to get our kids in school so they can socialize with other kids. We've had enough of their playing at home all day. They need an education. School, after all, is a great place for kids to learn how to get along with other people and follow structure—with someone else in control. It is, hopefully, a place where they will be able to learn self-discipline, self-control and cooperation, and will be exposed to how other children think, act, and feel about themselves and the world around them. That, too, is a part of school, the sharing of experiences, the "show and tell" days. Many parents want their children to form relationships and friendships with others along with learning from others how to act more grown-up.

Then, however, we find they are socializing with "those kids" from the other side of the tracks we have concerns about, sitting next to them in school and bringing them home. They want them to sleep over. We have tried to set our value structure and now others are trying to undermine it. Kids begin learning what lures to use in life from other kids, using school like a swap shop where everybody exchanges ideas about what "lures" to use on their parents and the world around them. No wonder kids usually run all the way home from school. *"I want to try out this new lure on my parents and see if it works as Johnny told me it would." "I wonder if my parents will jump for the temper tantrumming lure? The pouting lure? The whining lure?"* They are learning how to think, act and feel in ways we don't want them to.

I will never forget when we were doing the ancient ritual, dinner together, with the whole family—at a real table, not television trays—with everyone there at one time. My sweet daughter, Holly, let a burp out that lasted for at least a minute! She let it rip. She proudly looked at everyone around the table and began to smile. The food fell right out of my mouth. I remember saying to her in a stern tone of voice, *"Hey, hey, hey, you don't act like that in this home young lady,"* and she said, *"Well Jenny can do it at her house!"* That is the time when you feel the urge to take more control of your kids and keep them in a jar, with the lid welded shut and holes poked in the top. Once in awhile, you imag-

ine, you could let in a tutor to educate them, like those pickled people they used to sell in the souvenir shops. But, as we all know, this method is not realistic, so it's back to school for more lessons in life.

You can always tell that kids at the elementary school age are being controlled or molded by their parents thoughts concerning how **they** would like their kids to think, act and feel. If you don't believe, this take a look at how the kids are dressed. If you listen closely to a typical morning scene, you can hear parents sternly telling kids what to wear. I remember my own school days and saying, *"This is too big; it doesn't fit me,"* and the reply *"Trust me you look good; you'll grow into it." "Sure, when I'm 87!"* Are parents dressing their kids in the way they want them to be seen to meet **their** needs? How about yourself? Do you meet your needs **through your kids?** What is the potential problem with this?

As parents, we need to teach our kids how to dress themselves, for example, because they don't yet know how to match clothes, and the best way to teach them is by buying those clothes where they match the animals, giving them the opportunity to learn how to mix and match clothes. And allowing them to feel the power to choose which clothes go with what. Another dandy item on the market is children's underwear. Holly kept us informed of the day of the week by coming into our bedroom and sticking her butt out, proudly displaying her underwear to us. Staring us squarely in the face was Friday! Turn over the responsibility for choosing what to wear as early as possible. Let them come to you for suggestions regarding clothes. You will need to influence their decisions sometimes because they may want to wear a certain shirt every day, but this is where teaching them to be patient comes in. The truth is that their clothes are theirs and not yours. Later we will talk about teenagers choices regarding clothes. The choices that kids make regarding what clothes to wear are not going to kill you.

If you look at the elementary school period you will notice that group norms dictate behavior. In school, you go potty together, snack together, nap together, and line up for everything. The best example I can give you of this togetherness is when I coached my son's soccer team, trying to teach the kids to spread out and play their positions. But when the ball is dropped, they look like piranhas after fresh meat!

Another example was when I was lecturing around the country and was asked to please talk with kindergarten kids following my talk at the local high school. I love this age and made sure I could make time for them. The teachers were thrilled that I could come to their class. They tripled up the classes into one room with all the kids on the floor while I sat in that little tiny chair up front. My talk focused on taking control of your life, the choices we have and who really controls whom? I had the kids up on stage with me and used props and stories to make my points. I knew the information was being well received and thought I had these kids in the palm of my hand. Their eyes and ears were attuned to my every word and motion. They sat and listened attentively. You could have heard a pin drop. The teachers were amazed at my control, jealousy running through their veins at my ability to mesmerize these kids. When I finished my talk, I asked if there were any questions and will never forget the little boy who raised his hand right away, shaking it until I thought it would fall off. *"Yes, what question do you have?"*, I asked, and with that the boy asked very boldly, *"Do you own a boat?"* The three teachers in the back row on their little chairs fell backwards with laughter. A little girl blurted out, *"Well my Dad owns a boat."* So much for thinking they are listening.

CHAPTER 4

ADOLESCENCE: THE WONDER YEARS OR THE THUNDER YEARS?

I don't care what you say!
I hate you.
Quit hassling me about my hair, it's my hair.
I wish you were dead!
I can't wait until I'm 18!
Why do I have to pick up my room?
Why do I have to do my homework?
It's my life, why can't I run it?
My clothes are my clothes I should be able to choose what I want to wear.
Why can't I stay up later?
Why can't I do my homework when I want to do it and not when you want me to do it?
If I study better with the television or radio on, it should be my choice.
Why can't I date?
Why can't I go to an R-rated movie?
Why are there so many stinking rules?
Why don't you get off my back?

Welcome to the years of questioning everything in life—**adolescence.** Phil Collins hit the nail on the head concerning adolescence with his song titled "Land of Confusion." Confusion surrounds this period for both kids and parents. It's unlike any period in life. Numerous changes are occurring in both boys and girls. It's critical for parents to understand that adolescence is a period of time with a start and an end. You and I are most likely recovering adolescents ourselves. We lived through it. So will they, with our guidance and structure.

A new style of walk

You will notice that an adolescents' walk is changing from the same in-line elementary school walk to their own unique "cool" style. The kids, or adolescents, now look more and more like those Disney films that showed those silly birds trying to land on ice. Practice makes perfect and at this stage, there is plenty of room for practice. Kids are beginning to develop their own style. Varying from straight up and down to looking like a rap song in action. Slinky as can be.

A new style of dress

During adolescence, parental concerns about control over dress becomes almost comic. The parent, on one hand states, *"You are not going out of the house looking like that"* while the kid changes on the bus into what the parent did not want him to wear. The battle for control over clothes is incredible, as many kids tell me. This is the stage of life that I call the "dressing room." Kids are trying to find themselves not only in clothes, but in makeup, hairstyles and the like. Let them go through it by themselves. The more you control their choices in these areas, the more problems you are welcoming into your life. The more you allow them to muddle through this on their own, the better. Of course, you might want to buy a boot or towel to put it in your mouth during these dressing room times. At one time everything is in, but wait until the next day, because what was in today is out tomorrow. The styles are crazy. In fact, there is no style. The battle over dress has kids vying for independence and choice, while parents try to hold their own. *"I know what goes with what better than you, honey, so let me pick out your clothes."* Your child might say *"But I don't want to wear that, that's dorky."* *"You're going to wear what I want you to wear and that's final."* Can you relate to any of these? Are you allowing your kids the opportunity to muddle through on their own? Is it tough not to put in your two cents worth? But what are the prices for trying to control your children's decision during these times?

Who's under all that makeup?

Girls tell me that they put on their make-up on the bus or in the restroom and take it off on the bus on the way home from school. Their parents tell them not to wear make-up, but girls want to make their own decisions. At what age is make-up appropriate? At what point do we step in and let girls know how much is too much? Sometimes you would swear that girls put it on with an air-brush to begin with, and then later learn that there is a technique to it. In the programs that I have directed, we had people come in and teach young people the art of applying make-up. They loved it. As I have stated before, I am all for teaching people new skills, and this definitely is a skill worth teaching and one worth the kids' time too.

Hair, hair, hair

When it comes to hair style, chaos is the rule. Anything goes—from one side shaved to mohawks, tails, designs and so forth. Don't try to fix their hair at this age—you'll get your hand slapped or cut off! You may have done it when they were in elementary school and got away with it, but look out now. Kids want to fix their own hair. You may hear comments like "Quit messing with my hair" or "It's my hair, not yours!" If you want to take your life in your hands, go into the bathroom where a group of adolescent girls have been. The smell of hair spray will drop you to your knees. It seems as though everybody is trying to

get their hair to look like a radar dish. The wilder the style, the better. You will see girls coming out of the bathroom leaving a vapor trail behind them. As they walk through a doorway you will see them stop, stand sideways, inch their way through and then return to a normal walk because they can't fit through the doorway with all of that hair! The outcome is that hair is a precious commodity to almost every young person. How they choose to wear it is their choice.

Think about hair time for yourself. The Bart Simpson, four corners stand up look, was in style at the Thomson home back in the sixties. We had the 4 dollar haircut, 1 dollar for each corner. Four corners on the head with butch wax or Vaseline to top it off. My father was the butch wax king. He would scoop it out of that little container and like wall paste, apply an even coat to the hair. A hurricane would have been no match for that hair! Now, it is the styling salon for everyone, with everything from designs in the hair to perms, waves, mousse, etc. The days of the home haircut or the local dime store haircut kit are gone.

Earrings on boys!

The appearance of one or more earrings on boys has thrown many a parent off the bridge. The resulting argument is one I have heard many times over in my office. *"No kid of mine is going to wear an earring—over my dead body!"* One adolescent I worked with had of all places, an earring through his penis as his sign of uniqueness. That's unique? Ouch!

Our kids used to be so cute, so cuddly, so sweet. *"I love you"* came spontaneously. *"Our little helper"* is what we called our daughter, but she changed. Our little boy was such a sweetheart. What happened? Welcome to adolescence.

Physical and psychological changes

Kids change during this time both physically and psychologically. They're like a superball in a racquetball court—all over the place and so are their hormones. One moment they are sweet, the next they could make Sybil, Ted Bundy, Charles Manson or Jeffrey Dahmer appear well adjusted. Generally, you are going to see girls maturing earlier than boys, both physically and psychologically. Physically you are going to see them getting taller and taller with boys voices changing from a squeaky tone to a deep Arnold Schwarzenegger voice. My own personal experience of physical changes came with the junior high school experience in gym class when the gym teacher told us to *"Hit the showers"* fifteen minutes before the end of our class. I looked around and thought, are we going home to take showers? No such luck. A towel was thrown at me by the teacher. I began taking my shirt off and looking around at the other scared faces. Others were doing the same. Some were just ripping their clothes off—apparently they couldn't wait to get in that shower. Next come the pants, then the socks and last, the underwear—thank God I didn't wear the Scooby-Doo ones! With the towel wrapped around me, I waddled my way to the shower pit. We were herded like cattle into a large shower room. Moo! I was like everyone else, checking my toes out, starring at the floor. Then I looked up. I starred in amazement and did what I now call "comparison shopping!" I found out, that very day, that boys matured at different stages. Some boys looked like stand-ins for the "Planet of the Apes" while other looked like the fuzzy peach at the market. Oh God, what an experience.

Boys develop more muscle, girls develop breasts and voices change, hair begins in new places, and like it or not, sexual feelings. The adolescent has arrived.

What do they want from us?

In my lectures I always have fun talking about this stage of life. With various audiences I have been able to identify what kids want, and what parents and other adults want just by asking questions and listening to the answers. Here's what I have learned:

What kids want:

Responsibility
Children have repeatedly requested more responsibility for their own lives and for more in dependence from others.

Decision Making
Children want to make their own decisions about friends, music, money, what to wear, and when to study.

Control
Children want to take effective control of their own lives and take on that responsibility.

Power
Children want to have power in their own lives.

Choices
Children want to make their own choices and not be controlled by parents or other adults.

What is fascinating is that the adults want the same things for their kids. I ask the adult audiences if they want their kids to develop **Responsibility,** and I receive a resounding Yes! I ask if they would also like for their kids to develop good **Decision Making** skills by the time they leave home. Again, a resounding Yes! Then I get to asking the audience if they want their kids to have **Power, Control, and Choices.** It is amazing what I have heard, or should I say have not heard when I have asked this question. They give me a resounding Yes to every other question but allow their kids to have power, control, and choices. Some have stood and said that this is what's wrong with the country nowadays—giving these kids power, control, and choices! Adults are afraid that if we give those things to kids they will lose the control. Control over the kids. The control over their actions, their thoughts, and of course their feelings. Guess what? They never had it to begin with.

Children are dominated by their parents' wants and wishes. It follows that during adolescence kids push and pull for independence and power. Kids want that power. They want that control. They want those choices, even though many of us are afraid of giving it to them. At this point in my on-stage presentation, I have the audience raise their right hands and show me their palms. I tell them to put those hands on the back part of the head and wiggle their fingers. Everybody laughs and wonders what they are doing. I inform them that these fingers wiggling above their head are what I call "choice detectors" or "challenge detectors." We don't physically see them on kids' heads, but every adult living or working with kids understands what I mean. Those detectors challenge everything you want your kids to do, including how you would like them to think or feel. They are the ways in which kids tell to us that they want freedom in areas of power, control and choices. *"You can't make me do it." "I'm not gonna do it." "I don't have to." "You're not the boss of me you know."* Ever heard any of these? Those detectors are up and waving!

The good old days

A little old lady in Minnesota challenged what I am saying here. I had presented the information incorporated in this book in a two-hour presentation entitled "Kids, Control and Choices" and had time at the end of the presentation where it was open mike to Mike, so to speak. Out of the one thousand people in attendance, the old lady strutted up to the microphone and she was "hot under the collar." Her question started out as a comment on my young age and turned to whether or not my information should be presented to adults, let alone to kids. She did not like the fact that I was talking about these choices to kids and believed that all we need to do is go back to the **good old days** and *"Take the kid out to the woodshed and beat the hell out of him."* With that, she walked briskly back to her chair in the auditorium. As you can probably picture there was some giggling and then silence from the audience. There I was, in front of a thousand people, wondering what my response was going to be. My response to her was that from an early age we are taught that we have control over other people and that that teaching is wrong because it suggests that we have total control over our children.

After answering the lady, I shared with the audience an observation I made while growing up in my own family. I asked them if they had ever seen the movie "Vacation," with Chevy Chase. I explained to them that the only difference between that family, the Griswolds, and my family was that we did not have a dead aunt on the luggage rack! When we were eleven and fourteen, my father took my brother and myself over to the Sears store in Duluth, Minnesota to buy a surprise for my mother. This surprise turned out to be a pop-up tent trailer. My mother, as you can imagine, was surprised. My father proposed that we venture out to Disneyland for a two-week "Vacation." All in favor say yes, motion passed—we're off! To top it off, we pulled our surprise package all the way out west behind the classic Rambler station wagon, equipped with fold down back seats. My father is the kind of guy who when he gets in a car to drive, he gets in the car to drive. And drive he did. You stop at the rest area and he says, *"You have 3 minutes … ready, set, go!"* He is strictly a point A to point B kinda guy. My mother, on the other hand, is altogether different. She is the original sunshine girl with the Dots, Ju Jy Fruits, licorice, popcorn, peanuts and assorted candy in the front seat. She had a Mini-mart up there. She had the maps and the guides sprawled out on the dash and was always wanting to sing songs or play the world famous car bingo game. She had all of the historical places of interest listed on little stickers and placed on the dash in order of our route. I will never forget the moment when my mother noticed the first historical site on our trip— The Grand Canyon. She motioned for my brother and me to look at the site with words like, *"Now kids look—look at the pretty site,"* or *"This is the first and last time we will get to see this."* Of course, we paid no attention to her. Because of this, she raised her voice repeatedly with no response from either my brother or myself. Why, you may ask? Because we were engrossed in an All Star Wrestling match in the back of the Rambler station wagon, with the seats folded down, and sleeping bag spread out so we could either sleep or play. Play, my foot, we fought all the way out there! My mother passed over the brink of sanity after all her pleas with us to stop were to no avail. She reached over and elbowed my father in the ribs and said, *"Bob, aren't you going to help?"* It was then that my father slowed the car to warp speed 7 and reached around with that one hand that was really the **"hand from hell!"** That hand looked about the size of a large garbage can cover when it was coming toward me. When he grabbed me and slowly pulled me up to the front seat, you could hear him say calmly but sternly, *"Your mother said look,"* and with that I looked left then right and even asked for paper and pencil in order to take all the information down. When "Bullet Bob," as we called him in later years, grabbed you, you did pay attention, at least while he had hold of you. What I remember also is that he couldn't drive for long with one hand on the wheel and the other on me, so he would let go. My brother and I would go farther back in the Rambler and continue our wrestling match. My mother then wanted us to see the south rim of the Grand Canyon and again went through verbal requests, including raising her voice, with no luck. Again, Bob to the rescue. This time when he reached back he could not grab hold, because we were farther back in the Rambler. He would say, *"I'll stop the car if I have to,"* or *"I will chase you down,"* but we knew he had that old hockey injury and we could out run him.

It was at that moment that I knew that I had those detectors also, as well as **the choice to Think the way I wanted to, the choice to Act the way I wanted to, and the choice to Feel the way I wanted to.** It was the greatest feeling of power and control. It's also the worst feeling. **It's the worst feeling because knowing that you have control over your choices puts the responsibility on you for decision making, problem solving and life in general. No more blaming Mom or Dad for anything.** It's as if your parents or other adults take you up in an airplane, give you a summary of the airplane controls and then bail out on you. Before they jump you hear them say, *"It's your plane; fly it or crash it; it's your choice."* You realize that after your parents have floated down to earth in their chutes, they become the control tower personnel that will provide you with information about your flying, but at no time will they be in that seat with you. Teach this concept to your children. We will talk more about it in later chapters.

Kids are absolutely right about those detectors— they don't **"have to"** do anything in life except two things. Do you know what two things in life you "have to do?" No, not die and pay taxes. That is what everyone says to me. You are right on one of them. At one end of the spectrum, you **have to be born.** Christopher tried to prove us wrong on that. He sure took his sweet time, but he did enter the world, after all. At the other end of the spectrum, you **have to die**, unless you can find a way to prolong life! **Every-**

thing in between birth and death becomes choices— be they good choices or poor choices. The concept of good choices and poor choices is critical to keep in mind. We need to teach this point over and over to our kids. Bad kids? No. Poor choices made by kids? Yes.

What happened to those good old days? Remember the comment I've heard from parents? *"I wouldn't have been able to sit down for weeks if I had talked to my parents that way."* One important point to understand. People born before 1950 had these detectors also, but kept them in their pockets like the old lady in Minnesota because they grew up in a time where power, control, and choices were dictated by the adults and not questioned by kids. Sure they thought about talking back to their parents or making the choices that kids make today, but if they had taken those detectors out of their pocket and waved them, they would have had that hand cut off! They were literally a generation of "legends in their own mind," meaning they could live (or act out) only in their fantasies. What has happened since the late 60's is that those detectors have been gradually coming up to the point where it is unusual to find kids who don't challenge the rules or their parents or other adults. Kids who do not challenge are the odd ducks. Many tell me that my suggested age of 10-14 is too old and that it should be around 7-10 years of age when kids start using their detectors. What do you think? At what age do you see these detectors coming up? Do you think this change has something to do with why so many parents and adults working with kids are looking as if they are burned out? Is this why thousands of people come to hear my lecture, "Strategies For Saving Your Sanity?" Sure it is. Is this why parents are buying their kids luggage long before graduation? In my years of lecturing, I've run into college instructors who told me that they were frustrated with the lack of discipline and the attitudes of current college students. Their frustration becomes so significant that many of them went to teach at the high school level. Later, I heard high school teachers say that they were fed up with the disrespect, belligerence, lack of preparation, refusal to turn in homework or lack of participation in class, and that as a result, they were going to the middle school level to teach. After that I heard the middle school teachers say that the attitudes and the behaviors of the students were absolutely crazy. They went to the elementary level to teach. Now I'm hearing teachers at the elementary level say that they are going to work at the grocery store! I have heard repeated comments that responding to a kid with the "woodshed mentality" of old is like throwing spitballs at a battle ship. You can pull privileges, place them in detention, in-school suspension, or threaten them with other consequences, and in many cases they do not respond. At least not as quickly as people of the "old days" used to. The best example of the failure of this "do as I say—or else" mentality has come in Europe with the fall of the Berlin wall and the ensuing democracy in the Soviet Union. Even when there was a twenty-four hour take-over by the "hard liners" in the Soviet Union, in an attempt to return to the "old days," people fought back to regain the freedom of choice. The people made it clear that once you cross the line into democracy and offer people choices to think, act, and feel on their own, going back to "the woodshed days" is nearly impossible.

The "know it all" syndrome

It is quite normal for kids to go through a know-it-all stage during adolescence and even young adulthood. It seems as if you can't tell them anything. Hang in there. Mark Twain understood this process when he said, "When I was 14 it seemed to me that my parents did not know anything. By the time I was 21, I was impressed at how much they had learned." Teenagers can bring out the worst in all parents and those working with them. Many a parent has asked me, "Why are they so angry all the time? Why do they think I'm such a dummy? Why won't they listen to me? Why don't they do what I say?" How do we deal with the up-and-down mood swings? How do we teach them to be responsible and in control of their own lives? Adolescents, at this point in their lives, bring a whole new meaning to the word irrationality. Their mood swings seem to come out of nowhere. They make PMS look tame! They want us to be there for them, immediately. At the same moment, they want us to leave them alone. It's not only the land of confusion for them, but for us as well.

"Come in here and watch some T.V. with us." "With you?" "Yes, with us." "I will be up in my room listening to my heavy metal music if you need me." Mom and Dad begin to wonder, "Does he hate us? What's his problem?" "Just one night I would like it if he would spend some time with us." Is this a reasonable request from us as parents? Sure it is. Don't be surprised if you get a lot of yawning, fidgeting, rolling of the eyes and maybe even some comments like, "This is really a dumb show, can we watch MTV?"

Now you see them, now you don't. It's like a magician's vanishing act. Now you see them at the dinner table, now you don't. You turn around and they're gone. Up to the bedroom with the door closed and the stereo on at level 10. Out the door with their friends.

"Will you help us with the dishes, please?" This was a familiar statement made in our house when we were growing up. I vanished into the bathroom with **"Boy, do I have to go"** statements. It was amazing that during adolescence my bathroom trips could be predicted rather easily following any meal. My brother's favorite vanishing act was lying on the floor next to the stereo with the headphones on. These tricks worked wonderfully well for each of us. What do you remember about your adolescent years?

- ❏ What was your favorite kind of music?
- ❏ Who was your best friend?
- ❏ Who was your first date?
- ❏ What was your most embarrassing moment?
- ❏ Who were your girlfriend(s) or boyfriend(s)?
- ❏ What was your involvement in tobacco, alcohol or other drugs?
- ❏ What did you do later in life?
- ❏ What grades did you receive?
- ❏ What did school mean to you?
- ❏ What did you think about your parents?
- ❏ What did you think about your bother(s) or sister(s)?
- ❏ What was your reputation?
- ❏ Did you want privacy?
- ❏ Did you like to talk on the phone?

Are you able to generate some thoughts about these questions? Do they bring back good memories? Bad memories? Your thoughts about your own adolescence will direct how you are going to think about your son or daughter. These thoughts will then direct how you are going to act in response to your kids. If you were wild and crazy, you might be the type who wants to control their every move, based upon the moves you made. Is this true for you? You hope they won't give you as many sleepless nights as you gave your parents. These thoughts will also direct the feelings of insecurity or anxiety inside of you. You will see many examples of adolescent behaviors throughout the remainder of this book and more importantly what we can do to save our sanity when these behaviors arise.

CHAPTER 5

ALL BEHAVIORS ARE PURPOSEFUL

Why do kids pout, whine, cry, threaten, drink, drug, skip school, wear weird clothes, talk, refuse to talk or run away? Why do some kids choose to fail, to get in trouble with the school or the law, threaten suicide, succumb to peer pressure or choose to rebel? Why do adults drink, drug, whine, complain, anger, depress, attempt suicide or give up?

On the other hand why do some kids and adults make the right choice? The answer to these questions is that all people are attempting to meet one or more of their internal psychological needs with their best choices at the time. These choices result from frustration, which in turn, motivates them to make a choice to deal with this frustration. Choices can be good. Choices can be bad. Whatever works at the time to reduce the frustration becomes our best choice. Even if the choice isn't what others consider to be a "good" one, if it works for the person once, he will often keep using it. Just like the tiny fisherman we read about in the crib, these choices are like "lures" from the tackle box. They learn what "lure" to use to get them what they

want, which is to meet one or more of their needs. If it works, they keep on using it until something or someone intervenes. If uncorrected, these choices will lead to toddler, pre-adolescent, adolescent and adulthood behaviors that many of us are concerned with. If people knew of better options to meet their needs they would use them. The productive thinking strategy in this book will address these concerns and offer solutions to the problems we all want answers to. A basic premise that you should integrate into your brain was taught to me by Dr. Applegate:

Everything we think and do is purposeful, and is our best choice at the time to meet one or more of our internal psychological needs.

This chapter will help you look at problems as a lack of need fulfillment. In getting down to a need level, you will open up a whole new way of looking at behaviors and associated problems.

Both parents and kids have the following needs:

Security:	Having the skills to meet your needs in each of your environments.
Faith:	Having a positive belief in yourself and in a higher power.
Worth:	Feeling powerful and in control.
Freedom:	Knowing you can choose how to perceive or respond to the world around you.
Belonging:	Feeling love and caring with other people.
Fun:	Having joy and happiness in your life.
Knowledge:	Having information and input about yourself and your world.
Health:	Having physical, emotional and psychological balance in your life.

The word "need" creates some confusion. We usually hear it used in the context of, "I need a hug," "I need you in my life," "I need a car," "I need a job," "I need a hot fudge sundae," or "I need you to behave right now." We are all internally driven through the fulfillment of certain psychological needs. In fact these needs determine how we think and act. When you have what you want, you feel good. When you want something and you do not get it, you feel bad. How good or how bad will depend on how much you wanted what you want. These needs are dual-purpose. They not only create a sense of fulfillment in our lives when they are met, but they can also create a frustrating feeling when they are not met. The same things happens with our kids. Our kids feel good when their needs are being met, and, like us, they feel frustrated and in pain when their needs are not being met.

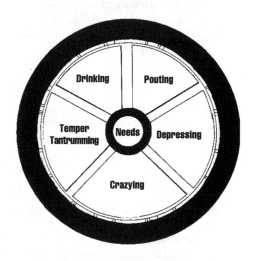

Wants are different from needs. Think of wants as spokes in a bicycle wheel that can lead to need fulfillment. Wants are pathways to meet needs. Angering is a "want" that can meet the need for Worth. Money is a "pathway" that can meet the need for Freedom. Depressing is a "pathway" that can meet the need for Belonging. We learn these choices through experience. They are taught or modeled by others we come in contact with, just as the baby in the crib learned that crying was a pathway to satisfy his needs. Kids will learn from their parents and other adults the pathways or choices they will use to meet their needs. They learn this by watching us. They observe the choices we make to meet our own needs in our lives. Most

people will teach typical choices. Productive thinkers will teach efficient choices. It's that simple. *"Where did we learn our choices?" "Were they all good choices or were they attempts to control people or situations?"*

In productive thinking it is important to understand that the behaviors you choose can be either efficient or inefficient in attempting to control the outside world to get what you want.

Efficient behaviors are:
- ❑ Behaviors that meet one or more of your needs.
- ❑ Behaviors where there is no loss of fulfillment in any other need areas.
- ❑ Behaviors where we control only for what we think and do.
- ❑ Behaviors focused on changing the present and the future.
- ❑ Behaviors that help us see the control we have over our own lives.

Inefficient behaviors are:
- ❑ Behaviors that meet one or more of our needs.
- ❑ Behaviors that cost us fulfillment in one or more of our need areas.
- ❑ Behaviors that attempt to control other situations or people.
- ❑ Behaviors that deal mainly with the past.
- ❑ Behaviors that lead to short term payoffs and long-term costs.

Notice that both sets of behaviors meet needs, which reinforces the idea that **"all behaviors are purposeful and are our best choices at the time to meet one or more of our internal psychological needs."** The significant difference is that efficient choices do not carry with them the consequences or prices that inefficient choices might have. Also, inefficient choices are used mainly to **control** other people, things, or situations. A parent who chooses behaviors like excessive yelling, threatening, physical harming or guilting is putting himself at risk of losing some need fulfillment by trying to change or control another's thoughts, actions or feelings. And he is usually responding to something that has already occurred.

It is important to recognize that behaviors themselves are neither efficient or inefficient; they are simply behaviors. Behaviors have a positive side and a negative side, based upon the prices they exact. Yelling, for example, might be viewed by some as inefficient, but when a person yells in support of his team or at his child as she runs into the street, it is efficient. You will know if your choices are inefficient if you are paying any prices in one or more need areas or if you continue to experience frustration.

From this point forward I want you to consider inefficient behaviors as just that, behaviors. But they are behaviors that tell a story. They are like waving flags in the air or shooting flares into the sky. They say, *"Notice me, I'm making choices that are meeting one or more of my needs."* These behaviors are also a clue to us that someone may be frustrated in one or more of his need areas and is making his best choices to alert us to this. *"Why don't they just tell us they are frustrated?"* For many, they can't, due to the controlling people around them. For others, they don't know how. As a result they use what they have seen others use to meet their needs. Does it work? Sure it does. Remember the man on the psychiatric unit who was fishing with the imaginary pole in the imaginary lake? He lured me down the hall, and when I asked, *"How many are you catching,"* he turned and said, *"You are the thirteenth one today."* The key is to rethink: **"All behaviors are purposeful and are our best choices at the time to meet one or more of our needs."**

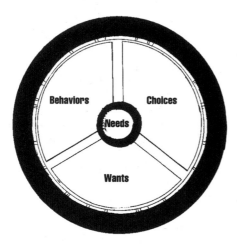

Pathways such as drinking start out as a small spoke in the bicycle wheel. Without intervention, the spoke becomes larger and thus takes up more of the person's life. Left untouched, the choice of drinking becomes drunking and finally addiction. Pathways such as depressing start out as a small spoke, many times in the form of pouting and if left

untouched, develop into major problems. Pathways such as angering start out as a small spoke, many times in the form of temper tantrumming and if left untouched, can develop into more aggressive behaviors such as criminal activity and/or violence. The longer the inefficient choice goes untouched, the more difficult it is for others to intervene. You can begin to understand that telling a person to stop a behavior that is need fulfilling is like telling them to stop breathing. It has been working for them for quite some time and they are not apt to stop on your request alone.

The typical response to a behavior is to try and stop it. The productive thinker, however, would step back and understand that the behavior is purposeful. A flag in the air. A flag that would signal them:

A. To **evaluate themselves** in two areas.
   1. Their relationship with the other person in terms of being either need reducing or need fulfilling.
   2. The environment they have created with the child as it pertains to need fulfillment or need reduction in such areas as Belonging (relationship with them), Freedom (allowing them choices, permission to talk, demonstrating trust, loyalty and sharing feelings), Worth (allowing them responsibility, decision making, control, and power).

B. To step back and **evaluate the other person** in four areas.
   1. What need areas the person is frustrated in.
   2. What influence their environment has on the behavior that he is choosing.
   3. What intervention is necessary to change the behavior.
   4. What alternative choices can be provided to the person to deal with his frustration.

Purposeful behaviors

Take a look at the following chart and see if you can identify which needs are being met by the behaviors listed and what costs might be expected. Please note that all behaviors should be viewed as being demonstrated excessively.

Behavior Exhibited	Needs Met	Needs you Pay Prices In
Pouting		
Angering		
Depressing		
Drinking		
Guilting		
Lying		
Cheating		
Threatening		
Promiscuity		
Crazying		
Refusing to talk		
Talking back		
Physical aggression		
Swearing		
Bragging		
Criminal activity		
Wearing weird clothes		
Wearing weird hairstyles		

This exercise will help you understand that **all behaviors are purposeful and are a person's best attempt at the time to meet one or more of his needs.** The problem with choices such as these is that they can cost a person in other need areas. A person who chooses to pout, for example, may meet a need for Belonging by pulling people toward him, Worth by being able to control others with this behavior and Fun by being manipulative. The cost may be in the areas of Belonging when people move away from them, Worth in their lack of power over others, and Freedom in their allowing others to be in control of their choices. Angering may well meet the needs for Worth and Security, but cost the person in the areas of Belonging and Fun. Using substances may meet your needs for Fun, Worth, Belonging and Security but cost you in the areas of Freedom, Fun, Health and Belonging. To gain effective control of your life, you must learn to satisfy what you believe is basic to you and learn to respect, not frustrate, others in fulfilling what is basic to them. Responsibility is finding ways to meet your own needs without depriving others of the same right. Conflicts occur when kids and parents have different ways of meeting their needs. Playing loud music might be extremely need fulfill-

ing for some kids but nerve-wracking for their parents. If, on the other hand, the parents like country and western music, the kids might moan and groan in the background. The key is finding a happy medium or a compromise. Finding a way to meet your needs without compromising other people's need-fulfillment is responsible choice making. Doing your own thing with no thought or consideration for other people is irresponsible choice making. This goes for adults as well as kids. Unfortunately there are a lot of kids who "do their own thing" as a part of adolescent behavior. Playing loud music, swearing, smoking, yelling and pushing each other around may be "choices" for kids to meet their needs but might be distracting to others in the area. Our role as parents is to teach them what appropriate and inappropriate choices are. We do this by setting up an appropriate structure first in our homes. In this way you both win. We can then discuss with our kids the choices they and others make as efficient or inefficient.

When working with the schools I came in contact with some tough kids. One group in particular comes to mind, a group of 10 ninth grade girls. They would walk around the halls of the school looking for their next victim—like lions stalking prey. They were looking for a girl that offended them in some way. Some insignificant way. Maybe somebody who looked at them in a different way. Said something about them. Or was just prettier than they were. The reason was not significant to them. Once they picked her out they would circle around her and one by one would go in and beat the hell out of her! Why? They always responded with, *"because it felt good."* These girls were demonstrating that choices such as these are need fulfilling to them at the time in such areas as Worth, Belonging and Fun. Need fulfilling at the time— because later they felt the consequences for their choices in the form of suspensions, eventual expulsions and even criminal charges being filed. They eventually paid prices in the areas of Freedom, Belonging, and Security among others. To some of these girls, this consequence meant very little, particularly in-school suspension or suspension from school which meant a three-day vacation for them. Their choices were very frustrating, not only to myself but to their victims. But now that I understand their choices from a different perspective— a need perspective—their choices make more sense to me. They were making their "best choices" at the time to deal with the frustration they were feeling in their lives. Many of them were from homes where there was a lack of Belonging, Worth, Fun and so on. Their choices in the form of fighting were like waving flags or shooting off flares. The bottom line, however, is that these girls did need to be held accountable for their actions.

Two cultural beliefs make it difficult for us to learn this new way of looking at our lives and gaining more control of ourselves. First, we have been taught via stimulus-response learning that all our behaviors are a reaction to what the world is doing to us. You may get mad because your kids don't appreciate you or get depressed because your spouse doesn't give you the positive attention you feel you deserve, or you may get angry because your kids don't do what you want. Secondly, and probably a consequence of the stimulus-response learning, is a belief that if you can determine with some accuracy who is to blame in any given situation, the situation will get better. This fosters the typical pattern of looking "out there" for the cause of problems. Looking "out there" will direct your actions and your feelings. It will put you in a position of finding fault with "out there" for how you are thinking, acting or feeling. It is very important to learn for yourself and also to teach and model to your kids that, **"It's your responsibility to meet your needs *with* others, not *through* them."**

Mick Jagger and the Rolling Stones said in their song, *"You can't always get what you want, but if you try real hard you can always get what you need."* Sometimes our wants are blocked. But if we look beyond our wants and identify the needs where we may feel frustrated, then we will be thinking on a need-fulfillment level. This level opens up a multitude of pathways or spokes to meet our needs. Let's take a look at a list to expand on this point:

What parents WANT	NEEDS fulfilled
❏ A child who loves them.	❏ BELONGING, SECURITY, WORTH.
❏ A child who listens.	❏ WORTH, SECURITY.
❏ A child who minds.	❏ WORTH, HEALTH, FAITH.
❏ A respectful child.	❏ WORTH, SECURITY, FAITH.
❏ An alcohol-drug free child.	❏ SECURITY, HEALTH.
❏ A responsible child.	❏ SECURITY, WORTH.
❏ A child knowing self-control.	❏ FREEDOM, WORTH.
❏ A child on the honor roll.	❏ WORTH, BELONGING, SECURITY.
❏ A law abiding child.	❏ SECURITY, HEALTH, WORTH.
❏ A pregnant married daughter.	❏ SECURITY, BELONGING, WORTH.
❏ A clean bedroom.	❏ WORTH, SECURITY, FAITH.
❏ A child on time for curfew.	❏ SECURITY, WORTH, HEALTH.
❏ A child who does his chores.	❏ SECURITY, WORTH, HEALTH.

When we want something and have it we feel good. We feel frustrated, though, when we want something and we do not have it. We need to understand that we feel good because we are not just getting what we want, but what we need. We feel frustrated because we are not obtaining what we want, but more importantly, we are not getting our needs met. As you read over this list I hope that you can see that when a parent wants something and gets it, his needs are fulfilled. When your needs are fulfilled, you will be happy. You will feel good. Let's look at the same list but from a different view:

of frustration is up to us. **If you are a typical person, you are attempting to meet your needs through your kids.** In that case the level of frustration is tied to whether your child makes the choices that will be need-fulfilling **for you.** If he doesn't choose as you want, you feel serious frustration! Sometimes you feel frustrated for them, perhaps over something important to them. If not, the frustration comes from not meeting your needs as a parent. This concept is very important. Go back over the list and ask yourself if you have ever been guilty of meeting your needs through the choices

What parents HAVE

- ❏ A child who dislikes them.
- ❏ A child who talks back.
- ❏ A child who is disruptive.
- ❏ A child who is disrespectful.
- ❏ An alcohol-drug using child.
- ❏ An irresponsible child.
- ❏ A child who blames others.
- ❏ A child getting poor grades.
- ❏ A child in trouble with the law.
- ❏ A pregnant teenager.
- ❏ A messy bedroom.
- ❏ A child who is late for curfew.
- ❏ A child who neglects his chores.

Frustrated NEEDS

- ❏ BELONGING, SECURITY.
- ❏ WORTH, SECURITY.
- ❏ WORTH, FUN.
- ❏ SECURITY, WORTH.
- ❏ SECURITY, FREEDOM.
- ❏ FREEDOM, HEALTH.
- ❏ FUN, SECURITY, HEALTH.
- ❏ BELONGING, WORTH, FAITH.
- ❏ WORTH, SECURITY.
- ❏ FREEDOM, BELONGING, FUN.
- ❏ WORTH, SECURITY, HEALTH
- ❏ SECURITY, HEALTH, FUN.
- ❏ WORTH, BELONGING.

You can see that when parents want something and don't have it, they are frustrated in one or more of their need areas. The frustrated needs listed are just examples. You may have other frustrated needs if you were the parent in these examples. If you read this list over again, you can almost feel the parents' frustration. Remember that the degree of frustration is related directly to how much the parent wants what they want. If they really want their children to listen and the children do not listen, their needs are going to be frustrated to the same degree. If they want their children to get good grades and their children receive poor or failing grades, the parents are going to be frustrated. The point is that all of us are going to be frustrated to some degree in our need areas; however, the degree

your child makes. If you are like most of us, you will acknowledge that you have. Be aware if you are frustrated because your child is not meeting your needs. Identify the needs that your child is meeting with his choices. Provide them with alternative choices to meet their needs where they will not pay prices. Evaluate yourself in those frustrated need areas to see if you are providing a need-fulfilling environment for your child.

Let's take a look at some commonly used parental behaviors. See if you can identify which needs the behavior meets and which needs parents pay a price in. Please note that all behaviors listed should be viewed as being excessively demonstrated.

Behavior Exhibited	Needs Met	Needs You Pay Prices In
Physically threatening		
Angering		
Physical punishment		
Criticizing		
Swearing		
Demanding		
Yelling		
Drinking		
Smoking		
Depressing		
Pouting		
Giving Up		
Drugging		

It doesn't take a brain surgeon to figure out what motivates people to do what they do and think what they think. In both cases the parent and the child want to meet their needs, but **unfortunately parents often meet their needs through and not with their children.** In meeting their needs through their children, parents control their thoughts or actions—or try to. You will notice that each of the parental behaviors listed above are controlling. Excessive physical punishment meets the parental need for Worth by controlling the child but costs them in Belonging, because the child avoids the parent as a result. When there is a lack of relationship between the child and the parent, problems will arise. Sometimes these problems will come up in such forms as purposely getting poor grades, getting in trouble at school or in the community, talking back to others, refusing to abide by rules and so on.

Parents as need fulfilling or need reducing

The question we need to ask ourselves is, *"How do I want my children to perceive me?"* More importantly, *"How do my kids perceive me?"* Want to take a risk? Ask your kids to be honest with you and tell you how they perceive you in the various need areas. Why? Well, from experience, you will find that kids will move toward you when they perceive you as someone they can trust and meet their needs

with. Think of your own life as an adult. Isn't it true that if you know someone who is an excessive complainer, a criticizer, or a downright snob you, too, will run for cover when you see them? Who wants to be around a "U-Boat Commander" if they have a choice! I rest my case when I hear so many kids saying to me, *"You would leave home too if you had a parent like mine,"* or *"The reason I shut down when my parents talk to me is that they don't talk— they yell and scream and say something like, 'don't you dare say a word!'"* *"My parents don't even listen to me."* *"My father has hit me several times in order to get me to mind."*

At one time, kids spent a large part of their time helping out with the family, satisfying their needs for Belonging, Worth, Security, Fun and Faith. When you feel need fulfillment and a relationship with your parents, major discipline problems are rare. Sure there are going to be the ups and downs of everyday family life, but excessive controlling and powering from both the parents and the kids are less likely if there is a sense of need fulfillment. It isn't, of course, the parents' job to do this alone, but we can look at our own need fulfillment first and take an inventory of how we are being perceived by our kids, especially with regard to providing them the opportunity to meet their needs with us.

In China, children are expected to contribute to the welfare of society while in school and to be involved in some type of productive work. This productive work can be in the form of community service, helping other people, the aged or the handicapped, or other forms of help.

Even my grandfather got into the business of building a relationship with my brother and me. We will never forget the days of fishing accompanied by a trek into the woods for berries. The day always started off with pancakes and juice for a "good start," according to Grandpa. The trip to the lake was pure pleasure in the Studebaker Lark. To save gas he would put it in neutral at the top of a hill and let it roll to a crawl before starting it. We will never forget the laughter he roared with from his toes when our lines were tangled up with the entire squadron of fishermen on all sides of the lake. Wherever I threw my line in, I was assured of getting it tangled up with someone else. By the end of the day we noticed the sunburned balding area on his head beginning to look like a pulsating beet. We will never forget the three pounds of worm goo on his hands and shirt from digging in the crawler box in order to help bait our hook. Couple this with stopping to pick juneberries, blueberries or strawberries in the deep dark woods, and you had a Grandpa right out of the textbook. During the winter it was ice-fishing accompanied by the roasting of apples over a small fire with the filler being cinnamon and sugar. What memories of a great relationship!

Take inventory for yourself. Look at your needs. Are you creating an environment that is need fulfilling for yourself and your kids? Are you yourself need-fulfilling to them? To others? You decide?

Remember this important point:
Everything we think and do is purposeful and is our best choice at the time to meet one or more of our internal psychological needs.

Need theorists such as Abraham Maslow, Clayton Aldefer, David McClellan, William Glasser and Gary Applegate have all supported this statement. The degree, method or pathway of need-fulfillment varies, due to genetic differences, environmental background and personal choices. How each person chooses to meet needs is a matter of choice. Reading a book may be need-fulfilling to one person and need-reducing to another. As you were growing up, perhaps the pathways you used to meet your needs were touching, kissing and hugging. Your family may have considered this to be very important. On the other hand, your spouse may have had very little touching, kissing or hugging, and her family may have used words to express caring. Or, maybe they had very little need-fulfillment with others. This is why the choices to meet needs vary from person to person and situation to situation.

Learning about the psychological needs that both motivate and frustrate us is an essential step in taking effective control of our lives as parents. There are eight basic needs that drive or motivate us. Unmet, these needs also frustrate us. The number of needs is not as important as the names. Understanding and accepting that we have internal needs that drive all of the behavioral choices we make is what's important. Understanding that our children are driven by these same needs is important also. They, too, become frustrated when their needs are not met. Creating a need-fulfilling environment for our children to grow up in is a critical task for parents. A synopsis of these psychological needs will follow in a later chapter. What we can do to create a need-fulfilling environment will also be explained.

CHAPTER 6

WHERE MOST PARENTS ARE

Where Most Parents Are—WhMPA for short (that's pronounced WOMPA)—can be described as a position that is neither weak nor strong. I explain to many audiences that WhMPA is not meant to be derogatory, but a description of virtually where most people are today. We want to begin by better understanding where most people are in regards to how they choose to think, how they choose to act and how they choose to feel.

The term WhMPA came from my professional work and personal friendship with the creator of the Skill Development Theory For Successful Change, Dr. Gary Applegate. When opening the Center for Skill Development in Sherman Oaks, Calif. with Dr. Applegate many years ago, we came up with the term by mistake, while talking about the uniqueness of our approach to helping people. We both believed that teaching the skills of productive thinking were different from where most people are today. It was our belief that we were teaching a new way of looking at yourself and a new way of viewing the world. If people were to put the information we teach into their lives, we believed that they would be thinking differently than most people. Because of this we believed that they would be equipped to deal more efficiently with the daily problems of living. As you will read, this term can apply to both parents and kids. In my presentations I use the term WhMPA to stand for Where Most People Are. Let's look at the thinking patterns related to WhMPA's.

WhMPA's have certain thinking patterns that are prevalent whenever problems arise. WhMPA's think the following thoughts about getting what they want:

- ❏ If I stop another person's bad habit(s), things will change.
- ❏ If I change my action(s), things will change.
- ❏ If I think positively, things will change.

- ❏ I want life to be comfortable and stress free.
- ❏ If only my kids would change, my life would be better.
- ❏ If I ventilate my feelings, I will feel better.

Stopping a bad habit

Many WhMPA's, to feel better or to change a bad habit, think they must stop something. A WhMPA states, *"My bad habit is yelling and screaming at my kids. I am going to stop yelling at my kid, stop nagging and stop screaming so much. I am going to stop some action, some behavior of mine, some negative thought and if I stop, then my life will be better. I'll be less frustrated."* Who could disagree? Have you said to yourself that you were not going to scream anymore? Not yell anymore? Not raise your voice? Not spank? Not lecture? If you stopped one of these, your life would be better. You know that. This is no news flash. Why is it so tough for us to just stop doing something? It is difficult to do because of Dr. Applegate's basic premise: **Everything we think and do is purposeful, and is our best choice at the time to meet one or more of our internal psychological needs.**

Our psychological needs are as follows:
Security—to feel a sense of security and the feeling of having skills.
Faith—to feel a positive belief in yourself and in a power greater than yourself.
Freedom—to feel you have choices.
Worth—to feel that power and control comes internally from what you achieve.
Belonging—to feel love and caring with people through friendship and relationship skills.
Fun—to feel pleasure and have fun in life.

Knowledge—to have information so you can build upon your present skills and develop new choices in your life.

Health—to be in balance in all need areas, both physically and psychologically.

These needs are dual purpose: they motivate and they frustrate. They motivate us to choose efficient behaviors to satisfy our needs. They frustrate us when these needs are not being met, and tell us that we better get going and make a choice to close down the difference between what we want and what we need. We will feel good when our needs are being met efficiently. We will feel pain and frustration when we are not meeting our needs efficiently. The key is to find ways to meet our needs, for our kids to meet their needs and for each of us to learn how to live together where we're not frustrating each other to the point that we want to buy luggage for each other as a gift!

To immediately stop screaming, yelling, drinking, drugging or getting others to do the same is tough at best. Just think of the "bad habits" we have: overeating, overdrinking, overdrugging, sexually acting out, smoking and so on. Can you relate to any of these bad habits? These choices, like others, are purposeful to meet one or more of our needs. If you choose to rethink in this way, you will see that these choices are purposeful and that they are very need-fulfilling, at the time. Notice I said at the time. They work at the time, but usually bring about long term consequences. Think of the last time, for example, that you wanted to lose weight. You know that you need to put less food in your system if you want to accomplish your goal. Simple, right? Wrong. You find yourself lapsing while at the local Dairy Queen with that Peanut Buster Parfait. It tastes so good—for a moment. As you are leaving the Dairy Queen you start to do what millions do. You start to FEEL frustrated because you made a choice that is not going to help you reach your goal of weight loss. You may get back on track right away and make better choices from that point forward. You may also choose what a WhMPA would do. You may continue to eat and figure it is a lost cause. But if you simply stop an action or thought that is working for you at the moment, the need will still be there. Stopping food consumption is not the answer. Meeting the needs that food met is the answer. Identifying those needs and then finding alternative pathways to meet

those needs in a cost-free way is the answer. Hard work? Sure, but you will get what you want out of life. You will be taking effective control of your life. You will not let the outside world dictate your thoughts, your actions or your feelings. If you manage to get your kids to stop doing what is irritating you, the needs they were meeting with that annoying behavior will still be there. If they choose to irritate you with certain behaviors, those behaviors are purposeful to meet one or more of their needs. Asking them to stop doing what they are doing is just as tough as it would be for us to stop eating. Doing so just puts this need on hold. Putting them in their bedroom for "time out" is like pushing the hold button. Eventually they will need to come out. Hopefully they will find another way to fulfill that need or they will return to the same old choice. Who teaches them another choice? We become the teachers of better choices and better alternatives that they can use instead of the choices that get them into trouble. Unless they can start meeting those needs in another way, a more efficient way, they are going to feel pain in the form of punishment or other negative consequences such as groundings, time outs, and/or loss of privileges at school, home and in the community. That is why teaching or modeling alone is not efficient in the long haul. They must learn what their poor choice was and learn what better choices are available. Learning that they have the ability to go beyond just stopping a behavior is critical. When we understand this better, we will begin to perceive ourselves as teachers and models of efficient choices to meet all needs in all environments. We will teach and model efficient solutions to all problems in life and at the same time, show that problems and problem-solving are part of it. Problems will become opportunities for growth and opportunities for seeking new choices. Not only for the kids but for us. They will see that we have problems also and that what is more important, we have a strategy that works. They will see through our modeling that they, too, can use this strategy for themselves. Look on the other side, too. We want to be able to get our kid to stop drinking and using drugs, to stop procrastinating, and start doing their homework, to attend school, and get better grades, to stop swearing, and so on. Why is it so difficult for our kids to stop these behaviors? They, like us, are choosing behaviors that, at the time, work for them to meet one or more of their needs.

Starting with actions

Another thought that WhMPA's have is, *"I'm going to start with an action without changing what I think about my kids."* These new action choices will be my best attempt as a parent to get them to be the way I want them to be. *"If I do something nice for them they should be nice to me."* These actions might be positive things like saying "Hi" to your kids in the morning, making them breakfast, cleaning their rooms for them, taking them to the movies, buying them something, or making their favorite food. Have you done any of these in order to be nice to your kids? In order to have them be the way you want them to be? Have they been nice in return? If you're like millions of others, sometimes it works, sometimes it doesn't. When it doesn't, WhMPA's get frustrated. These are all actions we choose. They are our best choices at the time. There's nothing wrong with them. Or is there? Think about what we are trying to accomplish with these actions. We are trying to get from our kids something that we want. But why start with actions? Whether it is successful depends on whether your kids want what you want. Our first inclination when frustrated with our kids is to try to do something "to them" or "for them" in order to get them to change or be the way we want them to be. Good intention, but poor choice. If you've ever been overweight, you've probably done what millions have done. You've probably dropped to the floor, done sit ups, push ups, aerobics, ran or walked until you thought you would die. Within a few hours or days you quit. Just look at health spas. They will tell you that very few stick with it. Why? Because most people want a "quick fix" and start with an action that will change their problem situation fast. Changing our actions is the worst place to start when we come across problems with kids. Yes, starting with actions in some cases works very well, but in the majority of cases, we would be better off using what I teach in the areas of productive thinking skills first before choosing certain actions.

WhMPA's sometimes are happy, sometimes successful, but just as often, they feel out-of-control and puzzled about how to get people to give them what they want. Notice the words "give them what they want." WhMPA's are usually working in some way to manipulate or control people around them to do what they want, think what they want or to feel how they want them to feel. Unfortu-

nately, their attempts do not always work, frustration sets in and the gates to controlling behavior open up. Kids do the same thing. They experience a problem in life and figure they will start with actions also. If they are lonely, they'll try to make friends, call someone up on the phone, try to go out and meet new people. If they are lucky, it will work out for them. If they are like many people, their attempts are met with frustrations when people are not at home, they don't want to go anywhere with them, or even be their friends. Hence, loneliness and frustration set in. They will not continue to use these actions when the results are poor. The problem is not the actions. The problem is how they choose to think. Overweight people try to stop eating. People with addiction problems try stopping their use cold turkey, as do others with similar problems. For some it works. Most, within a short period of time, return to the old choice that worked for them, even if they paid prices for that choice.

Just think positively

WhMPA's sometimes focus on changing their thinking to "positive thinking" alone. You have heard about the Power of Positive Thinking before. You know, wake up in the morning and think, *"Today is the first day of the rest of your life."* Positive, positive, positive! Telling your kids, *"Don't worry, think positive,"* *"When life gives you lemons, make lemonade,"* will only go so far. Thinking this way for ourselves has its limitations also. Have you told yourself or your spouse that you just need to be more positive around your kids? Have you gone to bed thinking, *"I will be more positive with them tomorrow?"* *"If I become more positive, then they will become more positive?"* Have you noticed that when you have tried to be positive with them it does not turn out the way you want it to. They look at you and wonder what is wrong with you. They might even roll their eyes in disgust. What do you think of then? Positive thoughts or negative thoughts? I've told many a person in my seminars that if you want all the positive you can stomach, then go to an AMWAY meeting. You will walk out of there humming, *"I think I can, I know I can, I know I will"* ... In just one hour, you will get so pumped up, you can't stand it. The problem is not AMWAY. The problem is that you'll go out to the world thinking positive, positive, positive and you won't always receive back from the world positive in return. So much for just thinking positive.

Working to be comfortable

WhMPA's work to be comfortable. Nobody wants stress in their lives. *"If we can just make it through the next year, everything should go smoother for us." "I hate it when my kids have problems." "I can't wait until I'm eighteen." "They think they can't wait until they are eighteen, what do you think we are waiting for?" "I hate it when I have to deal with all of their problems."* We are all looking for some time in our life when we will have it made. Some time when we are comfortable. *"I can't wait until I'm sixteen so I can drive." "I can't wait until I'm eighteen so I can vote." "I can't wait until I'm in my twenties so I can go out and make money." "I can't wait until I'm retired so I can relax."* If you look at each of these statements you will quickly see that people are waiting for something to make them happy. We see many parents trying to make sure that there are no problems that they must deal with in raising their children. Good luck! You're going to have problems in your own life. Your kids will have problems in their life. Welcome to the world of parenthood. Welcome to a world of frustration. Problems, as we will find out, can be viewed as an opportunity to learn and grow. Comfortable is not really where we want to be. Comfortable should be viewed as uncomfortable if we want to grow.

Comfortable is the guy who jumps out of the window on the fifth floor and you see him come by on the third floor and ask him how he is doing. He looks at you and says, *"So far, so good."* He hasn't hit yet! My other definition of comfortable is having one foot in an ice bucket and the other foot in a hot bed of coals—on the average you will feel "comfortable." The problem is that there will be "hot" days of screaming, yelling, fighting and arguing around the house, and "cold" days of avoidance of one another, not wanting to talk to "them," along with general dislike of their behavior. It's what I call the Holiday Inn syndrome where you check in at the front desk for messages, grab a towel, a bar of soap and generally stay in your own room. We may go to the lobby for a little socializing, but that is rare. We choose to avoid our kids when we feel angry with them and what they have done. The problem is that it's like putting a phone call on hold—eventually you need to answer it. Eventu-

ally, you need to come out of the room and deal with the problem you are having. Every time you think you have it made, the world around you changes. If you don't change your thinking with the changing of the world around you, you will think, act and feel negative because you are uncomfortable. If you always do what you always did, the results will always be the same.

If only my kids would change, my life would be better

WhMPA's work very hard to change "out there." I can't tell you how many WhMPA's have told me over the years, *"If only out there would change, my life would be better." "If my kids would change, if my spouse would change, if my boss would change."* Who can disagree? Their lives would be better. But how long have they been waiting for "out there" to change? For a very long time. Have you ever thought, *"I want you to be on time?" "I want you to be more responsible?" "I want you to do your homework?" "I want you to stop talking like that?" "I want you to spend less time on the phone and more time in your room studying?"* My concern is how much you want these things to come true for you. Do you want your kids to become a little more responsible or are you wanting them to become responsible by noon tomorrow? To what degree do you want what you want? If you are thinking *"If out there would change life would be better,"* you will most likely go out and try to change out there using a variety of manipulating and powering behaviors. The more you want "out there" to think, act and feel the way you want, the more you will CONTROL them through powering or controlling behaviors on your part. Have you ever had any of the previous thoughts? When thinking that way, WhMPA's use whatever means they need to in order to get what they want. Have you ever tried to change others with powering and controlling behaviors such as threatening through yelling, screaming or physical punishing?

In this respect, kids are no different. Kids will tell me, *"If my parents, or other people would change, my life would be better."* Who can argue with them about the wants they have? Sometimes parents and others aren't going to change. So who is left to change their thinking, their actions, their feelings? Do the kids **have to change** their thinking, change their actions or change their feelings? No. They can drink, drug, swear, pout, whine, complain, etc. as long as they choose to. We need to understand this with each and every behavior they choose. It is critical for them to see that their choices are attempts to get what they want for themselves. These choices can be good choices or poor choices. As a parent you can be the best manipulator, the best positive reinforcer in the whole wide world and sometimes your kids will just say, *"No, that's not a good idea, I'm not going to do what you want."* In psychology, we have many approaches that deal with trying to change "out there." Behavior modification is based on changing "out there." If I can give you enough reinforcers, as the theory says, you will change. That might be true if we lived in a stimulus-response world. But we don't. It is a world based on meeting our internal psychological needs. When the phone rings you answer it based upon something inside you at the time that directs your choice to pick it up. You have the choice. The stimulation of the phone ringing doesn't direct your choice. You have had the phone ring and you made a choice not to answer it. Right? You have chosen to run a stop sign or stop light. If I think of meeting my needs, you could wave a million dollars in front of my face, you could do anything you could think of, but if I don't want to do it, I may not do it. These tactics may be similar to the little old lady in Minnesota who wanted to bring back "the woodshed days" in an attempt to regain control over "these kids nowadays." The little old lady would view the WhMPA as the savior in robe and sandals. She would add a holiday celebrating WhMPA's. Unfortunately, attempts to gain or regain control may fall upon the deaf ears of kids and create more frustration for the person making the attempt. That is particularly frustrating to people from the "old days" who try to change kids' behaviors today. As you well know, if we as parents just sit around and ventilate our frustrations with parenthood, we will be worn out and depressed or angry. The same goes for our kids. If all they do is ventilate their feelings about their problems, they will end up in the same state of mind. Ventilating feelings does get us talking about our problems but WhMPA's stay stuck in this area, over and over and over.

How does that make you feel?

WhMPA's like to focus on expressing their feelings when problems arise in their lives. They want to let you know how they feel. The problem is that ventilating feelings alone does not and will not solve problems, it just puts them on hold. It allows us time to get the feelings out, but does very little to solve the existing problem. If you notice kids today, many have been trained by the adults around them to do the same. They sit around and simply complain or ventilate.

I have to admit that I was a WhMPA when I first started out in the people helping field. I must have been the king of WhMPA forest, the more I think about it. My first job was in the schools in Austin, Minn. My title was Education and Enforcement Liaison Specialist. Not a bad title for a first job. I was working out of an old vault in the assistant principal's office at the high school as the liaison between the police department, courts and the schools. My responsibilities were to work with tough kids and their parents. These were kids who hated school, hated other kids and especially hated guys like me who represented authority. I set up my office in the way I was taught in school. I created a therapeutic environment with the chairs set properly, the books faced properly on the shelf and, of course, my degree on the wall. It was dark and old, but it was my office. Everything was set for my first student. The call came over the intercom from Margaret, one of the secretaries, that a young lady named Gloria was there to see me. I quickly jumped to my feet, checked out the atmosphere and went out to meet Gloria. I could see that she had a problem just by looking at her. She was teary-eyed and looking down at her shoes. I presented myself in a friendly way by saying *"Hello,"* (I remembered that psychology class section on being empathetic), and escorted her back to the office. Initially I sat comfortably with my arms crossed and legs crossed. Quickly I unfolded my arms and legs because I remembered that that displayed the non-verbal stuff related to being unfriendly and uncaring. I didn't want that. So I sat arms open, legs open, leaning forward and either looked like a catcher or a guy who was ready to deliver a baby! I said, *"Gloria, tell me what I can help you with."* She began to cry. I said, *"Gloria, if you tell me what is going on I know that I can help you."* With that she unleashed a story that included a recent break-up with a boyfriend, failing in school, feeling hated by her friends, regularly using marijuana and alcohol, and fighting and arguing with her parents. To top it off she had repeatedly attempted to take her own life. When she finished she looked up to me and said, *"My friends* said that you could help me, can you?" I sat back in my chair with my mouth open, hands and legs still apart, and after a long silence said, "Gloria, How does that make you feel?" Four years of college and this is what came out. I looked at the wall, saw that degree in Psychology and thought to myself, now I know what the B.S. stands for! Boy was I in trouble. I didn't know what to do, other than say, "How does that make you feel" and that came as a result of my working in an alcohol-drug treatment center while in college. I was like Where Most People Are in wanting to solve this young lady's problems and looking for something "out there" to help me to do it. Boy, was I frustrated! I told Margaret, please, no more students for today.

I know that I can help you

I started to realize from that very first helping relationship that what I was doing was asking an out-of-control person to solve their own problems by just expressing their feelings and changing their actions. To begin with, expressing only your feelings is what many of us call ventilation. That is okay, but what I have found out in my personal and professional life is that the problem is still there. We only spent time talking about how frustrated we were with having such a problem. I spent 45 minutes with Gloria just ventilating and found out that both of us were depressed in the end. Ventilating feelings usually keeps us focused on just one of the components of our behavior—our feelings. Have you ever just expressed feelings about a problem with your spouse, children, your best friend or co-workers?

That is what I was taught in order to help other people with their problems. Get them to identify feelings, circle words from a list on a paper if they have to, then express them openly. That should help them. Well, it didn't help much. I found out that even colleagues in the school building were good at using this technique.

My first tour of the high school was provided by Mr. Lehrke, the assistant principal I worked with. He stood six feet two inches and was an ex-Marine drill sergeant. He paused on the second floor just outside the teachers lounge, pointed to the sign on the door and said, "Stay out of there if you know what's good for you!" I was confused because I wanted to meet the staff as well as grab a pop on my down time. I asked him why I should stay away

and he told me that, "They're nothing but a group of LL boys and girls." "What's LL boys and girls stand for" I asked. Mr. Lehrke said it stood for Lounge Lawyers, people who thought they had all the answers to the school's problems, and that they had their own law firm, Bitch, Piss and Moan! Even though Mr. Lehrke told me not to go in there, I did. Boy, was he right. With certain people you heard it loud and clear. "I only get one pack of dittos, how can I teach?" "The administration needs to change if we can ever teach around here." This story proves the point. Just expressing feelings about problems and issues will not solve those problems. Do you have one of those LL law firms at the place where you work? With certain friends you know?

Knowing that "feelings" work was getting me nowhere. I moved on to the actions component of Gloria's behaviors. Being a good problem solver, I focused on the problems she was having and suggested "problem solving" plans that would help her change what she was doing. Since I had been trained and certified in Reality Therapy as a primary method of problem solving or "giving fishes to hungry people," I decided to help Gloria change what she was doing. In regard to the break-up with her boyfriend I tried what I call "cheerleader therapy" and told her that she was really a pretty girl along with the old story of there being more fish in the sea. This seemed to work, because I saw her smile a little. I used another form of therapy I call band-aid therapy in regard to the fights and arguments that she was having with her parents. I suggested that she sit down with her parents that night and have a pow wow in order to express her feelings. That didn't work either, because she hated being around her parents, let alone talking to them. I then tried what I call bartender therapy with the problem related to her failing in school. I suggested some methods to help her improve in school: raising her hand, asking for a tutor, studying more and doing extra credit work. With the problem related to her lack of friends I suggested that she go to the local YWCA and join the teen youth group. The group would be a great place for her to meet other youth and form the friendships that she was looking for. Regarding the alcohol and other drug problem I suggested to her that she could do some reading in the Big Book of Alcoholics Anonymous, go to some Alcoholics Anonymous meetings and not drink anymore. These all sound like some pretty good plans for Gloria, right? Wrong! They are what we call Z plans on the alphabet scale. I was assuming that Gloria had all the "skills" prior to completing the plans, like the ability to go up to the Y and ask for the youth group, let alone introduce herself to other youth, or know how to have fun and friends when stopping her alcohol and other drug use. What a set up for failure! No wonder I had clients looking at me for years with what I call the "trout look." They would listen to my suggestions with a blank stare and mouths wide open as I suggested these plans of action.

For the alcoholics I worked with, I would suggest that they stop drinking because it was their drinking that was causing their problems, go to their support meetings and continue to read the Big Book. They would stare at me and say something like, *"How am I supposed to have fun on Friday night and who am I going to hang around with?"* I would smile and suggest that they go to more meetings to solve all their problems, and they would return fire with, *"What should I do the other 23 hours of the day?"* With that I might suggest that they might want to check out another meeting. It is common in the alcohol and other drug treatment field to suggest 90 meetings in 90 days. My attempts to treat these people were to change their actions through "forcing" them to do what I wanted them to do. They would talk the talk but not walk the talk. As a result, I saw many of them go back to drinking and drugging. My attempts were very controlling.

Using the best choice at the time

This story of my early attempts to help people does drive home an important point. In dealing with problems a person uses his **best choice at the time**. If we believe this, we need to understand that people like Gloria are making their best choices to solve their problems. We also are making our best choices at the time and so are our kids. By under-

standing this we can choose not to be "fish givers," as the saying goes, but **teachers of better skills** *"so that they can feed themselves for the rest of their lives."* I relied on the skills that I was taught up to that point as ways to solve Gloria's problems. Unfortunately, they were *provided for her* and not *taught to her* so she could solve her own problems throughout her life. If we continue to approach peoples' problems with the idea that we can "fix" them, then we will be approaching our children in the same way. We will be teaching our children indirectly that other people should be relied upon to solve problems for them and that someone or something "out there" with greater power has the answer for them. This fosters dependence when, in fact, we should be teaching independent living skills to our kids.

We need to also understand that many times the behavioral choices that people act out, like drinking, drugging, attempted suiciding and depressing are really the tip of the iceberg, as we look at a problem. What lies underneath the surface, as with an iceberg is critical for us to understand. You will understand in later chapters that behaviors are purposeful and in fact meet needs. Unfortunately, they carry prices with them. You can probably theorize for yourself what was going on underneath Gloria's behaviors, based upon what she said to me. What need was she meeting with her choices? Was it Security? Faith? Worth? Freedom? Belonging? Fun? Knowledge? Health? What needs were being frustrated?

After many years of seeing clients, conducting seminars and listening to people, I have concluded that what people are looking for is a strategy that will help them deal effectively with all problems that they come in contact with. Temporary solutions like cheerleader, bartender and band-aid therapies are not the answer; they, in fact, only prolong frustration.

CHAPTER 7

REGAINING OUR SANITY THROUGH PRODUCTIVE THINKING SKILLS—GOING BEYOND WhMPA

"We cannot always build the future for our youth, but we can build our youth for the future."
Franklin D. Roosevelt

Looking back, I now know that Gloria lacked the "skills" to take effective control of her life and move beyond WhMPA. No wonder she felt so awful. What she really needed was to feel **Secure** in her own ability and skills to deal with her problems, **Faith** in the positive in her life and the opportunity that problems bring to her, a sense of **Worth** in order to feel powerful and in control, to feel **Freedom** in the sense of having choices, to feel **Belonging** with her parents, peers and others, to have **Fun** and enjoyment, to gain **Knowledge** of the avenues to take control of her life and to feel **Health** in the sense of psychological balance. A discussion of the psychological need areas of Security, Faith, Worth, Freedom, Belonging, Fun, Knowledge and Health will follow in later chapters.

The new productive thinking strategy that goes beyond WhMPA includes seven principles:

1. WE NEED TO UNDERSTAND THAT OUR THOUGHTS ABOUT OUR PROBLEMS DIRECT OUR ACTIONS AND OUR FEELINGS.

2. WE NEED TO UNDERSTAND THAT OUR PROBLEMS ARE DEGREES OF DIFFERENCE BETWEEN WHAT WE WANT AND WHAT WE HAVE.

3. WE NEED TO SEPARATE PROBLEMS INTO WHAT WE HAVECONTROL OVER, WHAT WE HAVE INFLUENCE OVER AND WHAT WE HAVE NO CONTROL OVER. WE NEED TO APPLY THE CONCEPTS OF ACKNOWLEDGMENT, ACCEPTANCE, ALLOWING AND ADJUSTMENT TO ALL PROBLEM AREAS.

4. WE NEED TO IDENTIFY ALTERNATIVE THOUGHTS, ACTIONS AND FEELINGS IN THOSE AREAS WHERE WE HAVE CONTROL.

5. WE NEED TO IDENTIFY NEW CHOICES/PATHWAYS THAT WILL FULFILL NEEDS THAT HAVE BEEN BLOCKED OR ARE UNFULFILLED. WE NEED TO WORK ON CREATING A PERCEPTION OF NEED FULFILLING BEHAVIOR TO THOSE AROUND US.

6. WE NEED TO IDENTIFY THE PROCESS STEPS THAT WILL BE REQUIRED TO CLOSE DOWN THE DIFFERENCES.

7. WE NEED TO UNDERSTAND THAT ALL PROBLEMS CAN BE OPPORTUNITIES FOR GROWTH USING THESE STEPS.

The following chapters will present these productive thinking skills for parents and their children. I have led you up to this point in understanding some of the turmoil that parents often experience when raising kids. In the following chapters you will find exercises to incorporate these concepts into your own life along with activities that will aid not only you in saving your sanity but also serve as a resource for you to teach to your children. In order to teach new skills to kids we need to first learn these new productive thinking skills for ourselves. In that way we become the teacher and the model of better choices when the world does not give us or them what we or they want. Pogo, the philosopher, made the classic statement, *"We have met the enemy and they is us."* We, as parents, need to take some of the blame for how our kids end up in life. Are we the enemy? Are we part of the problem? Let's admit it, **kids are going to learn more from what we do than from what we say to them.** If this is true, then **we need to first evaluate ourselves in the areas of thinking,** and see if we are teaching and modeling appropriate skills to our kids to help them develop into responsible, capable adults. Are we teaching them what to do instead of what not to do in problem situations? Are we teaching and modeling that life is a series of problems that can be overcome, if we choose to think first and then act? Are we teaching them the power of self-control? Are we teaching them to rethink instead of react? After all, most of us did not have these strategies down pat before we had our kids and many of us will probably start figuring them out when our kids are about ready to leave home. Sadly enough, that is what I keep hearing from parents. *"Where was this strategy when my kids were growing up?"* *"If I had this type of thinking taught to me at an earlier age, I would not have been such a WhMPA!"* *"If I could only go back and change everything I said and everything I did."* None of us wants to suffer from that fatal disease of "shoulda, coulda, or woulda" after our kids have left the home. We need to focus on what we have control over, from this point forward. You had control over purchasing this book. You also have control over putting this information into your life from this point forward. You cannot change what choices you have already made up to this point.

It is important to understand that parents who have problems in their lives have differences between what they want and what they have. They want something they are not getting. At the present time, they do not have *enough* information or skills on how to think and act in order to close down those differences. I don't mean this in a derogatory way. I just mean that they do not have the necessary skills. When we are frustrated, **we do not have enough information to close down those dif-**

ferences. If we knew of better choices to close down the differences, we would use them. This book is an attempt to provide you with new choices that, with practice, will give you confidence, power, and a sense of control of your own life and as a parent. To help you understand this concept better, let me ask you some questions:

When your kids yell, do you yell back?
When they hit, do you hit back?
When they feel bad, do you feel bad?
When they do something wrong, do you do something immediately to discipline them?
When you want them to behave, do you threaten them with physical discipline?
When they don't do what you want, do you threaten them with consequences?
Do you take away privileges?
Do you send them to their room to think about what they did?
Do you spank?

If so, then join the millions of **people who react to the world around them.** You are reacting to what your kids are doing or not doing because you want something you are not getting. The problem is that you are **allowing yourself to be controlled by outside events, people or the environment.** When your kids or others do not give you what you want, you react. **They then become the controllers of your choices.** You are literally **giving away** your control to outside forces, namely your kids. You will begin to feel like a puppet with strings on several parts of your body—controlled by your children and/or others.

We all react to the world around us in various degrees. Some people react excessively, and as a result, feel a more significant degree of "upsettedness," anger, guilt and hate. Our child says, *"Shut up"* and we say *"Shut up."* They say, *"You're stupid,"* and we parrot back, *"You're stupid, too!"* For every emotion or action they throw at us, we counterattack with one of our own. After all, as parents we have more control than they do, right? We will **allow them** to control our emotions, our thoughts and subsequently our actions.

CHAPTER 8

PRODUCTIVE THINKING SKILL 1
Our thinking directs our actions

"Men are disturbed not by things, but
by the views which they take of them."
Epictetus - Stoic philosopher
from first century A.D.

The familiar cartoon of four people looking at a glass of water provides the backdrop for some of our discussion regarding how thoughts direct actions. It's the same glass of water that both people are looking at, yet one person perceives the glass to be half full and one perceives it to be half empty. The glass is the same size, the **interpretations** are different. No two people have ever read the same book. A teacher might ask a student, *"What was the author saying in the story that was assigned?"* rather than the more appropriate question, *"What was your interpretation of what the author was saying?"* Each person views the story as well as life events differently. People's interpretations of events are as unique as their fingerprints. There are virtually millions of fingerprint categories. There are also millions of interpretations. A persons' perception may be close or tremendously different, which is what makes our role as parents interesting. We think a situation occurred in a certain way and our kids see it in a different way. It is like viewing the event through a looking glass. Like ourselves, they view the same situation differently. William James, an American psychologist, said that *"Genius is little more than the faculty of perceiving in an unhabitual way."* If we want to follow his lead, we will begin to perceive our kids differently. In doing so, we will challenge the way we see things and ourselves as well. We will view the strange as familiar and the familiar as strange. How many times have we said to our kids, *"That's not the way it happened,"* or *"There is no way you were thinking that at the time,"* or the ever popular, *"You don't really think that way, do you?"* How about, *"You can't be feeling that way about the situation."* Are we using wide or narrow interpretations in what we are saying to our kids? Are we allowing them to express their interpretation?

There is a story of a man who was driving along a country road in his brand new car, enjoying not only the new car, but the drive and the scenery. All of a sudden a child stepped from the brush and threw a stone at his car. The man stopped the car, backed up in anger and disgust, and, as you can imagine, was "madder than hell" at this kid. He began to give it to the kid with both barrels when he was stopped by the kid who said, *"I'm sorry about throwing the stone at your car, but I didn't know of any other way to get you to stop. It's my brother, he's in the ditch and he's hurt very bad."* Would your interpretation change? Would you still be "madder than hell?" Would you choose to use different words with the child as a result? There are many times in our parenting that we view the glass as half full, when actually the glass might be half empty. How many times does the child indicate to the parent that he has a different perception or interpretation of a problem? *"You just don't understand, that's not what happened. You weren't even there!"* As an unknown writer wrote, *"I know you believe you understand what you think I said. I am sure you realize that what you heard is not what I meant."*

That is why it is critical for us as parents to **step back and evaluate our interpretations** about:

- ❏ What our kids are saying to us.
- ❏ What they are presently doing.
- ❏ What they have done in a given situation.
- ❏ What our thoughts are regarding our kids and others.

When your child comes home, for example, and informs you of something that the teacher did to them in school and goes on to say that the teacher put them in the hall for talking but they can't figure out why, a WhMPA might go into the school loaded for bear and want to tear into the teacher to find out what happened. The parent gained from his child only their child's perception of the glass.

The other parent, the productive-thinking parent, on the other hand, would take what the child said as one perception of the situation, and practice productive thinking by stepping back and wondering what the other side of the story might be. With the goal of **information-getting** in her mind, the mother would set off to school to **ask questions** of the teacher in order to help form an accurate interpretation of the problem. In this way, the mother would not jump to conclusions, find the teacher guilty at first and innocent later. With enough information, the mother could later question her child. Jumping to a conclusion before you have all the information is a common problem for many people. After all, you and I usually receive information, form an interpretation and then act upon it. That is literally where WhMPA's are. **I am trying to teach you to step back and rethink your information, which takes skill and patience on your part.** If I can go from being a WhMPA to productive thinking, you can, too, and save yourself many headaches. Your interpretation will be critical. Take the time to investigate what you hear and see to make sure you have all the facts before you act.

In many of my presentations, I use a slide that depicts a father and son at the breakfast table. The son is chomping away at his cereal while Dad is reading the paper. The caption above the Dad reads, *"What's this about a serious drug problem at your school?,"* while the son responds, *"Golly no, Dad, you can get all you want!"* This cartoon points out the fact that even with only verbal information, two people can have different interpretations. I would love to guess what the next cartoon might be. If the father perceives the son's comment in a negative way, he will say things like, *"I better never catch you using drugs!,"* followed by a lengthy lecture or sermon on the evils of drugs. If you choose to perceive the situation in a neutral way, you will act in a neutral way. Most likely you will choose to ask questions in a calm, information-getting fashion rather than an accusatory way. You can see that in a simple situation like this the father can think about the event in many different ways, or he can choose to RETHINK by asking more questions about his son's statement. ALLOWING the son to clarify his statement is critical in order to gain a better and more accurate interpretation of the event. Have you been interpreting the world around you in a stereotyped way? Have you allowed others to provide more information to you when an issue comes up in order to clarify your perception? Do you stop people when they say something you disagree with or do you ask them to clarify their interpretation? Can you relate to what has been said so far? Is there room for improvement regarding your interpretations?

I look at our behavior as being made up of three different, separate components. I believe that these three behaviors actually make up our total behavior as human beings. The following picture describes the three components of behavior: **Thoughts, Actions and Feelings.**

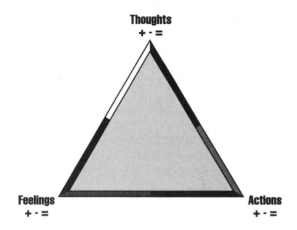

Feelings

Let's start with the feelings component first. Feelings give us constant feedback on how we are doing in terms of getting what we want in our lives. When we want something and we are getting it, we usually feel pretty good. When we want something we are not getting, we usually feel pretty bad. Feelings motivate us to change our behavior when we feel hurt or frustrated. Feelings then cause many of us to make changes in our lives.

Feelings such as anger, sadness, pain, hurt and joy, to name just a few, have the ability to generate a wide variety of responses and actions, both positive and negative. Although we cannot arbitrarily or abruptly change our feelings as simply as we can our actions, we need to understand and accept that we do have control over feeling negative or positive. So do our kids. We need to teach and model that to them at every opportunity. The world doesn't make us feel a certain way. WhMPA's would disagree with this, believing that the world around

them "makes" them feel the way they feel—either positive or negative. As a result they blame the world for the good or bad feelings they experience. Please do not teach your children that others control their feelings and set them up for a lifestyle of blaming.

It's not possible to always feel on top of the world, to lead a 100% "Feeling Good" life all the time. Remember Gloria? She was a good example of a young lady feeling very negative. I tried to get her over to the positive side by getting her to express just how she felt at the time. Remember the results? I was getting depressed too! Expressing feelings will just keep you in the "bitch bag." We all have been there. We have had relationship problems, financial problems, job problems and so on. Just expressing or ventilating our feelings only keeps us focused on our frustrations. Have you ever done this? Have you ever just complained to each other as a couple about the problems you are having at work? At home? With your kids? With each other? Did it solve anything? Did it relieve a little pressure inside? Probably. But it did not solve the problem unless you came up with a new way to think or act about it. We really need to build our skills in all components of our behaviors. We need to focus on whether our thinking is negative or positive. Is it helping us solve the problem or frustration at hand or not? We need to also evaluate whether our actions are helping or not. The more efficient productive thinking and action skills we have, the more alternatives and choices we have, the more control we have, and the more able we are to deal with negative feelings.

This does not mean that we deny the importance of our feelings. In fact, it is probably true that the only thing that is always real to us is how we feel. We may be fooled about who we are, where we are, what we are doing and where we are going, but we can never be fooled about how we feel.

Actions

Actions are what you and I do in our everyday lives in order to get what we want. We drive a car in order to get from point A to point B. We pick up the phone in order to answer it when it rings. We push our facial muscles together in order to frown and open them up in order to smile. We move our lips in order to create sound in the form of words. A simple behavior such as talking can be viewed as both negative and positive by people, depending on the tone we take. The choice in tone is ours to make. The choice to act or not act is ours to make. Actions we choose can be positive or negative. Actions such as hugging, kissing, laughing, touching, to name just a few, are considered to be positive. Of course these are open to interpretation. Some people, for example, like to receive hugs while others feel uncomfortable. Actions such as hitting, screaming, yelling, or physically threatening are usually viewed as negative in nature. If we lined up one hundred people and asked them how they viewed these behaviors, they would probably say that they are negative in nature. But what happens when these behaviors are used as a form of self defense in reaction to fear? Are they always negative? We will learn about and evaluate more behaviors later.

Thinking

In order to feel better and make better choices, we must first begin to evaluate our thinking about ourselves and our choices. Shakespeare stated it correctly when he said, *"There exists nothing good or bad, but thinking makes it so."* That is why thinking is listed on the top part of the triangle. To choose to think differently about the world, including our kids and ourselves, is critical. Choosing to think differently about events and problems is critical if we are to go beyond WhMPA. If we do, we will evaluate our own actions and evaluate how we feel. This is not a simple procedure because we are urged to "Just Do IT" as the commercial for NIKE says. With training in productive thinking, I believe that the results will be worth it. Not only in parenthood, but also in all kinds of life situations.

Our thoughts, too, can have a direct effect on the physiology of our bodies. Our thoughts about an event will trigger our bodies in a physical way. While watching a scary movie, we may become aware that our heart is racing much faster than usual. Dracula or the monster is approaching fast! As much as we try to talk in frightening situations, we can't. We can't because the fearful thoughts in our mind have sent a "speed-up" message to the part of the brain that regulates heartbeat. We feel paralyzed. Physiology can be viewed as the fourth component of behavior, but for now I want to focus on thoughts, feelings and actions.

The important point to remember when looking at the triangle of thoughts, actions and feelings is that our thoughts direct our actions and our feelings. How you choose to think about a problem you are having will direct how you choose to act and how you choose to feel. How you choose to think about another person will direct your actions and your feelings toward that person. Negative thoughts usually generate negative actions and negative feelings. Positive thoughts usually generate positive actions and positive feelings. Neutral thoughts usually generate neutral actions and neutral feelings. Which is best for you? Do you want to feel positive or negative most of the time? Is neutral a better option to consider? When frustrated, which thinking pattern do you think most people choose?

Four thousand years ago a Hindu mystic wrote on a scroll, *"As one's thinking is—such one becomes."* If we think we can, we will. If we think we can't, we won't. If we think negatively, we will act and feel negatively. The only thing standing between us and our capabilities is our perception of who we are and what we are capable of doing. WhMPA's believe that what they see or what they hear determines what they think. WhMPA's do not step back and rethink and evaluate information. The opposite is true for productive thinkers. Productive thinkers believe that what they think determines how they feel and act. Evaluating what you hear and see is important to a productive thinker.

I am reminded of a teacher that I knew in the school where I worked when I first started my professional career. She was a whiney sort of person, always complaining about something. She complained about the system (out there) and her inability to teach because she never had the right materials or the right students. I can't forget the time that I was walking down the hall, noticed her coming the other way and chose to duck into an open classroom in order to avoid her. I was not the only staff member who felt this way. She affected others negatively. She was interpreted by myself and other people as a negative influence.

For a moment, think of me as a positive, friendly, fun kind of person. Think of me as the type of person you would really like to get to know. What will you do? How will you feel? If you meet me, will you move toward me? Will you move away from me? If you think of me as a negative, hostile, critical person, what will you do? How will you feel? Will you move toward me? Will you move away from me? If you are thinking of me as a positive person, you will probably move toward me. If you are thinking of me as a negative person, you will probably move away from me. What causes you to move toward or away from me? Is it what I do? No. **What causes you to move toward or away from me is how you choose to think of me. Your thoughts will direct your actions to move toward or away from another person.** You will respond to me according to what actions or thoughts I choose.

Your response also depends on your value system. Some choices like drugging are viewed by most as poor choices. Some see alcohol and tobacco use as okay but the minute they hear of drugs such as marijuana, LSD or cocaine, they perceive the user in a negative way. They have developed a negative perception of certain drugs. Why? Where did that come from? Who put these on a continuum for them from "good" to "bad?" What a person wears is a personal choice, and one that might cause conflict between parents and kids, for example. Why is this so? Kids can choose one way and parents another. Who makes the value judgment about correct choices? Wouldn't it be less stressful for us to focus on the bigger picture in life? Wouldn't it be better for us to focus on which choices are going to be potentially dangerous or harmful to our kids and let the other choices fall by the wayside? If a kid wears a Rock and Roll T-shirt or attends a concert is he going to die? What about a male wearing an earring? Isn't the bigger picture that we want them to be responsible, make good decisions, develop internal power, control, and choices? We know that these are the key to a successful future life. Wouldn't it be better if we set a structure in our kids' lives that wasn't so constrictive? If they abide by that structure, however they are dressed, however long their hair, so what? Kids who are responsible, kids who make good decisions, kids who have power, control and choices in their life dress in a variety of ways. Some wear earrings, attend rock concerts, have long hair, and rips in their pants. Is hair the issue? Are the earrings or the clothes the issue? Do the choices your kids make direct your choices? Do they control your feelings? Your actions? Why? Why do you allow yourself to think, act or feel bad about these issues? Why do you even make them issues? Do you find your kids resisting your control in these areas? Are they saying things like, "*Get off my back, quit treating me like a kid, let me grow up?*" Who has the problem?

Take a look at the following list of typical situations in a child's life that you may come in contact with. Evaluate your thoughts regarding these situations, and think what actions and what feelings you might generate as a result. Will your thoughts, your actions and your feelings be negative, positive, or neutral?

❑ Other race dating or marriage?
❑ Earrings on males?
❑ Girls wearing excessive make-up?
❑ Dating?
❑ The playing of certain sports?
❑ Hanging out with older kids?
❑ Friends of another race or religion?
❑ Kids with long or multicolored hair or maybe a shaved head?
❑ Kids wearing "out of the norm" clothing?
❑ Heavy metal or rap music?
❑ Unchaperoned parties?
❑ A person who is alcoholic or addicted to drugs?
❑ A person who is a smoker?
❑ A person who is homosexual, bisexual, gay or lesbian?

Do you generate positive, neutral or negative thoughts in these areas? These are just words. What kind of feelings did they generate? What kind of thoughts did *you* generate? Did they bring back some memories related to your childhood? Where did you get your interpretations of these situations or words? From your parents? From other people? From the media? Do your interpretations or thoughts about these situations direct your feelings and your actions? Can you choose to think neutrally about these areas? Would that be hard for you? Can you choose to act neutrally about these areas? Would that be hard for you? Can you choose to feel neutral? What results will occur if you make these choices? Would it be better to get to know the person better before you judge him based on looks or what you may have heard? Would it be better to ask questions of the other person first to clarify your initial perception? **We are not born with prejudices, we develop them.** We are not born thinking negatively about other people or the world around us; we develop that from our experiences. If we can evaluate our own values and question why we think, act or feel the way we do, it will make our life and our life as a parent that much less frustrating. It will take time and contemplation on our part, but the time will be well worth it in the long run. We can also teach and model to our children that people are just people with different races, different jobs, different personalities, and other differences. These differences do not have to control our lives. We spend needless time and energy in responding negatively to differences. Evaluate your responses for yourself. Widen your lenses.

In my seminars, I have the members describe to others what makes them approachable and what makes them unapproachable in their day-to-day life with their kids. It is amazing how perceptive they are, if they put themselves in the role of their children and honestly answer the question *"What do my kids think of me?" "Do they think of me as approachable?" "Do I give them permission to express their thoughts? Their feelings?" "Do my kids perceive me as need fulfilling? Need reducing?"* These questions give parents valuable information in evaluating their kids' responses to them. Those thoughts motivate kids to move toward you or away from you as a parent. This kind of evaluation can help parents decide what they can do to change their kids' reactions and how they can perceive more positively than they presently are. How about yourself? What actions do you choose to use that just "irritate the hell out of your kids?" Are you willing to ask your kids or your spouse what actions could be on this list? Would you accept what they provide you without being defensive about it? If you could, you would be setting up an atmosphere where it is permissible for family members to talk about their feelings regarding each other in a constructive, non-critical, informative fashion. *"Mom, when you tell me to do my homework, you yell at me in a negative, critical tone and that irritates me." "Dad, you are always on my back about the clothes I wear or the style of my hair—what's the big deal about these anyway?"* The WhMPA would say, *"Don't you talk to me like that, I'm your Mother or I'm your Father, I know what's right for you; now get going and do what I say!"* The productive-thinking parent would take in the information from the child, ask for clarification and evaluate it. If they agree with the perception, they would make a conscious effort to change their actions.

We set the tone of our children's environment

Picture an elementary school. Picture the outside, then the inside. What you will probably find is a school with many kids and much energy. What

you will also find is a school where you have to duck your head while walking through the halls. Why? Because hanging from the ceiling is the art work of almost every kid in the school. Tied with a string is everything from paintings to rockets made of paper, animals, cars, etc. You will see and feel an environment that gives the kids PERMISSION to express their thoughts, their actions and their feelings not only in an artistic way, but in other ways also. This environment influences the kids in such a positive way. You will see the teachers giving the kids high fives, pats on the back, hugs and smiles as they come and go from the building. My kids went to Griffith Thomas Elementary School in Dublin, Ohio during the elementary years. What an environment! It was not the kids as much as the staff, from Mr. Staffilino, the principal, to the secretaries, the janitors, and of course the teaching staff and their associates. They made education come alive for the kids because they were alive with energy! Alive with creativity. Kids will follow the lead set by adults and a positive environment produces positive people while a negative environment produces negative people. When I teach a course at The Ohio State University on effective classroom discipline, I constantly talk about building a relationship first with the kids and not building discipline first. Setting the tone in what you say and what you do in the areas of care, empathy, friendship, and so on goes a long way with kids. Yet I always have some U-boat-commander-turned-educator in the class telling me that this won't work! While he is telling me this, he is frowning and his tone of voice denotes a negative I-give-up-attitude. I would give them a million dollars if they could prove to me that this attitude doesn't rub off on the kids in a day-to-day contact with them. Demonstrating friendship does not take money. Even if you don't have the classroom materials or if the levy failed, you are the keeper of empathy, caring, tone of voice and friendship.

The same can be said for the home environment where parents take the lead and set the tone. As mentioned before, many people grew up in families where the home environment was positive, while just as many grew up in families where the home environment was negative. But you and I can control the environment in our own homes. This is not the responsibility of our kids. We are the adults and we control the tone of the home environment. Our kids will receive permission from us to vary our structure as we allow them to. We may set out with a good plan for a positive tone and be-cause of a variety of issues, find ourselves sur-rounded by an environment that is negative, criti-cal, hostile or all of these.

Over the years many kids have said to me, "Why even try?" "They won't listen anyway." "There is no use in even talking to them." "They are always screaming, fighting, and arguing." "Our home environ-ment is so negative." "I hate going home, that's why I hang out with my friends so much." Our task is to cre-ate an environment that will give kids the motiva-tion and permission to approach us with anything they want. Our task is to evaluate our home envi-ronment and take an inventory of what makes it approachable. Ask your kids for help in evaluat-ing this. If you let them know that you are serious about their comments and that you want to make necessary changes, they will provide you with com-ments. Just by doing this, you will be sending out a message that you are open to discussing any issue and see it as important to the family. When the ball is in your court, will you evaluate what was said? Will you choose to improve your environment? Will you choose to improve your relationship with your kids? How about with others you live and work with? Could you take the same risk with them?

Earl Nightingale said, "We become what we think about most of the time." What do your kids think about most of the time? Is it positive or nega-tive? What do they think about when it comes to you? When it comes to your home environment? When it comes to their future? When it comes to life in general? Evaluation of what we do to set up our home environment is our first step in creating a better relationship with our children. It is an area that we have total control over. We need to look at ourselves first before we look to our kids for change. Sure, kids have areas that need to change also, but why wait for them to change? Why spend so much energy in trying to change them? Start with yourself first. Start with evaluating yourself and what you say or do to create a positive or a negative environment. How many times does your child hear the following messages?

"How come you never?"
"Not now. I don't have time."
"Shut up!"
"Where were you when the brains were passed out?"
"You never listen."
"You're so lazy."
"You're such a pig."

"Why can't you ever…?"
"Is that the best you can do?"
"You've been one problem after another all your life."
"I will never trust you again."
"You will never amount to anything in life."
"You are so stupid. How stupid can you get?"
"You will be the death of me yet."
"You don't know anything."
"Don't you have any sense at all?"
"Nothing is ever good enough for you."
"I can talk to you until I'm blue in the face and it never does any good."
"Can't you do anything right?"
"I brought you in this world, I will take you out."
"Can't you get it through your thick head?"
"When will you ever learn?"
"Nothing I ever say makes a difference with you. It just goes in one ear and out the other."

Have you said any of these to your kids? Did you hear any of these when you were growing up? In his lectures, Dr. William Glasser has stated many times that "Children find in the eyes of their parents the mirrors which they define themselves with in the re-lationship. Fill them with nothing, they become noth-ing. They have a tremendous ability to live down to the lowest expectations in any environment." If you set low expectation, they will set their sights at that level. If you set high expectations or reasonable ex-pectations, they will strive for those. The choice is yours. When they hear negative messages at home, kids' feelings and actions are bound to be negatively influenced. Children learn to program themselves from the messages they receive from others. Children are not born with attitudes about themselves. They enter the world clean and fresh, without any pre-conceived notions of the world around them. They are hungry for information. Their attitudes about themselves develop from the experiences they have, including the messages they receive from parents and others. The attitudes they develop about others and events in the world come from what they receive in the form of messages from us. Who has control over those messages? Who has control over providing information to them? We do. Look over the list of statements. **These statements are made only when we are frustrated with our kids about something that we are not getting.** Everything you do or say to your kids, in-tentionally or not, will have an effect on the three components of their behavior. It will affect their thinking about themselves, about the world around them, including you; it will affect how they choose to act in their own life, and it will obviously affect their feelings about themselves and the world around them. Did messages like the above affect your thoughts, your actions and your feelings when you were growing up?

How about changing some of our messages and sending these to our kids:

"I love you."

"You're a winner."

"Just let me know if I can help."

"The sky is the limit for you."

"You're going somewhere in life"

"Whatever the problem, you will be able to handle it."

"You're really making responsible decisions for yourself."

"You must feel real good about the choices you're making."

"You are not a bad kid; you are just making poor choices."

"You really take care of yourself."

"We can always count on you."

"You really are a pleasure to be around."

"I love it when you're so positive about everything."

"It's great to hear you singing around the house."

"I can tell that you are going to be very successful in life."

"Always remember that whatever you choose to do in life is your choice."

"It's great having a daughter like you."

"You're the best."

How we interpret events around us

Your feelings result entirely from the way you interpret events. Your anger, sadness, depression, loneliness, calmness, love, joy or other feelings are directed by how you **choose** to perceive an event. Of course our thoughts, our feelings and our actions are **influenced** by external events such as the weather, our kids, our spouse, our jobs, the government. Our physical make-up, intellectual ability, disease, handicapping conditions, past experiences in our childhood, last week, and yesterday also influence these thoughts, feelings and actions. Notice I chose to use the word **influence** rather than control. If we truly believe that external events

direct our behaviors, then we would be acting essentially like machines that have no ability to choose.

Your feelings derive from your interpretations of events; they are the result of your thinking—positive or negative. If you start with your thinking, you can analyze your interpretations. Your actions result from your interpretations. Developing productive thinking skills to view the world and ourselves in a different way is important. Our interpretations direct our actions and our subsequent feelings. Not all feelings are positive, of course, and it is appropriate and necessary to express feelings like sadness, depression, anger or hurt. The loss of a friend, the death of a loved one, the loss of a job, the yelling match with a child leaves most people with intense feelings. To express your feelings is to be human. The expression varies from person to person. Losing a spouse will generate a wealth of emotion. Losing a job may do the same. **The key question is how long you continue to talk about, display, or express these feelings about the event and to what degree you choose to do so?** Do you know people who continue to express feelings about something that happened quite some time ago? Some people continue to talk about the "raw deal" they got from their old employer or boss, about their spouse who separated or divorced them, or about the death of a loved one. Does it get a little old listening to them expressing these old feelings over and over? What are the potential prices or consequences you will pay for choosing to stay at just a feeling level? Will some people move towards you? Will some people move away from you? Will expressing your feelings move you closer toward solving your problem? If you just ventilate your feelings, how will that get you what you want? Do your children copy your behavior? Where did they learn it from? How can you influence them to go beyond WhMPA?

Evaluating our present thoughts, actions and feelings

The first step in taking more effective control in your life as a parent is to evaluate your thoughts, actions and feelings. Hopefully, you will be able to ask yourself personal value judgment questions about your present parenting such as, *"Is my thinking about my children affecting how I deal with them? Are thinking these thoughts going to help me as a par-*

ent or hurt me as a parent? Am I an effective model of choices to my kids? Am I feeling the way I want to feel as a parent? Is what I'm presently doing to solve my problems with my kids helping me develop responsible, healthy kids?" Change does not take place until "we" realize that what we are presently thinking and/or doing is not working enough. Challenging your present thinking about yourself and the world around you is a big step. It goes beyond WhMPA. WhMPA's evaluate others and the outside world first, not themselves. Answering these questions honestly will create the necessary motivation to look for better choices to close down those differences between what we presently have as a parent. By asking these questions, you will have started the strategy of change in the productive thinking process.

Evaluate yourself constantly. Ask yourself, "How do I choose to think today? How am I going to think about my kids today? Am I choosing to think negatively? Are my thoughts directing what I do? Do they affect how I feel? Are my actions negative? Do they affect my feelings and my thinking? Are my thoughts and actions working well enough to get me what I want in life? How am I choosing to think about others I live with or work with today? Are my thoughts positive, negative or neutral? Are these thoughts helping me enough?" The key word is enough. Enough to bring you what you want? If not, then you will take the next step into the productive thinking strategy. Once you get this strategy down intellectually, you can spend the rest of your life practicing it. You may say, "The rest of my life! I don't have that much time!" WhMPA's think that way. WhMPA's want quick results. Productive thinkers take one day at a time. Productive thinkers look at this as a strategy to practice first, and then to teach and model to others. It will take time. It took time to develop WhMPA thinking also. Productive thinkers think in a step-by-step process.

The A-B-C's of problems

Remember the statement made earlier? **The only people without problems are dead?** Are there certain problems of parenthood that are pushing you over the edge of sanity? Are you feeling down when hassles arise in your life? Are you using some of the negative thoughts listed previously? Have you paid prices for thinking these negative thoughts? Have you paid prices for negative actions

with your kids or with others? How have you solved your problems in the past? Is there a simple way to teach and model problem solving to others? We need to understand that there are basically two types of problems: emotional and practical. These are the two types of problems that our kids come across also. Emotional problems result from self-defeating feelings such as angering, depressing, worrying, fearing, and so on. We want something we are not getting, and we feel pain, sadness, depression and frustration. We may want love and caring from others and we are not getting it, resulting in negative feelings. These feelings tend to be a problem for the person experiencing them because they tend to minimize happiness and maximize personal pain. We all prefer happiness over pain. Negative feelings interfere with thinking productively and clearly, and they also affect the way you behave. Practical problems, on the other hand, are merely situations that you wish to change or solve. We want our car to start when it won't. We want the door to open and it doesn't. You may or may not have emotional problems in addition to your practical problems. The problem-solving form that will be discussed later is appropriate to help solve both emotional and practical problems.

The following model attempts to explain how we come to feel and act the way we do. You can see the connection with the previous triangle of thoughts, actions and feelings. This model was developed by Albert Ellis, one of the foremost cognitive-behavioral therapists in the world. Ellis once said, "I have long been convinced that people become and remain emotionally disturbed largely because they do not clearly define what their 'disturbance' is and what they can do to minimize it." The model uses a simple ABC framework in order to educate us as to how we come to feel and act the way we do. It can help us understand parenthood and a technique to share with our kids in a simple manner. It follows from the idea that our thoughts direct our actions and our feelings in a positive, negative or neutral way.

A ———————— B ———————— C

A   stands for an activating event or situation that has already happened, is presently happening, or hasn't yet happened but might.
B   stands for a belief or self-talk we have about a situation.
C   stands for the resulting emotions we

experience and the behaviors we choose. Productive thinkers believe that when something is happening at point **A** and you have a feeling and/or behavior at point **C**, it isn't the situation at point **A** that creates **C**. It is what you tell yourself at **B** that causes the feelings and behaviors at point **C**.

Productive thinking

B (Beliefs) about A (Events) creates C (Feelings)

The old saying that sticks and stones may break your bones and directly cause you physical pain might be true, but names, words, the environment and events in it do not hurt you emotionally. Does this make sense to you?

WhMPA's believe the opposite is true. WhMPA's believe that **A** causes **C**. WhMPA's believe that it is the event that caused them to feel the way they are feeling.

WhMPA belief system

A (Events) cause B (beliefs) and C (Feelings)

Contrary to popular belief, the only time that **A** causes **C** is when it is related to physical pain. If I take a hammer and hit you in the head with it, you will experience pain. If you fall off your bike, falling off the bike caused pain. The hammer or the fall (**A**) did cause the pain (**C**) and probable headache as a result. If a bee stings you resulting in pain, the bee represents (**A**) the event and the pain represents (**C**) the feelings. **But ninety-eight percent of the problems we experience in life are going to be emotional problems. The plain and simple fact is that you're not going to die when tackling the majority of problems you come across in parenthood.** You may think you will, but you won't. Think of problems as degrees of frustration related to the difference between what you want and what you have. In this way you are going beyond what WhMPA's think and beginning to view problems through a different set of lenses. You will start to laugh at the "old way" of viewing people and problems that you carried with you before. You are not going to die if your kids wear funky clothes or earrings, get pregnant, skip school, fail a class, receive poor grades, or do not make the team. You are not going to die if your kids get involved with tobacco, alcohol or other drugs, or date a person of another race. You may think that it is the "end of the world," but trust me, it is not. **These problems are the result of how you choose to think about the A's or events, that happened or could happen.** The framework again looks like this:

A - The situation occurs
B - You tell yourself something about **A**; you evaluate **A**
C - You feel something and usually do something

Three examples of the use of this framework are:

Example #1
A - Tom, a nine year-old boy, strikes out in a league baseball game.
B - *"I should have hit the ball; boy, I am really stupid; I just can't hit; I'm just a crummy player and I'll never get any better: this game really stinks."*
C - Tom feels depressed and sits around the dugout and mopes.

Example #2
A - Jim, a ten year-old boy, strikes out in the same game that Tom is playing in.
B - *"That pitcher should have pitched me a better one; that umpire is blind—that second ball was two miles high; I can't stand it when people are unfair to me."*
C - Jim feels angry and throws the bat and screams at the umpire after striking out, *"This game really stinks."*

Example #3
A - Bob, a ten year-old boy, strikes out, swinging at a third strike.
B - *"It's frustrating not getting a hit, but it's not the end of the world, unless I let it be; I did the best I could."*
C - Bob may feel disappointed, but doesn't believe he's a failure.

These three examples are provided to show you how the same event (**A**) can generate three different types of consequences (**C's**). The beliefs (**B's**) that caused uncomfortable, non-productive feelings at **C** in the first two examples are termed irrational beliefs. Let's look at a parent's belief system in the same set of circumstances.

Example #1

A - Tom, a nine year-old boy, strikes out in a little league baseball game.

B - *"He should have hit the ball; boy, he's really awful; he can't hit the broad side of a barn; he's just a crummy player, and he will never get any better."*

C- Tom feels depressed, angry and embarrassed.

Example #2

A - Jim, a ten year-old boy, strikes out in the same game.

B - *"That umpire is blind—that second ball was two miles high; coaches are terrible, they just set our kids up to swing at everything."*

C - Jim feels angry, and screams at the umpire, *"You really stink."*

Example #3

A - Bob, a ten year-old boy, strikes out while swinging at a third strike.

B - *"Well, he did the best he could; you can't hit all the time; I'll try to help Bob figure what he could do differently next time to get a hit." "It's frustrating, but it's not the end of the world, unless Bob or I let it be."*

C - Bob may feel disappointed, but to a lesser degree.

If you want to have some fun and at the same time learn about the WhMPA's in life, go to a little league sport of any type. Keep your mouth shut and your ears open, and you will know within moments who the WhMPA's are. The events of the game control their feelings. As a WhMPA would, they react negatively to every event that is not what they want it to be. You will also see at the game those parents who choose to view the game differently. They see that the coach is using his best choice at the time to substitute players or use certain plays, the referee is using his best choice, and so are the players on the field. A great movie portraying a WhMPA coach and a productive thinking coach is Disney's "The Mighty Ducks." It's a classic about a youth hockey team with Emilio Estevez as a WhMPA who, during the movie, turns to productive thinking and realizes the value of being a different kind of coach, not only in the short run, but in life. It is great!

Albert Ellis's rational emotive therapy techniques help us and our children analyze and connect thoughts and language with our emotions. It

is a simple process. Emotions stem not from external events, as children and many adults believe, but from a system of internal beliefs and ideas about those events. Our effort is to change unreasonable and irrational beliefs to thoughts that are more realistic and more reasonable, resulting in more positive feelings about ourselves, the world around us and other people, like our children. Sure, there are going to be times when it's not possible to get what we want, but we can at least choose to feel good about ourselves. The goal using this framework is to teach our children the thinking skills that will enable them to have an okay day in spite of what the world serves up to them. Some indicators of irrational and rational beliefs are that:

Irrational beliefs
❑ Do not stem from reality.
❑ Are not supported by evidence.
❑ Do not help you get what you want.
❑ Lead to inappropriate feelings (anger, depression, worry, fear, and guilt).
❑ Are extreme exaggerations of an event (awful, terrible, horrible).
❑ Are demands placed on oneself, others, or the world (shoulds, oughts, musts).

Rational beliefs
❑ Follow objective reality.
❑ Are supported by evidence.
❑ Lead to appropriate, helpful feelings (disappointment, frustration, sadness, concern, etc.).
❑ Are stated as preferences or desires.

Some examples of irrational parental thinking are:
"If my daughter uses drugs, I just know I will die."
"My son has a negative attitude and is spending time in his room alone just to irritate me."
"If my son goes to that party I know he will drink."
"If you don't study, you will flunk your test."

These can be irrational beliefs because there is **no evidence** to support them. There is such a thing as adolescent behavior. In fact I produced a popular cassette tape entitled "A Bad Case of Adolescence or Drug Abuse" to point out that many times, people will jump to conclusions regarding behaviors. Here are some more to consider.

"If my child does not play on the team this year

he will just get into trouble."
"My son will just waste his savings account money if we give him control of it."
"My son is going to be asking for more money later on if we give it to him now."
"If my daughter wears make-up, she will be considered sexually loose."
"If my daughter wears a bikini, she will be viewed as lustful and wanting to have sex."
"If my son hangs around with other kids who smoke, he will smoke."
"My child's friends are not responsible, so my child will be irresponsible."
"If he does not go to college, he will not make anything of his life."

These are irrational beliefs based on future events that cannot be predicted with any accuracy. Think about those beliefs regarding a kids' money. How is a kid supposed to learn the value of money, the responsibility of saving, the decision-making skills about spending money if he is not in control of his money? Does this occur only after he turns eighteen? Who teaches him this skill? If he comes back to you after his money is gone, don't give him anymore and tell him he owns the problem. If kids want responsibility, decision-making opportunities, power, control and choices, give that to them.

Understanding our self-talk

Self-talk will either build up or tear down a person's perception of himself as being capable or not of taking effective control of his own life. Remember all of those negative statements made to kids earlier? Those kinds of statements obviously tear down a child's perception of himself. Statements made by parents, teachers, friends, enemies and others will influence our beliefs about our power to control our own lives. Our interpretations are critical. Without teaching positive or neutral self talk, we allow our kids to fall prey to the world of negative thinking. That, in turn, creates the negative actions and negative feelings that are so common. Talk to your kids about the power of self-talk, and how our beliefs mold our views of ourselves and others. Talk to your kids about evaluating their thinking first when they are frustrated. Talk to them about the tremendous amount of power they will have if they choose to be thinkers rather than reactors. Ask them the same value-laden questions I used in the previous chapter to generate discus-

sion on this. Questions such as, *"Is thinking this way helping you to solve your problem?" "Is keeping those thoughts in your head helping you enough?" "If you continue to think like that, where will it get you?" "How long are you going to choose to think about what has already happened in this way?"* **These are the velvet hammer questions.** They thump you in the head and tell you to "get going, get off the pot, pick yourself up by the bootstraps, keep plugging along." Teach your children, or for that matter anyone you come in contact with, that thinking determines actions. Give them examples of how negative thinking in certain situations has kept you thinking, feeling and acting in a negative manner. Share with them the poor choices you have made in your thinking. They will not only see that it is human to think in negative ways about events, because we all do, but that, more importantly, it is not necessary to stay at that point. It gets us nowhere, fast. It is like putting the car in neutral and gunning the motor. Much energy is wasted without any movement. Teach them that our best friend is inside our head and that our worst enemy is inside our head, depending on how we choose to think.

It's important to address the beliefs that encourage unhealthy communications with others. Listed below are some of the irrational beliefs that can get in the way of people taking effective control of their lives:

- ❏ It's awful if others don't like me.
- ❏ The world should be equitable.
- ❏ Bad people must be punished.
- ❏ It's awful to make mistakes.
- ❏ It's awful to lose.

These beliefs can easily get in the way of meaningful relationships, and create bad feelings and poor choices. Which ones have you used? How about your kids—which ones have they used? The way we talk to ourselves significantly relates to how we feel and what we do. Notice that the irrational beliefs listed above contain absolutes in their statements. Notice the MUSTS, SHOULDS, OUGHTS AND AWFULS. This kind of self-talk, if we truly believe it, puts us in a sort of box, limiting our choices for how to feel and think. If we truly believe that it is AWFUL if others don't like us, then it is much more likely that we will make choices such as:

- ❏ Feeling and acting depressed if others don't approve of something that we did or didn't do.
- ❏ Feeling guilty because if others don't love

us or approve of us we must be doing something wrong.

These sure sound like WhMPA choices, don't they? How we think has an enormous impact on how we feel and what we end up doing. How our children choose to think has the same effect on their actions and feelings. Beliefs are the windows of perception through which we mentally view the world and everything in it. Beliefs are our ideas about how the world is or should be and how we want others in the world, including our own children, to be. In either case, these beliefs are powerful motivators of our actions and our feelings. In order for us to live effectively with others then, it is important to identify and weed out the irrational MUSTS, SHOULDS, OUGHTS AND AWFULS that run around in our heads. In rational emotive therapy, they call these irrational beliefs awfulizing, musterbizing, should've, could've, would've and can't-stand-it-itus. Once we have identified the irrational belief, the next step is to question the belief or put it on trial by questioning and disputing. Here are some possible questions you could ask yourself or your kids if you or they believe that it is AWFUL to not get love or approval **from others**:

❏ Why MUST I be loved by everyone?
❏ Is it possible for everyone to approve of me for everything that I do?
❏ Where is it written that everyone has to or will approve of me?
❏ What's the worst thing that can happen if others don't like me?
❏ Whose problem is it if others believe differently than I do?

The idea here is obviously for you to **step back** for a moment and reflect on just what it is that you are telling yourself and to see if it makes sense or if it's nonsense. *Are these thoughts productive for you? Are they helping you enough? Why is it awful? Is this the worst thing that can happen? Why can't you stand it? Are you in fact standing it now even though you say you can't? Where is the evidence that you must always get what you want? Will condemning this person make the situation better?* Another way is to examine these beliefs by stepping back and checking, or replaying the problem, as with a video camera. In this way you replay exactly what happened, who said what, where, and so on. You will be able to record it on tape and have the ability to push the rewind button, the play button and the pause button as you review the event in question. For some

of us, writing a scenario down on paper works better. It may take time, but getting information about the whole story will help you to look for the irrational beliefs or self-talk. It will save you from embarrassing reactions. As parents, it is important to teach your kids an emotional problem-solving framework such as this. Helping your kids to identify some of the self-talk that is interfering with their happiness and wellness will go a long way to establishing a mature, self-responsible adult. Stepping back and asking questions like, *"What was said?" "What was the meaning behind what was said?" "What are the various interpretations of what has happened?" "How could you choose to think about this?" "How could you choose to act about what has already happened?" "How could you choose to feel about what has happened or what has been said?"* or *"How long do you want to keep these thoughts, actions, or feelings?"* The best way to teach is to model. A good modeling technique in problem situations is to talk about and analyze the thoughts that led to the resulting events and feelings. Use yourself as an example. Use examples of what your kids have already been involved in. Using past events to teach can be beneficial because they are less painful or emotional and allow for clearer, more objective thinking. You won't be preaching or lecturing but teaching with a moderate or neutral tone of voice.

Choosing to think the way we want

Research indicates that over 12,000 thoughts enter our brain each day. If you can accept responsibility for how you interpret, then you have the opportunity to be more positive than negative in your outlook toward yourself and others. You can also develop a positive or at least hopeful world view that you can model and present to your children. As parents in the process of teaching our kids to be healthy, **we must provide them with opportunities to accept responsibility for what they choose to think, feel and do.** Think of life as a series of experiences in which we are involved. As we are involved with our experiences, we have perceptions and evaluations called thoughts that form into beliefs and finally lead to **choices** in our behavior. These beliefs about ourselves, others and the world are formed from the time that we can begin to think and are molded by our parents, teachers, friends, religious teachings, extended family members, and so on. Just as I stated earlier, we are not born prejudiced; we become so through our experiences and teachings. One of the most important lessons, then, for children to learn is the importance of taking total personal responsibility for their inner life, their thinking, and, as a result, their actions and their feelings.

Because everyone has the potential to look better, to feel better and to be more successful, it is important to teach our kids from a young age that it is not others **(A)** or outside events that make them feel the way they do or that force them to make choices. Rather, it is the person himself who chooses how to think, and how to feel and act. This is difficult to teach to people. Cognitively they may understand it, but when you tell someone that he has control over feeling positive, negative or neutral when something happens in his life, you come into conflict—conflict with previous messages heard from parents, from others, from the media, or messages that inform us day after day that the "world around us" controls our thoughts, actions or feelings. These messages are what I am trying to dispel, or at the very least, have you question. Again, this is accomplished by self-talk.

Now that some examples have been offered and some discriminations have been made between what is rational versus irrational in our self-talk, let's get down to the business of how we teach our kids to problem-solve in a productive and effective manner. The first step is to identify those irrational beliefs that create the upset feeling, be it fear, anger, depression or anxiety. The second step is to dispute or challenge the irrational belief through questioning, modeling, role-playing or storytelling. Dr. Virginia Waters, a cognitive-behavior therapist, associated with the Institute for Rational Emotive Therapy, identifies some common irrational beliefs she has noted in working with children and adolescents. Her key points are summarized below:

1. It's awful if others don't like me.

   Believing that one <u>must</u> be accepted by significant others is irrational for several reasons:

   a. <u>Demanding</u> that you be approved by all those whose approval you would like to have sets up a perfectionistic, unattainable goal. What happens when that one out of a hundred doesn't approve of you? You got it—bummer.

   b. You will have to keep worrying about whether or not the people you are trying to win approval from are approving of you or not.

   c. As a result you will give up many of your own wants and preferences and become considerably less self-directing.

   Teach that everybody does not have to like you.

2. I shouldn't make mistakes, especially social mistakes.

   a. No human being can be perfectly competent and masterful at everything.

   b. To <u>demand</u> that one <u>must</u> succeed is to make oneself prey to anxiety and feelings of personal worthlessness.

   c. Compulsive strivings for personal perfection or accomplishment usually result in needless stress and force one's self beyond one's physical or intellectual limitations.

   d. Over-concern with achievement often results in acquiring enormous fear of taking chances, of making mistakes and of failing at certain tasks—all of which tend to sabotage the very achievement for which one is striving.

   Teach that it is okay to make mistakes.

3. Everything should go my way; I should always get what I want.

   a. It would be nice if things were different from the way they are, but, the fact that it would be nice if this were so hardly makes it so.

   b. Getting extremely upset over a problem will rarely, if ever, make the problem change.

   c. It is not catastrophic when things don't go your way—inconvenient, maybe, but not catastrophic.

   Teach that you can't always get what you want; but you can get your needs met.

4. Things should come easily to me.

   a. How can you be good at everything you do?

   b. Everybody has strengths and weaknesses.

   c. Building your skills will increase your chances at success.

   Teach that life is filled with frustration and that learning to rethink about those frustrations is critical.

5. The world should be fair and just.

   a. Human unhappiness is caused by one's thoughts, appraisals, evaluations, or perceptions of events.

   b. Life isn't always fair and just.

   Teach that they can handle life's problems when things go wrong.

6. I shouldn't show my feelings.

   a. Showing your feelings is not a sign of weakness.

   b. Showing feelings is a part of life; wearing

them for an extended period of time is the problem.

Teach that feelings motivate a person to rethink the problems he is experiencing.

7. It's my parents' fault that I'm so miserable.

a. Blaming others for your feelings will get you nowhere.

b. How long are you going to use this as an excuse?

Teach that you are responsible for your happiness and your unhappiness.

8. There's only one right answer.

a. There are two sides to a pancake, two sides to a question, and two sides to a problem.

b. If life was so easy, we would not have any problems.

Teach that evaluating our perceptions about our problems is important in order to begin a productive thinking process towards problem resolution.

9. I must win; it's awful to lose.

a. Even the best of the best lose.

b. It's disappointing, but not awful.

Teach that life is a series of process steps toward an outcome.

10. I shouldn't have to wait for anything.

a. Stand in line and wait your turn.

b. Patience is a gift.

Teach that you can be flexible when problems arise.

Do you use some of these irrational beliefs with your children? Which ones are the most common in your house? Can you use some of the comments listed under the beliefs the next time there is a problem? Can you present your kids with a replay of what they are saying to themselves? Can you have them challenge those beliefs? Use the words control, influence, no control, and choices when doing so.

Parents' common irrational beliefs include:

❏ It would be awful if my children didn't like me.

❏ I can't stand it if others criticize my parenting.

❏ I'm totally responsible for everything my children do and if they behave obnoxiously or make poor choices, I must feel awful.

❏ I must be a perfect parent and always know the right thing to do in every situation.

❏ My children should always do what I want them to.

❏ If my child has a problem, then I have to feel terrible too.

❏ My children shouldn't disagree with me because I'm the parent.

❏ My children make me angry, depressed or anxious.

❏ If my children don't turn out the way I think they should, then I am a failure.

❏ Parenting should be fun all the time.

Can you relate to any of these beliefs? Have you held any of them in your brain and what are the prices for holding on to them? As you can see, the irrational beliefs that both children and their parents have are exaggerated demands or extreme evaluations of reality. In order to show how an irrational belief may be disputed in the context of a family meeting situation, let's go back to the baseball example. First, I will again present the **ABC's** of the problem, but this time will introduce the letter **D**, which will stand for DISPUTING the irrational beliefs. As Sherlock Homes said to the ever-bumbling Watson: *"It is a capital mistake to theorize before you have all the evidence. It biases the judgment."*

A - Tom, a nine year-old boy, strikes out in a little league baseball game.

B - *"I should have hit the ball; boy, I must really be stupid; I just can't hit; I'm just a crummy player and I'll never get any better."*

C - Tom feels depressed.

D - Why SHOULD you have hit the ball, Tom? I can understand you very much WANTING to hit it, but by saying you SHOULD have hit it, aren't you leaving yourself with no options as far as your feelings go? Does it make sense that striking out once means that you'll NEVER hit the ball? How can striking out once make you totally stupid? Are you bad in everything that you do? Can you find proof that striking out makes you bad or worthless?

This is a very useful way for parents to teach their children emotional problem solving skills. **By creating a dialogue through questioning, new thinking patterns about an event have a chance to emerge.** With this technique, you are teaching responsibility for emotions and behavior, and laying the groundwork for a solid foundation in effective problem solving that can be used throughout your lifetime. A note here: This technique works best with kids eight years old and older. At this age a child is able to use abstract reasoning, which is required to effectively solve problems using the model demonstrated. It's not that you can't use the model with younger kids, it's just that it will be quite a bit easier for the older kids to understand. Problem solving can be used with kids younger than eight but will take more patience and understanding. Using it with younger kids or cognitively deficient kids requires that you continue more slowly, repeating when necessary, asking them questions to see if they truly understand, and having them repeat back to you, using their language, to see if they do.

Ninety-eight percent of all problems in life will not result in death

Since ninety-eight percent of all problems in life are not fatal, we need to teach and model a framework to our kids so they can easily debate their problems in a productive way. My brother Brent is one of the Fellows with the Institute for Rational Emotive Therapy. As a clinical psychologist, he uses RET in his practice. Let's take a look at the steps that Brent uses successfully with children, adolescent clients and parents, one you may want to consider using when you have problem-solving meetings with your own children.

Step 1   EVALUATE UPSET FEELINGS

    C- Describe the upset feelings your child had in regard to the situation (depression-scared-angry-upset, etc.). Have your child answer:

    a) "I feel_____."

    b) Where do I feel this way?_____
Examples include: at school, during a game, at lunch time in the cafeteria, with friends in the hallway before school.

    c) What did you do when you felt this way?_____
Examples include: cried, hit, kicked, swore, stayed in my room

Step 2   ASSESSING THE EVENT

    A- Have your child describe the situation that he feels made him upset _____
Examples include: *"She hit me." "He called me a name." "I struck out" "I failed a test." "She turned me down*

for a date." "I had an argument with a friend." "You grounded me."

    B- What are you telling yourself, saying to yourself about striking out, getting an F on your test, being called a name? _____

CAUTION: It is difficult for children at first to cue in on what is going on at point **B**. Therefore, you may need to refer to the set of irrational beliefs described earlier in order to help them cue in on their thoughts. You may have to do some slow teaching at this point in order to help them understand this. For example, *"Is it possible that you're saying to yourself that you're really bad if you make mistakes?"*

    D- Once the irrational belief(s) have been identified, it is time to question them. Example: Where's the proof? How would that be so terrible? Why does it have to be so? Is it really awful? Are you really all bad? Prove it. Is this the worst thing that could happen? Is this belief getting you what you want? Is it true that you can't stand it?

    E- List your child's realistic alternatives to his upsetting beliefs. Enlist his support in constructing the list. What can he change about this situation? What could he do differently? How could he face this situation better in case it happened again? What could he do to prevent further problems?

Using the emotional problem-solving form with your children and yourself on a consistent basis will help you to learn the distinction and the relationship between your thinking, feeling and behaving. It will also help to identify your emotional and practical goals. It will help you examine and correct your perceptions and thoughts, and will aid you in making more accurate perceptions of reality.

Regular family problem-solving meetings can be beneficial. It may not be necessary to use the emotional problem solving form all the time, but if there have been some upsetting events in the last week, this time could be well spent to help your kids analyze the situation and learn their options for solving problems most efficiently. The old saying that two heads are better than one certainly applies here in regard to family problem solving. This kind of process allows the family to have a sense of focus. People helping other people to live more responsibly with one another in an environment that attempts to maximize happiness and minimize pain is the goal here. A second goal is to recognize each person as a contributor to the family system, establishing consistency and a sense of belonging. The rules for setting up and running family meetings are simple. The key is in making a commitment and sticking to it. Although one of the primary reasons for holding meetings is to discuss individual problems and possible solutions, it is also important to talk about positive happenings within the family. Acknowledgment of good behavior and planning family fun time is quite appropriate in order to prevent the meetings from becoming stale. I know some families who provide special treats, such as popcorn or sodas, during family meetings in order to develop a positive environment.

The following excerpt is from a session I had with a young person named Bob in which I challenged his irrational belief system using the **ABC** method:

Bob	*The kids at school are really getting on my nerves. I can't stand it anymore. They keep picking on me.*
Dr. Thomson	*What do they do?*
Bob	*They call me names.*
Dr. Thomson	*What do they say? What exactly happens?*
Bob	*One kid comes up and tells me, "You're stupid, you stink."*
Dr. Thomson	*What do you do then?*
Bob	*I tell him to get lost. I threaten to hit him.*
Dr. Thomson	*What happens then?*
Bob	*They keep calling me the names and I walk away.*
Dr. Thomson	*What are you thinking about at this time?*
Bob	*What do you mean?*
Dr. Thomson	*What are you thinking when these guys are saying this to you?*
Bob	*They shouldn't be doing this. They are really jerks. I can't stand them.*
Dr. Thomson	*Why shouldn't they call you names?*
Bob	*What, are you saying it's okay to call people names?*
Dr. Thomson	*That's not the point, Bob. Are these guys good friends of yours?*
Bob	*Are you kidding?*
Dr. Thomson	*Then what can you expect from these guys? I want you to think about something, Bob. Think with me that you have a baseball game planned with your friends for this weekend. Everything is set up and it rains the day you want to play—what would you do?*
Bob	*I guess I would make other plans to do something else.*
Dr. Thomson	*Would it make any sense to say it shouldn't be raining? Would it make any sense to say that you can't stand it when it rains?*
Bob	*No.*
Dr. Thomson	*Why?*
Bob	*When it rains, you can't change it. There is nothing you can do about it. You just have to change what you were going to do and make the best of it.*
Dr. Thomson	*It doesn't do any good to say it shouldn't rain when, in fact, it is raining. It's like putting your nose up against the window with a long sad face because of the rain. You might be there for a while.*
Bob	*Yeah, okay, you're right.*
Dr. Thomson	*It is the same with those guys calling you names. It doesn't do any good to say they shouldn't, when in fact they are. It doesn't do any good saying you can't stand it when in fact you can. It is frustrating, but you are not going to die from it. It might feel like it at the time, but trust me, you will not die.*
Bob	*But I don't like it when they do that, it's not fair.*
Dr. Thomson	*I didn't say that you do like it. I'm only saying that it doesn't help you to say to yourself, in your head, that they shouldn't, or can't do it, because they are proving to you that they in fact can do what they want to, just like it can rain and you can't stop it from*

	happening. *You don't have the control; they do. You have the control over what you think when they say what they say, what you do when they say what they say, and how you choose to feel when they say what they say.*
Bob	*Those guys are real jerks, though.*
Dr. Thomson	*I'm not denying that they are affecting you, but they aren't jerks, they are acting "jerky" There is a difference. They influence you. They do not control your thinking, your actions, your feelings. You are the captain of that ship. If you want to act negatively, you can. If you want to think negatively, you can. If you want to feel negatively, you can. I would just ask you, "How is this helping you?"*
Bob	*What?*
Dr. Thomson	*People can do many things to hurt other people, but that doesn't make them total jerks. These guys could be acting worse. They could be beating you up. Spitting on you. I could go on. People who call other people names usually have problems of their own. They hide their problems and what they are thinking inside by lashing out at others.*
Bob	*I never thought of that.*
Dr. Thomson	*It would be nice if you started thinking of the world like that. In that way, their comments to you would be like throwing spit balls at a battleship. The battleship doesn't even feel it. Of course you will feel some of the hurt associated with these names being hurled your way, but how much hurt is up to you and you only. If you believe this, then you are in control of whether you want to hurt. Don't misunderstand me, they are going to influence your thoughts, actions and feelings, but don't allow these guys to control*

those areas in your life. Once you do that, they will be yanking that chain a lot.

I hope you have learned the importance of your thinking as it pertains to your life as a parent as well as how it pertains to your children's lives. It is to your benefit that you become aware of your thinking, just as Bob did in the above session. While some thoughts work to our benefit and direct us towards positive actions, others work to our detriment and to the detriment of others. There is a tremendous benefit in letting go of such beliefs and replacing them with a system of beliefs that is more accurate, more realistic, and, above all, more responsible.

I haven't said much about the neutral aspects of thoughts, actions and feelings. That is because neutral feelings, actions and thinking take time and patience. Read on and you will gain added information to pull all of this together and the results will be worth the time and the effort you put into it.

Key points to remember

- ❏ Thoughts direct our actions and our feelings.
- ❏ Thoughts, actions, and feelings can be chosen as positive, negative or neutral—it's your choice.
- ❏ Our interpretations of events need to be challenged for evidence.
- ❏ Thinking, acting and feeling neutral is a productive thinker's way of stepping back and productively thinking versus a WhMPA's automatic reaction.
- ❏ The messages we provide to our children will influence their self talk statements in either a positive or negative way.
- ❏ Evaluating your own thoughts, actions and feelings first is the critical step productive-thinking parents take when frustrated.
- ❏ Productive-thinking parents make a value judgment as to the effectiveness or ineffectiveness of their thoughts, actions or feelings.
- ❏ Ninety-eight percent of all problems experienced in our lives or our kids lives may frustrate us, but will not kill us.
- ❏ Awfulizing, Musterbizing, Should've, Could've, Would've will keep you stuck

when solving problems.

- ❏ Can't-stand-it-itus is giving up; disappointment is a fact of life; we control the degree of our own disappointment.

Helpful hints

- ❏ Observe people around you and listen for their irrational statements.
- ❏ Try to identify how they are setting themselves up for frustration by what they are saying about the event they have experienced.
- ❏ Challenge and debate your own negative thinking.
- ❏ Keep asking *"Where's the evidence for keeping this belief?"*
- ❏ Keep asking *"What's the worst thing that could happen to me in this situation?"*
- ❏ Keep the **A-B-C** framework in your head when problems arise.
- ❏ Remember that **A** does not cause **C**. **A** INFLUENCES **C**. Your beliefs about what happened direct what you are going to do and how you are going to feel.
- ❏ Look for opportunities to teach and model these principles to everyone you come in contact with.

CHAPTER 9

PRODUCTIVE THINKING SKILL 2
Problems are degrees of differences between what we want and what we have

Unfortunately there is a widely accepted belief in our culture that it is good to suffer, that unhappiness and going through pain are good for us. Nothing is gained by spending time in unhappiness, since it only produces more of the same. This fatalistic view is best summarized by Alexander's mother in Judith Viorst's book <u>Alexander and the Terrible, Horrible, No Good, Very Bad Day.</u> Alexander had a rotten day through and through; he didn't get a toy in his cereal box; he had to sit in the middle of the back seat; he had to wear his railroad pajamas (which he hated) to bed. He moaned through his day as if he were totally helpless, simply being acted upon by overwhelming external forces, all of which appeared to "cause" him to have a rotten day. What a WhMPA. His is a story of victimization, capped off by his mothers' final statement that "some days are just like that."

Alexander's mother implied to Alexander that he just accept the rotten day as inevitable and beyond his control. Wrong! WhMPA parent alert! We need to challenge our kids. We need to challenge the belief that rotten days are unavoidable and beyond our control.

We can start by understanding that frustration begins with how we perceive the world around us.

WhMPA's (Where Most People Are), think the **CAUSE** of their problems is something "out there." They think other people—kids, machines, schools, teachers, governments and the environment—**CAUSE** them stress, frustration, pain and problems. **Thinking this way directs WhMPA's to act to change or manipulate out there** to get what they want in order to feel good. If out there doesn't change enough, WhMPA's feel bad. Either way, **WhMPA's allow "out there" to have enormous power over how they think, act and feel.** Just look around and you will see many examples of WhMPA thoughts and actions.

The second step in the productive thinking

strategy to regaining power or control over how you think, act and feel is to **rethink what problems really are.** Productive thinking provides you with power in life. Productive thinking provides you with control. Productive thinking provides you with new choices.

Negative thoughts, actions and feelings result from differences between what we want and what we have. We call these frustrations, stresses, problems, hassles, anxieties, depressions, etc. They all mean the same thing:

YOU WANT SOMETHING AND YOU'RE NOT GETTING IT.

You are experiencing a **DIFFERENCE** between what you want and what you have. It's the **difference, NOT THE ENVIRONMENT** that causes the negative feelings. The difference can be like shirt sizes—small, medium, large or extra-large. **The size of the difference or problem you experience depends how much you want what you want.** It is not based on out there (other people, things or situations) and what they are or are not doing. Can you relate to some of these simple everyday problems?

- ❑ Stepping on the scale and seeing a weight gain.
- ❑ Putting a skirt or shirt on and finding a stain on it.
- ❑ Ordering something from a fast food drive-up and later finding out they gave you the wrong order.
- ❑ Calling someone only to find the line busy.
- ❑ Asking a child to clean his room and later finding it unclean.
- ❑ Shopping for something and not finding it.
- ❑ Trying to find a parking place.

- ❏ Finding you overslept.
- ❏ Finding out your son was suspended from school.
- ❏ Finding out your daughter lied to you.
- ❏ Asking a child to answer you and getting no response.
- ❏ Having it rain when you wanted sun.
- ❏ Getting a speeding ticket.
- ❏ Getting laid off from work.
- ❏ Being stuck in traffic.

Can you relate to these frustrations, the difference between what we want and what we get? Can you imagine your frustration if you wanted a parking place and the lot was full, but you kept driving around the lot? Can you picture some of the behaviors that a WhMPA might use in this situation yelling, swearing and hitting the steering wheel?

Here are two examples I want you to think about. You are in a hurry to get somewhere. Do you want traffic to move at the posted speed limit (or maybe a little faster) when you need to be somewhere? When you **have** bumper-to-bumper traffic and you **want** to be at your destination on time, **how do you feel?** Are you frustrated? What degree of frustration do you experience (small, medium, large, extra-large)? What are you **thinking**? What **actions** might you display? Is the traffic the **cause of** your **frustration?** Of course, the traffic is an influencing factor, but it is not the cause of your frustration. Your thinking about the event (the traffic jam) determines the choices you make. Your thinking creates your choices! Can a driver be in the same traffic jam and choose to be less stressed? If he is less stressed, is it because he is getting what he wants or is it because he has rethought the situation? If you want a strategy you must first rethink your automatic responses in order to control your feelings and actions. The choice is yours to make.

The second example has to do with a daughter who has a messy room. As the parent, you want a clean room but what you have is a room where you can't even tell what color the carpet is! Are your initial thoughts negative? Are they something like, *"This girl will never learn to clean her room up." "She is such a pig."* What actions result from those thoughts? Do you attempt to control her by yelling at her, screaming at her, criticizing her for being such a pig? Do you threaten her with physical harm or with grounding? Can you relate to any of these? Has your daughter caused you to perceive the situation as you did or to respond in the way you do?

Take a look at some examples of the "want-have" differences some parents tell me about and see if you can relate to any of them.

What parents HAVE versus what parents WANT
- a. A child who dislikes them.
- b. A child who loves them.

- a. A child who talks back.
- b. A child who listens.

- a. A child who is disruptive.
- b. A child who minds.

- a. A child who is disrespectful.
- b. A respectful child.

- a. An alcohol-drug using child.
- b. An alcohol-drug free child.

- a. An irresponsible child.
- b. A responsible child.

- a. A child blaming others.
- b. A child having self control.

- a. A child getting poor grades.
- b. A child on the honor roll.

- a. A child in trouble with the law.
- b. A law abiding child.

- a. A pregnant teenager.
- b. A pregnant married daughter.

- a. A messy bedroom.
- b. A clean bedroom.

- a. A child who is late for curfew.
- b. A child on time for curfew.

- a. A child who neglects his chores
- b. A child who does his chores.

These are not unusual wants for a parent to have. Can you relate to having any of these parental wants? If you can relate to them, you will be able to compare the difference between what you want with what you have. In my workshops, I use the palm of one hand to represent what I want and the other for what I have. In an instant, the audience can see if there is a match or a difference. The problem is not in what parents want. The problem is whether the want is under our control or not.

Most of the wants that are listed above are admirable, but not always achievable. As you can see, what a parent actually has is often opposite. When that occurs, we feel FRUSTRATED. When we are frustrated, we must choose to think or act in some way to get what we want. The problem is that we are not taught to think or act in efficient ways to close down the differences. We have learned from our parents and from others around us to try to control what we cannot control. As a result, we generate WhMPA thoughts, actions and feelings. So when we are frustrated, we choose some pretty miserable options.

If there is a difference between what you want and what you have, you will feel frustrated or pain. When we speak here of what we want, we actually are speaking of what we need—needs that drive our system to think what we think, do what we do and feel what we feel. Whenever you have a difference between what you want and what you have, you have no choice but to experience frustration because basic needs are left unmet.

That is one way of saying your wants are your wants and you are entitled to them. The problem is that what you want might not be what others want. Make frustration your friend by learning how to take effective control of your thoughts, actions and feelings. Whatever the problem or frustration you are dealing with, remember the problem is not in the event, but how you view it. The problem then becomes what you choose to do to lessen the frustration in your life.

Pure thoughts, pure actions, pure feelings

Immediately following a frustration, you will experience a pure thought, pure action or pure feeling. For many a parent, this pure thought might be "I can't stand it;" a pure action might be "swearing or yelling;" and a pure feeling might be "anger or rejection" which lasts only a short while. The greater the frustration, the more intense the reaction. It is directly related to how much you want what you want.

The result of frustration is motivation, a pressure to do something to close down the difference between what you want and what you have. Whenever there is a difference between what we want and what we have, we will feel an urge to react. The problem with just being motivated, however, is that it does not tell us what to do. It does not tell us to think efficiently, act efficiently and choose to feel efficiently. Our reactions are usually the best choices that we know of at the time to close down the differences. We will continue to use them if we get what we want. If swearing gets us control over our kids, we will continue to swear. If yelling at the top of our lungs gets us what we want, we will continue to choose yelling. What happens when our choices don't work? What happens when every choice we use is like throwing spitballs at a battleship? What happens when your child stands there and says, "So?" What happens when he chooses to not talk when we ask a question? What kind of reaction do we come back with? We are back to frustration! Our frustration is now greater than ever. You may want to ventilate your feelings with those who will listen to you or you may want to give up. You may want to use alcohol or other drugs to blot out the frustration. You may just want to close your eyes, hope that you can tap your heels together and hope you get back to Kansas with Dorothy! But who taught us how to think, act and feel when we become frustrated? Our parents? Other people? Were they WhMPA's? Keep reading.

A good rule of thumb in dealing with frustration is to change what you HAVE in the environment, when you have total control over the HAVE. In the two previous examples you don't have total control over the daughter doing what you want her to do, or the bumper to bumper traffic freeing up. Productive thinking gives you the alternative of changing what you WANT. The rest of the steps in the following chapters will teach you how to do that. For now, it's important for you to begin thinking of problems as DIFFERENCES to get yourself in a motivated position to change what you want.

Problems and frustrations are really differences between what you want and what you have. It is important to make this point repeatedly because it gives you **new powerful alternatives** to solve problems. It is important because it helps you to understand other people and the frustrations that they also have. Remember, thoughts direct actions, so changing your thinking accordingly to "differences" gives you three ways to act to feel better instead of one.

In gaining your objectives, you can change:
(1) **What you HAVE.**
(2) **What you WANT.**
(3) **What you HAVE and what you WANT.**

WANT	DIFFERENCE	HAVE
(source of problem)		

CLOSE DOWN BY CHANGING WHAT **YOU HAVE**

CLOSE DOWN BY CHANGING WHAT **YOU WANT**

BY CHANGING **BOTH**

Frustration levels are like shirt sizes

One person will experience a traffic jam and react calmly while another explodes with anger and frustration. One parent deals with frustrations calmly and directly while another turns red, foams at the mouth, or swears, screams, yells and threatens. They respond or react differently because one of them knows that he has almost no control over external circumstances but total control over himself, while the other assumes and believes exactly the opposite.

Here's another example. Let's say you have been working very hard to build a relationship with your son and you believe you deserve some return on your investment. You took him where he wanted to go, you talked with him when he arrived home from school about his day and you asked him to go shopping with you. You really tried to foster a positive relationship. In return you received no "thank you" for the taxi service, a one word "O.K." response about the day in school and a resounding, *"Shopping with you? I'm not going shopping with you!"* Your return would not be what you expected and you would end up feeling very disappointed and frustrated. How frustrated would you be? Small, medium, large or extra-large? Suppose you feel like this is an extra-large problem, and as a result, you choose to yell, swear, guilt and criticize your son. *"Why don't you talk to me." "Why are you so ungrateful?" "Why don't you love me?" "I have been nice to you; why can't you be nice to me?" "I can't believe what a jerk you are!" "You make me miserable."*

This is how a WhMPA might unconsciously view the situation if he knew a little bit about productive thinking:

1. "What is it that I want?" — *A relationship with my son.*
2. "What do I have now?" — *A disappointing, frustrating situation with a son who has an attitude problem.*
3. "Is there a difference between what I want and what I have?" — *Yes, definitely.*
4. "To what degree?" (small, medium, large, extra-large.) — *Extra-large.*
5. "Is it 'out there' that makes me unhappy or is it the difference between what I want and what I have?" — *It's 'out there' it's my son.*
6. "Are the thoughts that I'm choosing helping me enough to solve this problem?" — *No, they are negative thoughts, but what would you expect? You would think the same.*
7. "Are the actions I am choosing to use helping me enough to solve this problem?" — *No, they are negative actions, but my job is to get this kid to accept me, to respect me. I'm his father.*

If you were to practice the **productive thinking process** you would ask yourself the following seven critical questions:

1. "What is it that I want?"

   A relationship with my son.

2. "What do I have now?"

   A disappointing, frustrating situation with a son who has an attitude problem.

3. "Is there a difference between what I want and what I have?"

   Yes, definitely.

4. "To what degree?"
   (Small, medium, large, extra-large.)

   Extra-large.

5. "Is it 'out there' that makes me unhappy, or is it the difference between what I want and what I have?"

   It's the differences I have.

6. "Are the thoughts that I'm choosing helping me enough to solve this problem?"

   No, they are negative thoughts.

7. "Are the actions I am choosing to use helping me enough to solve this problem?"

   No, they are negative actions.

If you have answered these questions honestly, you will no doubt find yourself with a problem that is frustrating to you, and that is affecting your thoughts, your actions and your feelings. Don't worry. If you notice, the significant difference between a WhMPA's and a productive thinker's approach is that the WhMPA believes that the son "out there" has caused the problem, and the negative thoughts, actions and the miserable day.

Stepping back and redefining the problem in the above terms and using the questions provided, will give you power and control over yourself. Letting go of areas you have no control over is critical in this situation. Your son is someone you might have influence over, but, as you can see, absolutely no control over. Frustrating? Yes. Don't do what many WhMPA's do in wanting to "do something" first in order to solve the problems they experience. You will set out to change the kid first and if he doesn't change, you will try harder until he does. At best, this will have only limited success.

How WhMPA's react when frustrated

❏ WhMPA's see a problem, feel frustrated and want immediate changes to occur.
❏ WhMPA's think, *"How can I change my child to get what I want?"*

❏ WhMPA's try to get "out there" to change by using manipulation, threats, coercion, rules and consequences or punishment.
❏ When these choices work for WhMPA's, WhMPA's feel reinforced and powerful, and attribute their success to their power over their children.
❏ When these attempts to gain control do not work—that is, when "out there" does not change—a WhMPA becomes more frustrated and tries even harder to manipulate the situation by:
   • Threatening physical harm.
   • Psychological intimidation.
   • Increasing negative consequences.
   • Emphasizing rules that "must" be obeyed or else.
   • Offering rewards as incentives.
   • Bribing with money or material possessions.
   • Excessively yelling, screaming, threatening and other powering behaviors.

These choices will lead to loss of control, feeling miserable and thinking negative thoughts. This is where some parents throw in the towel and choose to give up and let the kid do whatever he wants. Unfortunately, many parents are doing just what the kids demand of them.

Most parents will see a problem as something

that needs to be changed. There are three choices one can make when problems arise:

1. Change what is going on in the environment (the children's behavior) using manipulation, coercion, threatening, intimidation, as noted above.

2. Change your physical state to perceive the problem differently (with the aid of alcohol and other drugs). You might be happy or comfortable temporarily, but as you may have already experienced with the use of alcohol, the solution is only temporary. When you sober up, you will still have the same old problem staring you in the face.

3. Change your thinking first, rethink and begin to evaluate yourself using the questions listed earlier. Focus on what the problem is and identify the difference. Begin to focus on the ways in which you can take more effective control of your own life first and what choices you need to implement in order to close down the differences.

Obviously, I am suggesting that you choose to implement the skills associated with the **productive thinking strategy** in order to be more effective parents and at the same time develop a strategy to save your own sanity. This strategy, remember, is for you to put into your own life first and use in all of your daily affairs. You can then teach and, most importantly, model better behavioral choices to your children.

The choices people make when frustrated

Even if you understand what has been explained so far, you probably find it difficult to believe that people not only choose most of the unhappiness they suffer, but that choosing unhappiness almost always makes good sense at the time for that person. Again, **everything we think and do is purposeful, and is our best choice at the time to meet one or more of our internal psychological needs.**

When a person wants something, he is not getting, he makes the best choice he can at the time. If we understand this, we understand that our choices can be evaluated by asking ourselves if we are paying any prices for our chosen thoughts, ac-

tions or feelings.

A WhMPA believes that when he doesn't receive love from his children, he deserves to feel miserable. An irrational belief? You bet. There is nothing in the WhMPA's mind that even addresses the idea that their choices aren't realistic and aren't working.

In powerful situations like this, the most important question to ask ourselves is "Is *what I am thinking or doing about this situation helping me enough?*" The key word is enough. Sometimes people will say it is helping them to depress at the time, but in the long run that accomplishes nothing. They may say that drinking to deal with the stress works at the time, but later the consequences of drinking become a problem and not a solution to the original problem.

Unhappiness is a choice

There are five reasons why we choose depressing and unhappiness when we are not in control of our lives, are not getting what we want and are frustrated.

First, depressing and unhappiness are better than angering, the most basic reaction to frustration. Our society views angering as okay for small children, but as we develop, we learn that angering has great cost and doesn't get us what we want. In fact, angering usually diminishes our ability to better meet our needs.

Of course not everyone gives up on angering when frustrated. Our world is full of violence, particularly by men against women and children, and as we now see, violence between children and other children. Angering gives some people the illusion of having power over others but over time they lose this power, ending up in jail or otherwise powerless.

The second reason we choose depressing and unhappying behaviors is that there are more acceptable ways to subtly ask for help without actually asking for it. Our society has a strong value that we call "rugged individualism," which means that asking for help is a sign of weakness. Depressing works because it arouses the attention of those around us, and gaining attention is purposeful and powerful, but it carries a price.

Depressing is probably the most powerful of the help-getting behaviors we have in our choice system. It is hard to ignore an obviously depressing stranger, much less someone we know. What we are really saying by depressing is: *"If others only knew how upset I am, they would want to help me."*

The ultimate choice connected with depressing is to threaten or attempt suicide. The threat of committing suicide is a very controlling behavior that works. I have seen many clients in my office that use this as a way to receive attention and control of others around them when not getting what they want. Kids use it to gain power over their parents. It works. It is their best choice at the time, but a choice that carries consequences with it.

A person who is committed to actually taking his life is locked into a belief that his unhappiness is externally CAUSED. He has probably used depressing behavior for a long time and eventually came to the conclusion that all of the people who have attempted to help him couldn't make his unhappiness go away. When one's life is full of unhappiness and no one's attempts are successful at relieving the unhappiness, suicide SEEMS reasonable to them. It SEEMS to be the only choice that will relieve the pain.

The third reason people find it difficult to ask for help is fear of being refused, especially if we have been refused before. Many of us, making a request that we fear may be denied, tend to blend a little depressing into our requests, as if to say, *"If you turn me down, you are going to make me upset."* This adds a little power or manipulation to what we ask. Just think of the numerous ways in which kids today manipulate their parents and other people with subtle depressing—whining, pouting, begging or complaining. Remember the child in the crib rapping the bottle on the bars? If he could talk, he might have said, *"How long do I have to keep this behavior up? … Get in here right now!"* It worked wonderfully well to get him what he wanted. He will continue to use this behavior whenever he wants something that he does not have.

The fourth reason we continue to choose unhappiness is that it offers us an excuse for our unwillingness to do something more effective. In other words, when we believe that we are not in control of our lives, it is better to stay stuck (unhappy) than try something potentially better and possibly fail again. At least that is how most people think.

This process is particularly clear when we choose long-term unhappiness over ending a relationship with somebody important to us. Most of us choose some depressing when a relationship ends, particularly if the relationship was a very

meaningful one for us. The abrupt loss of being able to meet our need for Belonging is certainly painful and finding another person with whom we can share belonging is the only way to more efficiently meet this need. However, the fear of forming another relationship could mean being hurt again, so we stay with unhappiness and depressing instead of having to risk failure again. Through counseling kids, I have noticed that more females fall into this pattern in their early years of relationships with the opposite sex. Staying with a male because he "takes care" of them is the wrong reason in the long run. The female gives all of the control over her thoughts, actions and feelings to the male. None of us should allow others to gain this much control over our lives. We are setting ourselves up for trouble if we do.

When we choose unhappiness-related behaviors because some Belonging is lacking, we will get some short-term Belonging with those who spend time with us because of their own concern for our unhappiness. Over the long haul, however, unhappiness will be all we have because the people interested in helping us will not stay forever in a relationship with a depressing person.

The fifth reason we choose long-term unhappiness and depressing is that as painful as unhappiness and depressing are, they give us powerful control over others, particularly family members and other close associates.

Most of us all have an Aunt Matilda type of person somewhere in our family constellation, who is and has been for years, a "professional" depresser. Her expert abilities allow her to control any and all members of the family, and anyone she gets close to. She is like a talented general in her ability to always steer the conversation around to the theme of her life, her unending unhappiness.

No matter what people do for her or to her, it is never enough. At the same time, she subtly but clearly announces that she doesn't know why anybody even bothers with her, why they don't just leave her alone with this "dreaded curse" that has invaded her body and her life. She doesn't want to ruin anybody else's day or life. You can hear the violins in the background!

Aunt Matilda is one of the illustrious members of the "misery martyr club," what we commonly refer to as "the self appointed merchant of doom." Her unhappiness is real to her and her depressing behavior is what she has found at the time to be her best choice to gain some control in her life. She has not consciously chosen this role, but it is a choice just the same. If you tell her that her unhappiness and depressing are a choice on her part, she might hit you! Do you know some adults like her? Do you know some kids like Aunt Matilda? Are you yourself like Aunt Matilda? There are numerous other choices that do not carry the prices that this choice carries with it, both short and long term. We should never let someone else's behavior gain control over us, even our relatives, because it just provides an audience for the performer. Without an audience, most performers would not perform.

It is not easy relating to unhappy and depressing people, especially if they are family members. They make it especially easy to start "guilting" because we receive the message that although we might not be responsible for their unhappiness, we should feel responsible to either help them feel more happiness, or at the very least, feel miserable "for" them. Have your kids ever tried guilting and depressing behaviors on you? Have your kids been successful in using these behaviors with you or with others?

What we can do when we are around people who make these choices is to put limits on the amount of unhappinessing or depressing we will listen to. We can make ourselves available for limited periods only, doing constructive, non-miserying activities. With our kids, we can let them know that we understand that they are frustrated, but that depressing and miserying about a problem is not going to get them anywhere. We can also cease running to that person each time he or she chooses depressing or controlling behaviors. We don't want to alienate ourselves, but we also don't want to allow ourselves to be a doormat for them to walk on. We need to call time-out, so to speak, and to set and demonstrate the structure if we are to regain some control and sanity. **Knowing that people we live with and work with choose depressing and other behaviors will help us understand the concept of choices.** Understanding this can help us learn how to not get sucked into their choices. We will understand that they are capable of making better choices. Knowing this frees us from the pain of feeling guilty for their unhappiness, for their depressing and controlling behaviors. The behaviors they use are attempts to control others, but we can choose not to be controlled by these behaviors. I choose not to be controlled. How about you? We must first recognize the choices others make as controlling and then we must choose to respond in ways that place the responsibility back on them.

As miserable as depressing and unhappiness are, they can, at times be useful. The question is for how long? After the loss of a significant person in your life, particularly with death, depressing or mourning helps keep inappropriate anger in check, and helps us gain support from family and friends. Depressing is a better choice than angering in many situations. **The key, as stated already, is how long is too long?**

Babies learn to choose the behavior of angering as their first means of control. They learned, soon after making their grand appearance, to generate a variety of angering behaviors such as crying, thrashing about or turning red to control the world around them and in turn get what they want. Babies do not give these learned behaviors up as readily as we would like them to. They cannot give up their "effective choices at the time"—crying, whining, pouting—until they can replace them with more efficient behaviors. Remember, these behaviors are the lures they have used over and over to catch the most fish. Looking for a better behavior, the baby taps into his creative behavioral system and soon learns depressing, another powerful behavior, to replace angering. Like a fisherman's favorite lure, it goes on his hat, to be used again and again.

Unlike adults, children often consciously choose to use depressing behaviors in the hope of getting what they want. One young lady in our neighborhood was the queen of pouting. Whenever she wanted something and did not get it, she was on stage with the spotlight in her face. Her face would drop to the floor, she would look like a basset hound and proceed to cry. When pouting didn't work, she was even better at depressing. Unfortunately, not only kids but adults bought into this behavior, which kept her using it over and over in order to get what she wanted. Talk about a fishing lure that worked for her every time she wanted something! She then taught her pouting and depressing to her sibling with wonderful results. Many of the choices we learn in life are taught to us by the people we live with.

Depressing, however, has serious drawbacks. For one thing, it needs to be kept at a certain intensity level in order to be effective. Aunt Matilda, for example, has a "depressing intensity knob" on her belt; one that she can turn up or down depending on how much she needs to intensify her depressing and controlling behavior to get what she wants. Think of the Queen of Pouting. Does she have a control knob that she can turn up? Do you think she was pretty good at pulling in many fish? Do your kids use lures like pouting or depressing? Do they turn up the volume when it isn't working at one level?

Depressing, angering, complaining, crying, and guilting are all behaviors in which feelings are both predominant and painful. They exert powerful control over our own lives and the lives of others. Depressing, pouting, or any other type of behavior is our best choice at the time to regain control over the frustrating situations in which we find ourselves. Hard as it may be to accept, we are all more than willing to pay the price of severe pain and unhappiness to regain control. We will use whatever choice we need in order to get what we want regardless of the price or cost of that choice. Unfortunately we will do anything except take control of our own lives in order to control others.

The last thing that I want to be aware of when I am depressing is that I have chosen it. If I am aware of that, I lose control of myself and others which was my motive for depressing in the first place. We can't comfortably ask for Belonging (sympathy) if we and others look at our behavior (depressing) as a choice. We lose our justification for not doing something more effective. Finally, we no longer have a buffer to protect ourselves from our own anger because our lives are not as we want them to be in certain areas. Everyone really knows this, but few will admit it.

The reasons for choosing unhappiness

We know the four reasons that we choose unhappiness, but we also need to better understand why we are usually unaware that they are choices. There are three strong and logical reasons for our lack of awareness that we are making these choices.

1. Some immediate and intense, but very short-lived feelings do happen "to" us.

They are called pure feelings. When I'm driving in my car and I come up over a hill and notice a highway patrol automobile with radar pointed in my direction, I do not choose to feel the immediate, intense knot forming in my stomach. When I receive a certified letter from the IRS, I do not choose my nausea and upset stomach. When I receive a phone call from the school, from the police department, from the hospital or a "Dear John" letter, I do not choose to feel panic. Some feelings do happen to us.

We tend to jump to the logical but wrong conclusion that all of our feelings happen to us, when in fact these immediate feelings are only a small part of all we feel.

What we feel is divided into two distinct categories which always occur in sequence.

First, as I explained before, we experience an immediate, usually intense, short-term feeling which occurs at the moment of great frustration or pleasure. When I want something and have it, I experience pleasure or happiness. When there is a difference between what I want and what I have, I experience frustration or pain. I want to drive along the road without the highway patrol monitoring my speed. I don't want calls from the police, the schools or the hospital. Depending on how much I want what I want determines the intensity of my good or bad feelings. This **pure feeling** is a burst of good or bad feelings. We don't choose them, they come **to** us. They last from several seconds to several minutes. What occurs afterwards is **a feeling choice,** which we are in total control over.

Second, to deal with the frustration or prolong the pleasure, we almost always choose a long-term behavior such as depressing or form a close relationship with another person. These behaviors may last for a long time, even a lifetime, and the short term feelings (pure feelings) begin to subside as soon as the choice feelings begin. These long term feeling behaviors are called choice feelings.

Pure feelings obviously have a purpose, giving us messages that tell us we are safe or in danger. They initiate adrenaline production to help us in our flight or fight choices. Although few people today need to run or fight for their survival, the process and the purpose are the same: to tell us whether we are in control and if not, to help regain control. We choose what to do, think, and feel, but we do not choose the pure feelings that precede any of these behaviors.

The difficulty with this process is that when we switch from pure feelings to choosing feelings, we cannot easily differentiate one from the other. Because of this, we tend to think that the long-term pain of the feeling behavior (feeling choices) happens to us, just as the pure feeling did.

2. Our choices have become a part of our daily routine.

All of our behaviors have a purpose. When I walk to the kitchen to get a glass of water, I might be well aware of the purpose of my walk, but I am not attentive to the movement of my feet.

How aware are you of your movements as you drive to work? When you drive home? You might be thinking of many issues—your family, your boss, the weather, your plans for the weekend—but will you be focusing on putting your foot on the brake or accelerator pedal, or turning the steering wheel? Probably not. We do these behaviors automatically.

Similarly, if you have been depressing for a long time, you will have no more awareness of your choice than when you put one foot in front of the other walking to the kitchen. The fact that depressing is a complex behavior does not make us more aware that it is a choice.

Young children are more aware that sulking or angering are choices because they are just learning which behaviors work for them in getting control. I've observed kids looking at themselves in a mirror, practicing their best forms of crying, pouting, whining or temper tantrumming. If you say to your child, *"That choice isn't going to work,"* or *"You can use that choice all you want, my decision still stands,"* you'll be amazed at how quickly their choices change. Like the baby in the crib, if no one comes in and pays attention, he will eventually have to think of another behavior to get what he wants. The baby is no different from many of us who are constantly searching for the choice that will work. That is why it is critical to understand these concepts before we tackle our children's specific concerns. We often see children quite obviously deliberating which behavior to choose—crying, pouting, angering, or laughing. As adults, we are more sophisticated. Childish sulking becomes depressing because sulking as an adult is not "acceptable."

Whining becomes complaining, temper tantrumming becomes angering. Giving up becomes burning out.

3. To acknowledge depressing and unhappiness as a choice would be disastrous.

To be in control and in a powerful position is important to all of us. You lose some control in your life if you admit that what you are choosing to do or think doesn't work. It's like the alcoholic in Alcoholics Anonymous who admits that he is powerless over alcohol when he admits that he uses behaviors to change others and not himself. Additionally, if depressing is partially to control others, you must believe that your unhappiness is happening to you. People would rather suffer than appear to be asking for help.

If those around me, as well as myself, are controlled and directed by the belief that my unhappiness is "happening" to me, my apparent vulnerability is my strength rather than my weakness. Acknowledging my unhappiness as chosen would blow my cover.

The next time you or your children use depressing or any of the unhappying behaviors long past the time that they may be effective, ask yourself, *"Is choosing to depress (or whatever choice you may be using) my best choice to get what I want?"* Ask your children this very question when you see them choosing these behaviors. Here are some other questions to ask of your kids when they choose certain behaviors of concern to you.

"If you continue to cry, will the problem go away?"

"How is getting so angry about this going to help?"

"How long are you going to choose to be depressing over this?" *"Think of what prices you'll have to pay for the choice you're making."*

"Is your choice helping you to get people off your back?"

These are **comparison questions** that ask us to evaluate what we are thinking, what we are doing or how we are feeling. Is what we are thinking, or doing or feeling helping us enough to get what we want? In asking these questions "we" make the comparison instead of being "told" by others, as so often happens, that what we are thinking, doing or feeling is not "good." When others "tell" us that our choices are not working, the hair on the back of our neck stands up and we become defensive. We are more apt to make changes if we first make the comparison instead of having others make it for us.

When we grasp that, depressing, angrying, paining, complaining and all the related behaviors become "poor choices."

When I first came in contact with Dr. Applegate, I was told that what I was about to learn from him was going to "screw up my life." He was right. It has. For the better. Now I know I have choices, and I also know that if my children choose inappropriate behaviors, I can help them understand that the results will be short term at best and extremely frustrating at worst. Asking them simple questions like, "*Is what you're choosing to do helping you enough to get what you want?*" "*Are you at risk of paying any prices for your choice?*" "*How long are you going to choose to think like this?*" "*What can you do to regain control?*" These questions tend to wake them up to reality.

In any severely frustrating situation (whenever we experience an extra large difference between what we want and what we have), a short period of non-martyr depressing—several minutes to several hours—can help us avoid hasty, angry behaviors that might make any out-of-control situation considerably worse. Depressing puts us on hold. It provides us an opportunity to step back, take a little time, rethink what has happened, and what we want to do with our thoughts, actions and feelings from this point forward. It is obviously better to use depressing than angrying choices, such as suiciding behavior, in dealing with the pain of frustration.

It can be useful if we begin to look at our behavioral choices as a continuum rather than as absolutes. Depressing is neither always good nor always bad. Sometimes it is better than other choices, such as angering. The big question we need to ask ourselves and others is, "*How long am I going to choose to use depressing to deal with my frustrations?*" "*What prices am I going to pay in my thinking, in my actions and in my long-term feelings if I continue to depress?*" "*What are my other choices?*" "*Will those choices carry with them the consequences that depressing does?*" "*What am I going to choose to do?*" These questions expand our vision and our choice of options.

Self awareness exercise

Identify five problems you have in your life as a parent either at the present or in the recent past. Please list the (5) PROBLEMS, (5) WANTS and the (5) HAVES that you had in each problem.

PROBLEM _____
WANT _____
HAVE _____
    To what degree were you frustrated?
    sm___med___lg___xlg___
    What is or was the cause
    of your stress?_____

PROBLEM _____
WANT _____
HAVE _____
    To what degree were you frustrated?
    sm___med___lg___xlg___
    What is or was the cause
    of your stress?_____

PROBLEM _____
WANT _____
HAVE _____
    To what degree were you frustrated?
    sm___med___lg___xlg___
    What is or was the cause
    of your stress?_____

PROBLEM _____
WANT _____
HAVE _____
    To what degree were you frustrated?
    sm___med___lg___xlg___
    What is or was the cause
    of your stress?_____

PROBLEM _____
WANT _____
HAVE _____
    To what degree were you frustrated?
    sm___med___lg___xlg___
    What is or was the cause
    of your stress?_____

Did you complete this exercise? Research verifies that if you chose to complete the exercise, your improvement in productive thinking will be greater than of those who chose not to complete the exercise. The big question is do you want to be a better parent? A better teacher and model of more efficient skills so your children can take more effective control of their own lives? If yes, then complete the exercise before going on.

Now, identify five recent problems your son or daughter had using the same exercise format. Identify the problem, what they wanted and what they had.

PROBLEM _____
WANT _____
HAVE _____
    To what degree were they frustrated?
    sm___med___lg___xlg___
    What is or was the cause
    of their stress? _____

PROBLEM _____
WANT _____
HAVE _____
    To what degree were they frustrated?
    sm___med___lg___xlg___
    What is or was the cause
    of their stress? _____

PROBLEM _____
WANT _____
HAVE _____
    To what degree were they frustrated?
    sm___med___lg___xlg___
    What is or was the cause
    of their stress? _____

PROBLEM _____
WANT _____
HAVE _____
    To what degree were they frustrated?
    sm___med___lg___xlg___
    What is or was the cause
    of their stress? _____

PROBLEM _____
WANT _____
HAVE _____
    To what degree were they frustrated?
    sm___med___lg___xlg___
    What is or was the cause
    of their stress?_____

Key points to remember

- ❑ The only people without problems are dead.
- ❑ Problems are differences between what you want and what you have.
- ❑ Our degree of frustration is related to how we are thinking about what we want.
- ❑ WhMPA's work to change and feel better by: a) stopping a bad habit; b) starting an ineffective action plan; c) working to change someone else; d) excessively expressing or ventilating their feelings alone.

Helpful hints

- ❑ Tape the word **difference** to the bathroom mirror, refrigerator door, the dashboard of your car, in your workplace or any other place where you spend time.
- ❑ Observe people around you and try to **identify the difference** they are having when they are frustrated.
- ❑ Talk to and teach your children that **problems are a part of life.**
- ❑ Teach your children the **critical questions** to ask themselves when problems arise.
- ❑ Share how thinking **difference** gives you three pathways to solve your problems.

CHAPTER 10

PRODUCTIVE THINKING SKILL 3
INCREASING YOUR CONTROL OVER FEELING GOOD BY THINKING FROM "OUT-OF-CONTROL" TO "IN-CONTROL"

THE SERENITY PRAYER
"God grant me the serenity to accept the things I cannot change, the courage to change the things I can, and the wisdom to know the difference."
Author unknown

Ask yourself these questions:
Do you feel responsible for what your child does or does not do?
Do you feel excessively angry when your child doesn't do what you say?
Do you get upset when your child doesn't do what you want him to do?
Do you get excessively angry when your child does not take your advice?
Do you lecture your children on what they do or do not do in their lives?
Do you try to please your children all of the time?
Does it frustrate you when your child does not respond positively to the assistance you provide?
Do you take care of your children more than you take care of yourself?
Do you give things like rides, money, or presents to your children in order to get cooperation from them?
Do you feel frustrated when your child doesn't appreciate your efforts?
Do you believe your children determine how you feel?
Do you lose sleep over the problems your child encounters?
Do you try to make sure your child is not late for activities or school projects by helping him time after time?
Do you live through your children's activities?
Is your child's involvement in sports or extracurricular activities for you or for him?
Would you allow your child to choose to be in these activities?
Do you push your children into a lifestyle "you" want them to live?
Do you tolerate physical abuse or excessive verbal abuse from your children?
Do you physically hit or punish your children when they don't do what you want them to do?
Do you bribe your children to be good?
Do you lie to other people in order to protect your children from natural consequences?
Do you worry about your children's responsibilities like getting up in the morning, doing their homework, getting good grades, etc.?
Do you control your child's choice of friends?
Do you excessively control your child's participation in activities outside the home?

If there is one word that summarizes the conflicts arising from "yes" answers to these questions, it is the word **Control**.

"*I don't have to take this from you.*"
"*I'm not gonna let you run this house one more minute.*"
"*You cannot talk to me like that.*"
"*You will do what I say or else.*"
"*I demand that you do what I say.*"
"*I insist that you look at me right now.*"
"*You will answer me this instant.*"
"*I'm the parent here and you will always do what I say.*"

Any of these sound familiar? They are examples of parents trying to **gain control** of their kids' behaviors.

What do parents want?

We found out in an earlier chapter that kids want Responsibility, Decision Making, Control, Power and Choices. What we also found out is that parents agree with kids on the first two areas, but disagree with the last three areas. Particularly with the issue of control. Why do we as parents think we want control? It's need fulfilling for us. Why do we want our kids to be responsible and make good decisions? Because it is need-fulfilling to us. We get hung up on the issue of control. Why? Because as adults we want control not just over our kids but over our finances, our spouses, when the light turns green, the weather, other people and so on. The list is endless. Parents want what they want when they want it. Kids, in turn, are also trying to gain control of their parents' behaviors. Kids want what they want when they want it also. As a result, we have a constant tug-of-war. Who's going to win?

A baby bird learning how to fly needs a certain kind of stability. So do our children. They need **Security** and **Knowledge** of how to actually venture out there and try. They also need to feel a sense of **Faith** and **Freedom**, to believe that they can do something themselves. We have all seen the ups and downs and the poor landings, not only of the baby bird, but also of our own children as they attempt to venture out of the nest or out of our home.

Our main role in the early years of our child's life is primarily that of a nurturer. With time, our role changes to that of a teacher of skills to manage the daily problems of living. We continue to nurture, but not as much. Our roles as parents become re-defined on a regular basis as our children grow older. We begin to understand that, as parents, we become less in control, and our children become more and more in control of all facets of their lives.

Forms of controlling behavior used commonly by parents are yelling, physical punishment, locking kids in their rooms or out of the house, and threatening physical harm. **These behavior choices create just one more problem on top of whatever it is that you are disagreeing about.**

Excessive yelling will not help your child learn anything but to use the same behavioral choice when he feels frustrated. Furthermore, you may pay a price in **Health**, in the form of high blood pressure and increased pulse rate. Remember from the previous chapter that the problem is not with what your child is thinking, doing or feeling. The problem is that you want something from him you are not getting. As a result, you feel frustrated and you use your best choice of the controlling behaviors you know of to try to reduce the frustration. When your best choice doesn't work, what should you do?

Some parents use various forms of physical punishment in an attempt to gain control. Physical punishment "may" control a child's behavior in the short run, but in the long run, the damage and the resentment become incredible. Physically controlling a person of lesser size is easy to accomplish. But it comes with consequences for yourself as well as for the child. Many kids have told me of their parents hitting them in attempts to control their behavior. It may control their behavior "at the time," but resentment toward their parents builds and with time, comes out in the form of angrying, depressing, pouting and temper tantrumming.

Locking kids in their rooms, the "out-of-sight-out-of-mind" method, teaches kids that they are **bad kids** instead of **"kids making bad choices at the time."** Sitting in their bedroom, many a child has thought *"What jerks my parents are"* and not what we thought they should be thinking.

Other forms of controlling behavior are sarcasm, criticism and name calling. We can create negative perceptions in a child's head just by what we say to him. These perceptions will direct not only their thoughts about themselves and the world around them, but also their actions and their feelings. Many parents and adults believe that sarcasm motivates others to do what we want them to. But it only influences their thinking in a negative way about themselves, others, the problem at hand and life in general.

Start taking control as a parent by eva**luating** what it is you want. You notice I said start taking control of you, not the children or other people. This takes effort on our part. Trust me, the effort and time will be worth it. Everybody is looking to gain more positive feelings in life, regardless of what their role is.

Let's define positive and negative feelings

Positive Feelings
Getting what you want.
Negative Feelings
A difference between what you want and what you have.

As we learned earlier, this word **difference** is the key between having a problem and not having a problem. Differences are degrees of frustration. You can create minimal differences by changing your wants from those you cannot control, or have only minimal influence over, to those you can control. The following guideline should help you understand this concept better.

Change from wants that are beyond your control to wants that you can control

CONTROL
(100%)

_____

INFLUENCE
(50%-85%)

_____

NO CONTROL
(0 - 50%)

Parental self-awareness exercise

While working on the exercise below, think of some problems you have experienced in the past or are presently experiencing in various environments. Are they problems with parenting or in other areas? Next in each area, list at least two wants you can control, two you can influence and two over which you have no control. If you need help, go back to the self-awareness exercise in Chapter 9 and see what you listed as problems. **PLEASE NOTE:** Practicing this exercise each day for at least three weeks will change your thinking.

Problem at home that you would like to have resolved

_____
_____
_____

Problem at school that you would like to have resolved

_____
_____

Problem elsewhere that you would like to have resolved

_____
_____

What do you want as a parent regarding

Home
School
Other

What do you have as a parent regarding

Home
School
Other

Would practicing a process of changing your wants from **out-of-control** to **in-control** be helpful? For example, change from wanting your children to change their actions or attitudes (out of your control) to wanting to demonstrate caring to them, asking them questions, giving them guidelines and providing them with alternatives, along with allowing them the freedom to think, act, or feel the way they want to, and working on building a positive relationship with them. All of these are within your control regardless of what your kids do or how they choose to think. You have control over setting up expectations regarding their behavior at home, school and other places. You have control over allowing them freedom to choose to follow your expectations—i.e., coming in on time, not using tobacco, alcohol or other drugs, getting passing grades and being honest. You also have control over asking them if they are reading their books each day, taking notes in class, asking the teacher for help, asking for a tutor or asking you questions.

Now, list what you have **control over, influence over and no control** over in each problem area.

What you have control over
HOME PROBLEM

_____
_____

SCHOOL PROBLEM

_____

_____

PROBLEM ELSEWHERE

_____

_____

What you have influence over
HOME PROBLEM

_____

_____

SCHOOL PROBLEM

_____

_____

PROBLEM ELSEWHERE

_____

_____

What you have no control over
HOME PROBLEM

_____

_____

SCHOOL PROBLEM

_____

_____

PROBLEM ELSEWHERE

_____

_____

You know that you feel good when you get what you want. Yet you can see that many of the things you want are things you might not get. Are you willing to admit that what you are presently doing is not working well enough, that what you are presently thinking is not helping enough, that how you presently feel is not how you want to feel? Learning how to get more of what you want is in your control.

Take a look at the following lists that contain just a sample of situations we have control, influence or no control over. As you start to rethink about parenthood, and to use the words, control, influence and no control, you'll feel much more secure.

WHAT I CAN CONTROL
- ❏ The feelings I choose to have.

- ❏ Giving a compliment.
- ❏ Giving a hug.
- ❏ Smiling and saying "Hi" first.
- ❏ What I think of my child, myself and others.
- ❏ What questions I ask.
- ❏ Demonstrating caring.
- ❏ My tone of voice.
- ❏ How I view situations.
- ❏ How positive my attitude is.
- ❏ How long I feel frustrated.
- ❏ Providing alternatives to problems.
- ❏ Becoming a teacher of new productive thinking skills.
- ❏ Making statements of what I want or expect.
- ❏ Modeling efficient thinking, acting and feeling skills.

WHAT CAN YOU ADD TO THIS LIST?

_____

_____

_____

WHAT I CAN INFLUENCE
- ❏ My child making good decisions.
- ❏ Helping my child with his homework.
- ❏ Building a better relationship with my child.
- ❏ The home environment I create.
- ❏ My child's attitude.
- ❏ My child's feelings.
- ❏ My child's choices.
- ❏ The security of my child.
- ❏ My child acting responsible.

What can you add to this list?

_____

_____

_____

WHAT I CANNOT CONTROL
- ❏ My child's ultimate choices.
- ❏ The way my child ultimately chooses to think, act or feel.
- ❏ Hereditary or genetic effects.
- ❏ Disease.
- ❏ Injury.
- ❏ The weather.
- ❏ The past.
- ❏ Living forever.

WHAT CAN YOU ADD TO THIS LIST?

_____
_____
_____

WHAT YOUR KIDS HAVE CONTROL OVER

- ❏ How they choose to think.
- ❏ How they choose to act.
- ❏ How they choose to feel.
- ❏ Doing or not doing what you or others say.
- ❏ Getting up on time.
- ❏ Going to bed on time.
- ❏ Their grades in school.
- ❏ Doing or not doing their homework.
- ❏ Their attitude.
- ❏ What they say to others.
- ❏ Their tone of voice.
- ❏ Who their friends are.
- ❏ The choices leading to being grounded or losing privileges.

WHAT YOUR KIDS HAVE INFLUENCE OVER

- ❏ How you and others choose to think about, feel about or act toward them.
- ❏ Whether or not you trust them.
- ❏ Whether or not they choose to earn back lost privileges.
- ❏ Grades they want.
- ❏ Their friends' decisions.

WHAT YOUR KIDS HAVE NO CONTROL OVER

- ❏ The natural or logical consequences for their choices.
- ❏ The way others choose to act, think or feel.
- ❏ The past choices that they have made.
- ❏ Hereditary or genetic effects.
- ❏ Disease.
- ❏ Injury.

Ask your kids to read over this list and see if they agree or disagree with it. They will probably debate some of the items on the list. That's great! You will have allowed them an opportunity to re-think with you what they have control over, what they have influence over and what they have no control over. This is a great way to open up dialogue about these critical productive thinking areas.

Self awareness exercise in roles other than parenthood

A. Think of the problems that you are having at the present time, whether personal, in business, with your family, in your marriage, in your finances, another relationship, or something else.

Personal problem you would like to have resolved

_____

_____

Business problem you would like to have resolved

_____

_____

Family problem you would like to have resolved

_____

_____

Financial problem you would like to have resolved

_____

_____

Marriage problem you would like to have resolved

_____

_____

Relationship problem you would like to have resolved

_____

_____

Other problem you would like to have resolved

_____

_____

Ask yourself these questions: What is it that **you want** in each situation?

What do you want regarding
Personal problem_____
Business problem_____
Family problem_____
Financial problem_____

Marriage problem_____
Relationship problem_____
Other problem_____

What do you have regarding
Personal problem_____
Business problem_____
Family problem_____
Financial problem_____
Marriage problem_____
Relationship problem_____
Other problem_____

In each area, decide whether it is something you have control over, something you have influence over or something you have no control over. Now, list what you have control over, influence over and no control over for each area.

WHAT YOU HAVE CONTROL OVER
PERSONAL PROBLEM
_____
_____

BUSINESS PROBLEM
_____
_____

FAMILY PROBLEM
_____
_____

FINANCIAL PROBLEM
_____
_____

MARRIAGE PROBLEM
_____
_____

RELATIONSHIP PROBLEM
_____
_____

OTHER PROBLEM
_____
_____

WHAT YOU HAVE INFLUENCE OVER
PERSONAL PROBLEM
_____
_____

BUSINESS PROBLEM
_____
_____

FAMILY PROBLEM
_____
_____

FINANCIAL PROBLEM
_____
_____

MARRIAGE PROBLEM
_____
_____

RELATIONSHIP PROBLEM
_____
_____

PROBLEM
_____
_____

WHAT YOU HAVE NO CONTROL OVER
PERSONAL PROBLEM
_____
_____

BUSINESS PROBLEM
_____
_____

FAMILY PROBLEM
_____
_____

FINANCIAL PROBLEM
_____
_____

MARRIAGE PROBLEM
_____
_____

RELATIONSHIP PROBLEM
_____
_____

OTHER PROBLEM
_____
_____

B. Using this format, think about other problems. **What do you have control over, what do you have influence over and what do you have no control over?** Remember, a problem is a difference between what you want and what you have. Once you identify what you want, you can quickly determine if it is in your **control**, something you can **influence** or something that is **out of your control**. Now, list **the thoughts, the actions and the feelings** you have control over in each situation.

THOUGHTS, ACTIONS AND FEELINGS YOU HAVE CONTROL OVER

PERSONAL PROBLEM
Thoughts_____
Actions_____
Feelings_____

BUSINESS PROBLEM
Thoughts_____
Actions_____
Feelings_____

FAMILY PROBLEM
Thoughts_____
Actions_____
Feelings_____

FINANCIAL PROBLEM
Thoughts_____
Actions_____
Feelings_____

MARRIAGE PROBLEM
Thoughts_____
Actions_____
Feelings_____

RELATIONSHIP PROBLEM
Thoughts_____
Actions_____
Feelings_____

OTHER PROBLEM
Thoughts_____
Actions_____
Feelings_____

C. What is the benefit of using this method to assess and control your thoughts, actions and feelings as opposed to the behavioral choices you have made in the past? How would a WhMPA choose to think, act or feel?

Repeat this exercise daily and you will find you have a tremendous amount of control in all your environments. **Use this productive thinking strategy at work, at home or any place you go.** Identify your want-and-have-differences, and immediately ask yourself the questions if you have control, influence or no control? You will find you worry less, become less anxious, angry, depressed **and guilt ridden.** You will then be able also to help your children with their problems and to teach them an incredible skill that they will be able to use for the rest of their lives.

Here is a list of behaviors that kids choose or problems they get into. Read them over and decide which ones **you** have control over, which ones **you** have influence over and which ones **you** have no control over.

- ❏ Homework.
- ❏ Sexual activity.
- ❏ Drinking.
- ❏ Alcohol and other drug use.
- ❏ Angering.
- ❏ Temper tantrumming.
- ❏ Pouting.
- ❏ Swearing.
- ❏ Lying.
- ❏ Crying.
- ❏ Stealing.
- ❏ Dress style.
- ❏ Hair style.
- ❏ Choice of friends.
- ❏ Occupation.
- ❏ School attendance.
- ❏ Getting up in a.m.
- ❏ Going to bed.
- ❏ Being on time.
- ❏ Getting a job.
- ❏ Saving money.
- ❏ Spending money.
- ❏ Feeling happy.
- ❏ Whom they date.
- ❏ Whom they marry.
- ❏ Attitude.
- ❏ Their friends.
- ❏ Tobacco use.

As you can see many of these are, at best, areas we can influence. You can have a lot of fun with this list, using it to observe problems and events in new and unexpected ways. You will see others trying to control things they have absolutely no control over. Take a moment and sit down in a busy area, like an airport or a shopping mall and watch people, see them act out their problems in futile, frustrating and often funny ways. The amount of energy that you and I waste trying to control what we cannot control is incredible. No wonder there is so much burnout. No wonder people give up and give in.

Like everyone else, parents must let go of issues they have no control over if they want to save their sanity. This does not mean that we surrender, but it does mean that we become realistic about our wants. Children may refuse to do what we say or ask of them. They may talk back, swear, use alcohol, tobacco, or other drugs. They may choose to engage in sex. At best we have only influence over these behaviors. Unless we put our kids under armed guard twenty-four hours a day, we can only influence, not control them. Frustrating as it may be, that is reality.

UNDERSTANDING, ACKNOWLEDGING, ACCEPTING, ALLOWING AND ADJUSTING

Acknowledging, accepting, allowing and adjusting provide the key to a life with minimal frustration.

Acknowledging

Acknowledging a difference between what we want and what we have is usually not a problem for most of us, unless we are denying that we are frustrated. In that case, with time we will eventually experience the frustration we are trying to deny. As with many alcoholics I have worked with, a good question cuts to the heart of the matter: *"Will continuing to drink get people off your back?"* The person may choose not to answer, but he will think about your question. With time, it will take hold.

Accepting

When it comes to a problem we are experiencing, most of us have a difficult time accepting what we cannot control. The higher the level of frus-

tration we experience, the less likely we are to accept that we cannot control our problem. A king size WhMPA will, of course, fight to the death at the thought of accepting defeat. A productive thinker, on the other hand, looks at and accepts the areas of his life that he has no control over. The serenity prayer becomes a daily part of the productive thinker's life. In developing a strategy to save your sanity, it is important to know where you have control, influence, or no control.

Allowing

Allowing others to take control and make their own choices is difficult, especially with our children. On one hand we want them to be in control. On the other hand we want to be in control. We want them to think, act, and feel the way we do, but as productive thinkers, we need to allow them to make mistakes and allow them the opportunity to correct those mistakes, providing them with an opportunity to believe that they can take control of their lives. To the WhMPA, allowing them to have choices is goofy.

Adjusting

Once you acknowledge and accept that you have a problem, adjusting thoughts, actions and feelings is vital to your sanity. The larger degree of difference between what you want and have makes it more difficult to adjust your thoughts, actions or feelings. Difficult but not impossible. The more you want things that you have a good chance of getting, the better you will feel. Remember, you always decide what **"wants"** you put into your brain.

Productive thinking gives you control

Let's go back to the start of the book and recall my indoctrination into the world of parenthood. What did I want? I wanted my kids to think, act and feel the way I wanted them to think, act and feel. What did I have? I had kids who cried, screamed and threw up on me. They whined, pouted, burped and talked back. Did I experience a difference? Certainly I did, a big difference. Was I frustrated? Yes, I was frustrated. Did I think and act like a WhMPA back then? Absolutely. Did I look at what I had control, influence or no control over? No. At that time in my life I hadn't been exposed to Dr. Gary Applegate and the skills of the Skill Development theory for successful change. I used the best choices or skills I had at the time. If I knew then what I know now, I would have used different skills. So don't damn yourself for being human, and thinking, acting and feeling like a WhMPA. You will lose your cool from time to time and find yourself angering or screaming, but with practice, your time in WhMPA forest will decrease.

Frustration provides us with motivation but gives us no direction. We just feel a signal to "do something." We can **CHOOSE** to think negatively, choose to act negatively, and choose to feel negatively. We can also **CHOOSE** to think, act, or feel neutrally by stepping back and thinking productively first. This **productive thinking** will direct our actions and feelings in a positive and controlled fashion. WhMPA's react; **productive thinkers step back.**

In this connection, I will never forget a counselor I supervised in a drug treatment program. She made the classic WhMPA statement at a staff meeting, *"If my patients are having a good day and they are sober, then I am having a good day also!"* To put your happiness in the hands of other people is like putting strings on all of the components of your behavior and handing the strings to anybody who walks by. You become the puppet and they are the puppeteer. They direct your every movement. You go up and down as they see fit, not as you want. They have the control, not you. You give the control of your own life away to them.

Having worked in the field of alcoholism treatment for many years, I had the good fortune to learn what creates healthy thinking and what creates absolutely bizarre thinking. A client recovering from alcoholism told me one time that, *"The reason I am depressed is that it is my Higher Power's plan for me."* What a wonderfully built in, *"I'm-not-responsible-for-my-life"* belief this is. The problem was that it was not only she who believed this. Her therapist had taught her to believe it! The therapist told me that the lady needed to believe this because she was in an unstable position. *"To gain control over her life was not for her to decide. It was for her Higher Power."* The therapist, of course, should be helping this woman understand that she is the one who has control over the way she thinks, acts and feels. Many people in the helping professions often look

into a person's background for underlying causes of misbehavior, believing there is a **cause** for the choices a person makes and the subsequent behavior they exhibit. You often hear helpers saying, *"What can you expect, he comes from an alcoholic home?" "She comes from a broken home." "She was an abused child." or "They are really poor."* I don't want you to think that I don't agree that these conditions exist, but I do believe that these and similar conditions only **influence,** and not control our choices. Some people come from homes where one or both parents were alcoholics or drug addicts, or where the parents were physically, sexually or emotionally abusive. Some parents were homeless, out of work, single, divorced, and so on. What amazes me and proves my point is that these people acknowledge their past environments, and accept it as part of their past, acknowledging in effect that they are only influenced by experiences and not controlled by their experiences. They do not allow the past to control their present or future choices. They have made a choice to adjust their thinking. Even the most oppressive early environments only influence us; they do not rob us of the power and responsibility to choose.

But what if your own parents were WhMPA's. I mean extra large WhMPA's. They were mean, cruel or abusive. In order to be the best parent that you can be, you will need to let go of the resentment that you have over the way in which your parents raised you. Your parents used the "best skills that they knew of at the time." If they had known other alternatives, they probably would have used them. An abusive parent is really using his best skills at the time to deal with the frustration he is having in his own life. Where did he learn to be abusive in dealing with frustration? From the environment he grew up in. Nevertheless, he is responsible for his choices and should be held accountable for his actions. But this reconfirms the theory that we do in fact make our best attempts at the time to meet one or more of our needs.

That is why my association with Dr. Applegate and the Skill Development theory changed me from a problem solver to a **teacher and a model** of better choices. Remember the saying, **"If a hungry man comes to you, you can give him a fish and he can feed himself for the evening; or you can teach him how to fish and he can feed himself for the rest of his life."** I prefer teaching everyone I come in contact with how to fish. I want to teach people productive thinking skills to effectively manage their own lives. I want them to evaluate how they have attempted to control other peoples' thoughts, actions or feelings, and to give them new skills to effectively think, act or feel about themselves and the world around them. They will then look at what they have control over, what they have influence over and what they have no control over. By doing so, they will be stepping back and **thinking productively** first and then looking at the choices that they can make in any situation.

Increasing our influence over kids

How can we influence our kids to be responsible and capable? What can we do? Our influence over others, which ranges from fifty to eighty-five per-cent, is based upon the four areas that all of us have total "control" over in any relationship. Read these over and use them in your daily life with your kids. Teach and model these concepts using your own life problems as a backdrop. I'm convinced you will see results.

Demonstrating caring

We can **demonstrate caring** to our kids and other people through our touch, hugs, kisses, high fives and other kinds of physical contact. We aren't compelled to demonstrate caring to our kids. We have the choice. We have the control. Listening is the most important component of demonstrating caring. It is not by chance that God gave us two ears and one mouth. Unfortunately, many people use their mouths and not their ears. To be more effective in this area, you need to train yourself to be more of a sensor and less of a thinker when responding to others. Most of us think about what we want to say in response to our children and miss the importance of what they are saying to us. As kids can tell you, it does no good to even ask a question if no one is willing to listen to the answer.

You can demonstrate caring to anyone—even the biggest jerk in the world! Many people ask, *"Why on God's green earth would you ever want to bother?"* Because they, like everyone else, have the same internal psychological needs that we all have, and their needs will move them toward us or away from us based upon how they interpret our actions. If we demonstrate caring to them for the sole pur-

pose of building a relationship, and not to change some "jerky behavior," they will eventually perceive us as need-fulfilling people, move toward us and listen to us. As a result, they will work with us and not against us.

Many people, of course, have a hard time with this. They think in a negative way about the thoughts, actions and feelings expressed by others. Their negative perception of others' thoughts, actions or feelings then directs the typical WhMPA behaviors—controlling, arguing, criticizing, threatening, and so on. **If you perceive your need-fulfillment as coming from your kids, you will perceive them negatively whenever they don't think, act, or feel the way you want them to.** If you want them to be nice to you and they are not, then you will probably say to them or to yourself, "To heck *with you!" "Why should I be nice to you when I don't get nice back from you?"* **You are setting yourself up for being frustrated.** In the second step of the productive thinking strategy, we have a difference between what we want and what we have, which motivates us to attempt to change "out there." In the third area of productive thinking, the parent wants the jerky behavior to stop or wants the kid to change. At best this is something they can only influence but not control. Thus, the set-up for **Parent Burnout.**

Burnout is characterized by three primary symptoms:

An incredible physical reaction: When, for example, your child talks back to you, refuses to answer you, brings home a failing report card or cries uncontrollably, you take away their privileges and they respond with "So?," or when the IRS has informed you of an audit, you experience an incredible physical reaction that feels like it hits every part of your body, from head to toe. This occurs when we want something we are not getting, whether from our kids or others. The greater the difference, the more extreme the physical reaction. When it is extreme, your whole body tightens up in frustration—with people in a traffic jam, when a phone number you need to reach stays busy, when you spill something on your clothing, or you open a can and the pop top breaks off. Can you feel it?

A knot in the knickers: People develop "knots in their knickers" over many situations that they have practically no control over or at best can only influence. You would swear that your clothes are tightening from the reaction to what is happening. You want something you are not getting. You experience the frustration, the physical reaction, and the knot in the knickers. Traffic jams, the flushed toilet when you're in the shower, kids not doing what you want, other people frustrating you. These are all problems. These are all differences. Some people I've met are going to be strangled by their own Fruit of the Looms! Their underwear become a necktie. A necktie that is self strangling.

Optical Rectitus: Al Lehrke, the assistant principal I first worked with, told me of the people in the world suffering from optical rectitus. He went on to say that optical rectitus occurs when your optic nerves get tangled up with your rectal nerves and you begin to have a crappy outlook on life! You're wearing negative lenses through which to view the world and your kids. You will perceive them in a *"why-don't-you-why-can't-you-how-come-you-never"* frame of reference. You might even be saying things like, *"The only good kid is a dead kid!"*

If, as a parent, you interpret your need fulfillment as not dependent exclusively on what others do, then if they do not respond in the way "you" want, you will feel okay. Of course it would be nice if when you said "Hi," they said "Hi," and when you were nice, they were nice. But welcome to the real world and what you can only influence. You can, however, control the degree of frustration you experience in your life.

But, if you are counting on some type of feedback from your kids when you demonstrate caring and you don't get it in return from them, you will feel frustrated, hurt, rejected, angry or spiteful. This is the give-to-get syndrome as opposed to giving to give, which does not depend on the outside world around us to make us feel good. **If your thinking is the reason for your frustration, if you want something you have no control over, don't set yourself up. Choose to rethink, not react.**

A critical component of demonstrating caring is your tone of voice. In many instances you can convince yourself and others that you are demonstrating caring, when in fact, you are yelling at your child, telling him something like *"I am yelling because I care about you!"* Our tone of voice is proportional to our frustration. Listen to people around you and you will see what I mean. If you say "Hi" to your kids, you want a "Hi" in return. If you don't get it, repeat "Hi" an octave higher. If you don't get a response, you raise the volume. Say something like, *"I said 'Hi,' aren't you going to say 'Hi' back?"* Observe people wherever you are and you will see what I mean. View them in a new way.

Try to figure out what they want, what they are getting, the possible thoughts they are generating and observe their action choices. Listen for the tone of voice. You will be amazed at what you see and hear.

Asking questions

All of us have control over asking questions of anyone we are in a relationship with. The problem is not in asking questions as much as in receiving answers. Have you ever asked a question of a child who chose not to answer? Were you frustrated? Did you press again and again, raising your tone of voice with each question. If you think others must answer when you ask a question, stop and rethink. Your problem is not them. **Your problem is you.** You have control over how you choose to think, over demonstrating caring, asking questions, making statements and providing alternatives. Their unresponsiveness and your subsequent thoughts, actions and feelings of frustration are the result of your thinking and nothing else! Don't give away control over your feelings.

There are three basic types of questions we have control over asking:

OPEN-ENDED QUESTIONS:
These are what we call information gathering questions. We ask them to get more information about what others are thinking, doing or feeling.
"What happened?"
"Tell me your side of the story."
"What are your feelings about this problem?"
"What are you thinking about when you are having this problem?"
"If you continue to anger, will that help you with this problem?"
"What negative thoughts do you have about this problem?"
"What do you choose to do when this problem comes up?"
"What have you done in the past to deal with a problem such as this?
Was that effective?"
You are in control of asking questions, not getting answers. Most parents have problems when their kids either don't answer their questions or **the answer is one that parents don't want to hear.** An example is asking your teenage son the question, *"Do you think that drinking alcohol under the legal*

drinking age is okay?" He might answer, *"Yeah mom, everybody does it, don't be so square."* Perhaps you wanted a simple, *"No"* or *"You're right,"* but instead you get what you consider to be the wrong answer. If you are frustrated when your child answers your questions his way when you know what the answer "should" be, who really owns the problem? By deciding the right answer in advance, you are not allowing your child to meet his need for **Freedom,** to make his own choices and to give his own answers. Once he gives you an answer, you can challenge it with questions, but remember a productive thinker does this by demonstrating caring through tone of voice and allowing differences of opinion. The critical point here is that we look at our **tone of voice** and how we ask the question. The louder your voice becomes, the more you are trying to control the answer. If I had a dime for every time a child came into my office and said, *"They always yell at me; they never talk,"* I would have a boat load of dimes by now.

CLOSED-ENDED QUESTIONS:

Very simply, these questions are information giving as well as teaching questions we can use with our children. They are questions that can be answered, if the child chooses to answer, with a simple "yes" or "no." These questions begin with phrases like:

"Do you step back and rethink about what you have control over?"
"Are you in control of what you say?"
"Are you in control of coming in on time or earlier?"
"Are you in control of doing or not doing your homework?"
"Can you choose to follow rules or to disobey rules?"
"Do you choose to be unhappy?"
"Do you choose to think negatively about yourself or others?"
"Do you approach your friends and say 'Hi' first?"
"Do you choose to say 'Hi' first to others?"
"Do you create fun on your own?"
"Do you choose to think that all people have problems?"
"Do you bring your books to class with you?"
"Do you think of problems as opportunities to learn and grow?"
"Do you think about the process steps that it will take to solve a problem?"

If you become upset when you don't receive an answer, go back to the productive thinking steps. What were you thinking? Do you have a difference between what you want and what you have? If you are frustrated because others choose not to answer your questions, ask yourself these questions, *"Do you have control over their answering?" "Can you influence them with your questions?" "Does your tone of voice increase or decrease your influence?" "What do you have control over?"* In order to save your sanity, you can choose from this point forward to **rethink** that people will not react as you want. They may cover their eyes, stare into space, roll their eyes, plug their ears, mimic your mouth movements or respond with silence. Choose to **rethink** that what you are attempting to accomplish is to help others **think** about:

1. The problem they have.
2. The choices they are making or not making.
3. The potential outcome of the choices they make.

Change takes place on the thinking level first. It makes sense to help the other person rethink his thoughts, actions and feelings. You can visualize yourself like the airplane in the movie **"Top Gun"** that comes in, lets its rocket (questions) go, and gets out of there. **Allow** your rocket (questions) to penetrate the target (the child). Give it time and it will go to work. **Ask your question and allow the other person the opportunity to process the information on his own.** We can aim our open-ended and closed-ended rockets without controlling for them further. Many WhMPA's, however, take a **Rambo** approach, starting out with good intentions by asking questions, but ending up criticizing, threatening or turning up their voice volume, all in an attempt to change "out there." If you ask them why they do this, they will usually point out the child's "resistance" to answer correctly as the reason for their choice behaviors.

COMPARISON QUESTIONS:

Constructive change does not occur until people evaluate their present thoughts and actions. Comparison questions open up the gap between what we want and what we have by evaluating our actions and thoughts. Perhaps you know someone who wants to lose weight. You've asked them open ended questions and found out that they want to weigh or look a certain way. They have a difference between what they want and what they have. You can ask closed-ended "do you" questions such as, *"Do you exercise on a regular basis?" "Do you have* control over what you choose to eat?" "Do you drink at least eight glasses of water everyday?" "Do you monitor your food intake?" "What excuses have you used to prevent yourself from taking control of your weight?" These are **"velvet hammer"** questions because they are like getting a whack on the side of the head. These questions open up differences. They cause us to connect our thoughts and actions with the consequences or feelings that result.

Some velvet hammer questions that we should ask ourselves as parents are, "Is yelling at your children helping you enough to gain a better relationship?" "Does telling your daughter that she is a no-good, lazy jerk build a better relationship with her?" "Does threatening your kids with physical punishment work enough?" You can also use comparison questions with your children: "Is choosing not to follow the expectations in our home earning you the loss of the car?" "Is hitting your brother the reason you are sitting in your room?" "Is your choice to not come home on time the reason why you are grounded?"

You can also ask your children these questions: "Is crying about your problem helping you enough to solve that problem?" "Will choosing to depress about your problem help you to solve it?" "How long do you plan to stay angry?" "If you continue to use alcohol, do you think others will continue to be on your back?" "If you choose not to study, will that result in poor grades?" "If you choose to go to school instead of skipping, do you think the assistant principal will be off your back?" "If you continue to swear at me, do you think I will allow you to earn back the use of the car?"

These three types of questions seem a little awkward to ask at first, but practice, practice, practice. Think of yourself as a conductor: Bring in the "What," "Do You," and "Comparison" questions in a flow that is appropriate to the situation.

1. Identify what the person wants. Ask, "What do you want?"
2. Compare this to what they presently have. Ask, "What do you presently have?"
3. Discuss the degree of difference that exists. Ask, "Is there a difference between what you want and what you have?" "To what degree?"
4. Identify and listen for the thoughts, actions or feelings they have chosen to solve their problem or get what they want. Ask "What have you been thinking in relation to this problem?" "What have you been doing to get rid of this problem?"

5. Take each choice and ask comparison questions, such as:
"Is choosing to helping you enough to solve this problem?"
"Will you get what you want if you continue to?"
"What prices do you pay for choosing to _____?"
"If you focus on changing 'out there,' how will that give you more long term control?"
"Would you say that choosing to is getting people more on your back or off your back?"
"If you continue to think, act and feel the way you presently do, whose choice is that?"
"Is choosing to helping you meet those needs you identified as being unfulfilled?"
"If you continue to will you get what you want without paying any prices?"

It is critical to ask these questions in a mellow tone of voice. I used to ask these questions in a slanted way when I first started working with people. My tone of voice fluctuated, and I said things like, "Thinking or doing_____surely isn't going to help you, is it?" "You can't sit here and tell me that thinking or doing_____is going to get people off your back?" "If you continue to drink, you will get more and more people on your back; don't you understand?" "You better not do what you say you are going to do or you will be in trouble." You can almost feel my "leading-the-witness" slant here. You know what answer I want. If I didn't get that answer, I would argue my point with the person. People hate being controlled, and I was trying to control their thoughts, actions and feelings. What a WhMPA I was.

VERBAL
(7%)

TONE
(38%)

BODY LANGUAGE
(55%)

Studies have shown that in face-to-face contact, only seven percent of communication is verbal content, thirty-eight percent is tone and a whopping fifty-five percent is body language. Many researchers classify tone (paralanguage) in the non-verbal code; thus ninety-three percent of communication is nonverbal. Body posture, gesturing, eye contact and facial expressions often speak much louder than words.

In my workshops, I put people in small groups and send one person out into the hall to prepare for his part in a role-play when he returns to the small group. When he comes in, he plays the part of an obnoxious kid who displays passive-aggressive behavior in the form of eye rolling, not responding to questions, and even scratching his forehead with his middle finger for dramatic effect. This always drive the people in the group who are playing the part of the teacher, the parent or the adult figure nuts! Why? Because they want the kid to stop the behavior and, more importantly, listen to them when they talk to him. Many people comment that kids "must" answer their questions and give them respect. Wrong! If you want to set yourself up for tight rectal muscles, undies in a bundle and optical rectitus, try to control others' thoughts, actions and feelings.

Making statements

Everybody has control over making statements to other people. **The critical component here is how you control your tone of voice and how you present yourself, both verbally and non-verbally.** Many parents have very good information that they are trying to get across to their kids. The statements they make to influence them are rational and sensible. But when the parent presents his information, the child stares blankly, rolls his eyes or talks back, and the parent loses control by losing his temper. Think of some of the statements parents make: *"You better do what I say." "You are going to listen to me, if I have to make you!" "If you don't listen to me, I will take your privileges away."*

Remember that you are influencing your children with your statements. You are trying to help them evaluate their thinking about their problem(s), before they choose to change their actions. Your tone of voice and presentation are important:

"If you choose to do what you want, this is the choice I will make."

"If you continue to skip school, I will continue to inform the school that you are choosing to skip today."

"If you continue to come in late for dinner, you will continue to eat your dinner cold."

"Doing your homework is your choice and your problem."

"I don't have control over your choices, but I do have control over your privileges."

"If you go against the expectations, then you will be the one who is grounding yourself or losing the privileges you choose to lose—it will not be us taking these away from you."

Providing alternative choices

There are two ways in which we can provide alternatives to our children and to others:

a) **Teach your children** other alternatives based upon your experience with similar situations in your own life. This doesn't mean going through the "old days" when you were a kid, but relating to them in a way that presents them with the impression that you, too, were human at one time. Yes, human! Sit down with your child in a calm manner and discuss with them what they can do in the future. They have no control over the choices they have already made. They do have control over evaluating those choices and coming up with new and more efficient choices to use in the future if the same situation should arise again. How you present yourself to your children is important.

b) **Model better choices for your children**. Do as I say and not as I do is the WhMPA way. Your children will learn more about life from your actions than from your words.

It is critical for us to admit that we have made poor choices ourselves in order to influence our own kids. Think for a moment about the poor choices you made when you were growing up. Did you lie, steal, smoke, drink, cheat or talk back to your parents? Did you make poor choices in school, in the community, at work, in relationships or with money? Acknowledging them will keep us humble. We do not, of course, have to share each and every poor choice we have ever made with our children. Kids will learn that we are human. They will understand that we, too, have made poor choices. They will also understand through our guidance that we have learned about the prices we paid for making those poor choices, and how to make better choices in the future. And better yet, we will be able to teach and model to our children to solve similar problems in their lives.

When it comes to modeling choices, values, ethics and decision-making, we are not doing such a hot job. Look what we have delivered in the form of famous celebrities and politicians. The sad thing is that positive role models are few and far between. Just when we think we have someone to look up to, a controversy proves otherwise.

Did you receive praise from your parents when you made good choices? Did they tell you that you had made a good choice? Did they turn the problems you had into learning opportunities? Did they teach and model better choices for you to use? Did they make you feel like you were in total control of your life, that you had the power, control and responsibility? That you had the decision making ability? Or did nothing happen? How important is it that our kids hear praise from us for good choices? Think about how many times they hear, *"What the heck are you doing?"* *"That is really stupid."* *"How many times are you going to do it wrong?"* *"Are you brain dead or what's the deal?"* Kids after all, respond just like you and me when it comes to praise, criticism, ridicule or psychological or physical intimidation. Think about how you respond to your kids and whether it works in your best interest or your child's. If you decide that what you are choosing to think and/or do is not effective, that you are paying prices for your choices, don't worry. You're human, and you can think and act differently in the future.

I am not, of course, faulting anyone. We are all doing what we have been trained to do and many of us do very well. I have no reason to believe otherwise that the vast majority of those in the helping profession are dedicated, conscientious, and genuinely motivated to the alleviation of pain and misery in the lives of others. The problem is how we view the problems presented to us. The lenses through which our

parents viewed their world worked for them, but they are not working for us because they make things more frustrating.

What I am suggesting is that some of the classical, basic assumptions that form the foundation of our efforts to help people improve the quality of their lives hinder, although unintentionally, the effectiveness of our efforts.

If, for instance, our efforts consist mostly of doing things "to" or "for" our children, we either induce more dependency in our children or perpetuate the notion that life is essentially an ongoing battle with our environment. Neither process directly addresses the goal of teaching people, including ourselves, the productive thinking skills we need to better meet our own needs. These needs are internal to each of us and drive us from within, not from the outside world.

The belief that I have control over others, including my children, is false. At times if I tell them to jump, they will jump and even ask, "How high?" or say "Sit" and they sit, or say "Talk" and they talk. But there are many times when I said "jump" and they didn't even budge, or "sit" and they refused, or "talk" and they didn't even flutter their lips. At times we appear to have control over other people in getting them to do the things that we want them to do. **But the reality is that they jumped or responded to what we wanted because they believed that choosing to do that was the right choice for themselves at the time.** They made the choice, not us. It was not because of our power over them or because "out there" made them think, act or feel in any certain way.

In Jack Benny's classic scene, he is walking through a park during the evening hours when a robber approaches him, sticks a gun to the back of his neck and says, *"Give me your money or your life."* Benny stands quietly while the man repeats in a louder and more stern voice, *"Your money or your life!"* after which Benny places his hand to his jaw, stares blankly into the night sky, and says, *"I'm thinking, I'm thinking."* The point is that Jack hasn't decided in his own mind whether he wants to be 1) alive and poor, or 2) dead and rich.

Even though our choices at times can be really rotten or miserable, we always have a choice. We can think and act and feel the way we want. The same goes for our kids.

We do not have total control over anyone. Nor do our kids have control over us. As parents, we might think, *"I will be a good parent if I can get my children to change and do what I say."* When I first started in the field of counseling, I really believed this applied to me as a counselor. After all, I had my degree in psychology and my job was to psychologize or fix people who came to see me. They weren't just in the neighborhood and thought they would stop in! They came to me because they were in trouble in some area of their life and they wanted someone or something to help them out with their problems. I believed that if the clients changed the way I thought they should, I would feel good and they would feel good. If they didn't, I said things to myself like, "bad client" or "typical client" and might have referred them on to someone or someplace else. Referral, for me, was a nice way of saying "I give up." Have we given up on our kids? More and more parents come to me with children ages twelve and up, saying, *"I can't take this anymore, I give up."* They are waiting for the day when their kids turn eighteen so they can get them out of the house and out of their hair.

Let's look at an example. Robert was a confused young man. He came from a split family with a wealthy father. Mother had numerous problems, one of which was her own use of alcohol and other drugs. Robert was shipped from one house to another every three months, per the parents' divorce agreement. Father, focused on his professional career, had little time for him. Mother had even less. Robert, lacking in need fulfillment, as you probably guessed, turned to anyone to fulfill the void. Turning to a clique of peers involved in wearing all black clothes, cutting their hair extremely short and wearing pounds of earrings was his choice. They accepted him unconditionally. His parents didn't.

Robert chose to become involved with these friends for various reasons, but mostly because he found a sense of **Belonging** with them that he did not with his parents. It became more and more apparent that Robert chose his radical dress and weird behaviors at home, at school and in the community to counter the controlling behaviors of his parents. Robert refused to talk when asked questions, refused to mind his parents' rules, and refused to do what they said or what they wanted. Of course, Robert's parents were not interested in looking at themselves first. They were only interested in figuring out how to change Robert!

But which area do we have more control over changing? Ourselves? Or our children? Like the counselor I used to be, we start out by listening to problems our kids bring to us and then we come up with solutions for our child. But that solution is **our** solution. Not theirs. **If kids don't believe in the solution to a problem or feel ownership, the likeli-** **hood of their following through is slim.** That is what typical therapy is like. Problem solving, as you remember, should be used only when someone is in jeopardy of killing himself or someone else. We want to focus our attention on a productive thinking approach to problems.

We all want our children to believe that they have the power within themselves to change whatever they want in their lives. If they are unhappy, they can choose to be happy. If they are depressed, they can choose to feel better. If they have problems of any type, they should have the productive thinking skills to resolve them. Believing that you possess this power frees you from the confinements of the world around you.

Recently I watched a re-run of "The Wizard of Oz." When the scarecrow asked for brains, the wizard replied, *"You've always had a brain. You don't need a brain ... experience is the only thing that brings knowledge, and the longer you are on earth, the more experience you will have."* When the lion asked for courage, the wizard replied, *"You have plenty of courage; I am sure that all you need is confidence in yourself."* The wizard who turned out not to be a true wizard, after all, was truly a wizard because he realized that the cure for our weaknesses and maladies comes not from a "magic" source "out there" but from tapping our own inner power. The cure lies in getting down to the power that is within each of us. Just as the wizard could provide no "magic" cure, neither can all the "helpers" in the world. Not even from ourselves as parents. Only productive thinking skills can produce new actions that will enable us to get what we really want in life: the fulfillment of our own internal psychological needs.

That's why, when we want to either help ourselves or our kids with "their" problems, we look beyond the presenting problem and into what **needs** are being frustrated. The more efficient skills you have in meeting your internal psychological needs, the more choices you have, hence the more power and control you feel in your life. Isn't this what we want our kids to have in their own lives?

Key points to remember

- ❑ Separate problems into areas where you have control, influence and no control.
- ❑ Teach and model this strategy to your children with every problem they present to you.

- ❏ Acknowledge that life is a series of problems to be solved
- ❏ Accept that we have problems in life that we will have either no control, or at best, influence over.
- ❏ Allow others to take control over their own lives.
- ❏ Allow others to take responsibility for their own choices.
- ❏ Be willing to adjust your thinking and your actions in order to get what you want in your life, or to lessen the degree of stress you experience.
- ❏ Understand that you have control over four areas in any relationship: 1) demonstrating caring, 2) asking questions, 3) making statements and 4) providing alternative choices.
- ❏ Your tone of voice is critical in increasing your influence over other people.

Helpful hints

- ❏ Rethink problems in terms of control, influence and no control.
- ❏ Work on using the words control, influence and no control in your everyday language.
- ❏ Teach your children to use these words when they are frustrated.
- ❏ Look for opportunities to teach and model these skills to your children and others you come in contact with.
- ❏ Identify areas where you may be controlling for things, situations or people.
- ❏ Begin to view movies, plays and the world around you in these terms.

CHAPTER 11

PRODUCTIVE THINKING SKILL 4
THINKING FROM NO-CHOICE TO CHOICE

I Choose:
To live by choice, not by chance;
To make changes, not excuses;
To be motivated, not manipulated;
To be useful, not used;
To excel, not compete;
I choose self-esteem, not self-pity;
I choose to listen to the inner voice, not the
random opinion of others.
author unknown

Changes in time

"For all of those born before 1945—you were the survivors. Consider the changes you have witnessed: You were born before television, before penicillin, before polio shots, frozen foods, Xerox, plastic, contact lenses, Frisbees and the Pill.

You were born before radar detectors, credit cards, split atoms, laser beams and ballpoint pens; before panty-hose, dishwashers, clothes dryers, electric blankets, air conditioners, drip-dry clothes and before man walked on the moon. You got married first and then lived together. How quaint could you be! In your time closets were for clothes, not 'coming out of.' Bunnies were small rabbits and rabbits were not Volkswagens. Designer jeans were scheming girls named Jean or Jeanne, and having a meaningful relationship meant getting along well with our cousins.

You thought fast food was what you ate during Lent, and Outer Space was the back of the Riviera Theatre.

You were born before house-husbands, gay rights, dual careers and computer dating. You were born before day-care centers, group therapy and nursing homes. You never heard of FM radio, tape decks, electric typewriters, artificial hearts, word processors, yogurt, and guys wearing earrings. For you, time sharing meant togetherness—not computers or condominiums; a 'chip' meant a piece of wood; hardware meant hardware, and software wasn't even a word!

In 1940, 'made in Japan' meant junk and the term 'making out' referred to how you did on your exam. Pizza, 'MacDonalds' and instant coffee were unheard of.

You hit the scene when there were 5 and 10 cent stores, where you bought things for five and ten cents. Isaly's sold ice cream cones for a nickel or a dime. For one nickel you could ride the street car (trolley), make a phone call, buy a Pepsi, or enough stamps to mail one letter and two postcards. You could buy a new Chevy Coupe for $600, but who could afford one; pity, too, because gas was 11 cents a gallon!

In your day, cigarette smoking was fashionable, Grass was mowed, Coke was a drink and Pot was something you cooked in. Rock music was Grandma's lullaby and AIDS were helpers in the principal's office.

You certainly were not born before the difference between the sexes was discovered but were surely born before the sex change: you made do with what you had, and you were the last generation that was so dumb as to think you had to have a husband to have a baby.

No wonder you are so confused and there is so much of a generation gap today!"

Source unknown

Out-of-control parents

In a recent study published in the "American Journal of Orthopsychiatry," Richard J. Gelles found there were "*an astoundingly large number of children who were kicked, bitten, punched, beaten up,*

*threatened with a gun or knife or had a gun or knife ac-
tually used on them"* by their own parents. These
are, to say the least, frustrated and out-of-control
parents! If you asked these parents how they were
feeling, I suspect the majority would describe their
feelings in negative terms like angry, frustrated,
hurt, rejected, depressed or just plain "burned out."
Burnout occurs when we are attempting to control
something or someone we have no control or only
influence over. WhMPA's are always talking about
being burned out from dealing with someone or
something outside of themselves.

Out-of-control kids

The top problems in the public school as iden-
tified by teachers in 1940 were:
- ❏ Talking out of turn.
- ❏ Chewing gum.
- ❏ Making noise.
- ❏ Running in the halls.
- ❏ Cutting in line.
- ❏ Dress code infractions.
- ❏ Littering.

and 1990 they are:
- ❏ Drug abuse.
- ❏ Alcohol abuse.
- ❏ Pregnancy.
- ❏ Suicide.
- ❏ Rape.
- ❏ Robbery.
- ❏ Assault.

It is estimated that over 135,000 kids in this
country carry a gun to school on any one day. By
the time a kid reaches age eighteen, he has witnessed approximately 200,000 acts of violence and
25,000 killings on television. Today's curriculum
is reading, writing and retaliation. Many kids have
been able to convince their parents not to impose
any kind of structure, believing that they should not
have a curfew imposed on them, that the use of any
kind of language they feel like using is normal, and
that we should accept them as the new generation
and *"just get a life."* Many kids have told me that
treating parents as they please is *"where it's at."*
They believe that seeing any movie they want to
regardless of the rating is *"their right"* and is something *"everybody is doing."* Going where they want
to, including *"spring break"* at such places as
Daytona Beach, Cancun, or other exotic places,
unchaperoned of course, is also their *"right."* This
has led many a parent to wonder "Who's Raising
Whom?"

Every day, parents are confronted with situations where they want their children to behave in
certain ways. It starts out in the morning with, *"Get
out of bed, it's time for school,"* followed by *"I'm only
going to say this one more time, you're going to be late,"*
or *"I have to be at work right now and you haven't even
dressed yet,"* and continues after school with *"You
have to do your homework now,"* *"You had better be
in this house on time or you will get it,"* or *"Go to bed
this minute."* These are accepted ways for parents
to express their expectations. When these requests
fall on deaf ears, many parents yell a little louder
in order to be heard. They yell louder and the kids
continue to disobey. The frustration level rises with
each attempt. Because they don't know of better
ways to deal with their kids, the inevitable occurs:
Parent Burnout!

When lecturing to kids I ask them if they have
ever heard one or more of the following when their
parents are trying to **get them** to do something:

> *"You are going to do it because it's the rule around
> here, that's why!"*
> *"Because I said so, that's why!"*
> *"Because I'm your mother, that's why!"*
> *"Because I'm your father, that's why!"*
> *"Because I'm the adult and you are the child."*
> *"Fine, don't do what I say …you just wait until
> your father gets home!"*
> *"Okay (holding out fingers) … one … two … if I
> get to three, that little butt of yours is going
> to shine!"*

The kids go wild! They have their hands and
even their feet raised in response to all of these
questions! This tells me that parents today are using many of the same choices their parents used on
them. Parents have admitted to me that they, too,
have used these techniques repeatedly and have
had to turn up the volume knob in order to gain
more control of their kids' behaviors. Unfortunately, many parents have confirmed that when
they raised their voice, threatened or even physically grabbed their kids, their kids did what they
wanted. I say unfortunately because it creates the
blowfish syndrome that many WhMPA's suffer
from today.

Think of the scenario at bedtime. The kid
doesn't **want** to go to bed. The parent **wants** the
kid to go to bed. The kid complains, the parent

threatens, increasing the volume if necessary. The parent gives the one or two-finger routine. The kid stomps reluctantly up the stairs and into the bedroom. The parent stands at the bottom of the stairs, feeling so in control, so in power, with a little grin on his face, puffed up like a blowfish with great power. Power over the child. Power to get them to do as they were told. It gives the parent the same feeling that Barney had on "The Andy Griffith Show" when Andy was out of town in Mount Pilot and Barney was left in charge of Mayberry with one bullet in his pocket. He was the acting sheriff. He was in charge. He was king of the hill! If you remember the series, you will recall that the bullet in Barney's pocket gave him a false sense of security and power. When problems arose, and they always did, Barney needed more than a bullet in his pocket to help him out. When we experience problems with our kids, we need more than one-bullet control methods.

Why don't kids listen to their parents? Parents often tell me that they become scared of their kids because they are getting bigger, as well as getting tougher, to control. When I tell them that they never had total control in the first place, they want to hit me over the head. They want control. When the kids get older and bigger, the parent tries the same techniques that worked earlier but finds them to have little or no effect. What happens is that suddenly the parents feel power**less**. When their kids were younger and didn't go to bed, the parents could pick them up like luggage and take them to bed! But what about now? Where's that bullet?

Gaining control through punishment

What about punishment? Does it work with today's kids? Is it okay to hit? To spank? To threaten? What do we teach our kids by hitting them? By kicking them? By throwing things at them? Threatening them with physical harm? It worked for our parents—and their parents. Or did it? Should we keep on using it? How much is too much? If it doesn't work at 20 mph, should we go to 40 mph? Or maybe even 100 mph if we have to?

Punishment has been around for a long time. There are verses in the Bible that allude to the need for punishment or the need for "correction" of the child who disobeys. "The Old Woman in the Shoe" states that when the kids were bad, she "whipped them soundly and put them to bed." Many believe in punishment as the only form of discipline that works with kids. Others disagree.

Punishment is not usually effective for several reasons. First, punishment teaches a person what "not to do" instead of "what to do." It is more concerned with stopping a behavior then looking at other choices. Punishment is not primarily concerned with teaching better choices but with control. Punishment is attempting to control another person, period. Secondly, to be effective, punishment needs to be immediate and severe. In some cases punishment does work, which quite frankly is the worst thing that can happen. We spank, hit, physically threaten and control our children to let them know "who's in charge." It becomes the worst thing that can happen if it is reinforced through success. When it works, it produces the "blow fish syndrome", because just like the blowfish, we swell up with **power over others**, leading us further into the illusion of control. What we accomplished indirectly is to teach our children that control through punishment works. All they learn is how to punish instead of how to make better choices. But we really begin to think that we are omnipotent. Raising the volume, getting our eyes to bug out, popping our veins, and, of course, getting the saliva to run out of the corners of our mouth are all ways that we try to "control" our childrens' behavior. But if kids behave the way "we want them to" out of fear of punishment, they will never learn how to behave normally without us around them. They will only get sore necks from watching to see if we are listening. Punishing and controlling may work with some kids some of the time. They will do what you want, when you want. But with some it doesn't work at all. Does it work with your son or daughter? What prices do we pay for believing we have total control over others? The price many parents pay for their choice of behavior is a loss of relationship with their children because kids hate controlling parents and other adults. Just ask them if they will move toward or away from those who try to control what they think, do or feel. Which direction would you move in?

You're not the boss of me!

"What do you mean, 'you're not the boss of me' … I'm your father … I'm your mother. You must re-

spect me. I demand that you do! I brought you in this world and I will take you out! And I don't mean for pizza!" **The bottom line is if you are a controller, you believe you can force others to behave the way you want them to.** Good luck! In some cases it may even work. But in most cases, today's children know control better than we did at their ages. They can beat you up psychologically with expressions such as, *"You can't make me." "You're not the boss of me." "I can do whatever I want to."* In the past, parents met very little resistance from their children. In the past, those "don't-have-to detectors" were in their pockets. Out of one-hundred children, ninety-nine towed the line. They had the detectors in the pockets playing with their spare change. Today the opposite is true, those detectors are up and waving. Ninety-nine out of one-hundred own the line today! What happened? Is it the kids? Is it us? Is it society? Should we just let them do whatever they want? Give them total freedom?

Freedom for kids? Let them do what they want? No rules? Anything goes? How about the other extreme of corporal punishment? Out to the woodshed with them? The "tough love" approach? From one end of the pendulum to the other. Since the beginning of time, there have been many, many approaches to "controlling" other peoples' behaviors.

If you asked one-hundred parents I am sure you would find out that all of us **want** our kids to behave, get good grades, act responsibly, make good decisions, do what they are told, and so on. Admirable as they are, they are all desires that are OUT OF YOUR CONTROL. They are, at best, areas that you have INFLUENCE over. So how much do you influence? No longer do kids conform or change merely because of rules, deterrences, consequences, or threats of physical or psychological nature. The fulfillment of our internal psychological needs has become equally important. More will be discussed on this in the next chapter.

We all know some kids who seem to make more poor choices more often than others, but if you were to follow them around for twenty-four hours, you might be amazed at the number of good choices they make. Your kids will make it through, just like you did.

Leading the horse to water

You have heard the old saying, **"You can lead a horse to water, but you can't make him drink,"** and I have seen huge numbers of parents around the world who have said that **they will make the horse drink,** even if they have to drown it! I have seen parents paying tremendous prices for their punishing and controlling choices in the short run. They may make their kids act the way they want, but at what price in the long run? Who is really controlling whom? Some kids have been like the stubborn horse with their lips closed so tightly nothing could get in there. They purposely chose to go against their wishes as a way of showing their own power. You say sit, they stand. You say talk, they shut up and close their eyes or plug their ears. The kids perceive the parents in a negative and controlling way and as a result, choose to act in a negative and controlling way themselves. The vicious cycle begins. Who's controlling whom?

The strategy within this book is intended to get your kids to rethink their poor choices. **It is an attempt to lead the horse to water by putting salt in the oats!** Ask questions instead of demanding immediate change or action. You have control over *asking* questions. Ask comparison questions regarding choices they are making. Connect their choices with what they want. *"Will you get enough of what you want if you continue to act _____? Will people be more on or more off your back if you con-*

tinue to make the same choices you have been making?" These questions will motivate them to rethink. The best part is that you will be thinking as a productive thinker does and understand that you are controlling for the questions, not the answers. What a difference this will make. You can try the other way, the threatening, voice-raising method, but after years of being a WhMPA myself, I can tell you that it just is not worth it. The prices outweigh the rewards. When we practice productive thinking in this way, we can begin to see that what we have is a difference between what we want and what we have. We will also begin to see that the problem that our child has is also related to a difference that they have between what they want and what they have. As a result, we can begin to see that we are motivated to rethink our problem, or the difference, in terms of what we have control, influence and no control over. By using this strategy for ourselves, we can be in a good position to teach and model to our kids what they have control, influence or no control over in relation to their problems. We teach these areas through asking questions. We do not control their responses, but merely view our information as a way to influence them. We now are the teachers of better choices and not the controllers they dislike.

Controlling through punishment is always done **to a person** by someone with greater power, leaving the receiver with the impression that *"I'm a bad person."* They connect the choice they made with either being a good person or a bad person.

The television show "20/20" did an excellent program on discipline in which the researchers pointed out that in the long run punishment does not work. Punishment does not help people develop into who we want them to be. In a twenty-year follow-up study of parents who had punished their kids, they found the following to be true:

❏ Punished kids were arrested more often.
❏ Punished kids suffered more depression.
❏ Punished kids did worse academically.
❏ Punished kids earned less money.
❏ Punished kids had more difficulties in relationships.
❏ Punished kids tended to not like themselves.

From what we see here, punishment is not only ineffective, it produces the opposite of what we want. We want control. It produces and fosters lack of control. We need to go beyond punishment. We need to begin to create, within our own head, the vision that all people are capable of making good and poor choices. If we can understand that people are always making their best choice(s) at the time, it will make us teachers of better choices. We will not view our kids or others as bad people, but simply as people making poor choices at the time. This statement may sound a little confusing, but stop for a minute and think about the last time you made what you considered to be a good choice at the time, then moments later said to yourself, *"What a dumb thing to do."* Have you made some choices like this? What about those times you have said or done something you regretted later? Perhaps later you evaluated that choice and decided it wasn't such a great one after all. If you were punished everytime you made poor choices, would that help you learn or would you get angry over being punished by someone with greater power?

Many parents have felt the effects of insecurity and resulting burn-out because their kids refuse to do what they want. These same parents have told me that whenever they are around their own parents and their kids demonstrate inappropriate behaviors, they hear something to the effect, *"I wouldn't put up with that!"* *"You never would have said or been able to do that when you were growing up!"* *"What's wrong with you? Why do you let them do that?"* Of course hearing this from our parents or others makes us feel insecure and we begin to wonder if the "old style" of punishment is a better way to go. We begin to rent those old-time movies featuring Adolf Hitler, Jim Jones or Charles Manson, and watch every move in their attempts to gain control over other people. We even begin to sound like them, saying such things as, *"We have ways of getting you to do what we want."* *"We will fix this kid's wagon!"* **It's now "us" versus "them" in the quest for control.**

Punishment, unfortunately, continues to live on in the parents' quest for control. The WhMPA's who read the techniques and strategies explained here or provided by the experts will say, *"It doesn't work!"* *"It takes too long."* *"I'm not going to give in to a little kid."* This is followed by the frustration we experience when punishment doesn't work. We want our children to behave. They do the opposite. We have a difference. We experience frustration. If we choose the WhMPA way, we are looking for any way to "get" them to behave. Unfortunately, any way may include physical or psychological punishment—choices that always carry consequences. That is why a better approach is needed.

That is why productive thinking skills go beyond WhMPA.

There is a story of a frustrated man who was trying to move a very stubborn cow. He pushed, shoved, swore, kicked and prodded, all to no avail. He tried everything from positive reinforcement to punishment, but nothing worked. A young girl saw the man struggling with the cow. She went up to the cow and shoved a finger in its mouth and the cow moved ever so gently in the direction of the girl. People are like the cow. You can poke, prod, promise, threaten and push them, but they may not budge. If you give them a good reason, one of their own reasons, they will follow you wherever you want. The difference is getting into their world and finding out what motivates them, what makes them do what they do, think what they think, or feel what they feel. This is a productive thinking skill that goes beyond WhMPA.

In time, punishment or consequences may not produce the results that the parents want, creating more frustration for parents which, in turn, motivates the parent to "step on the gas" in regards to the punishment or consequences. This is when you hear the parent giving a kid five minutes of time out in the bedroom, with the kid smiling and saying *"Doesn't bother me,"* and the parent responding, *"Okay, now it's 10 minutes,"* and so on and so forth. You ground them for one day. They respond with, *"So. Whatever. That's cool, doesn't bug me,"* and you respond with one day extra for each response. It's like firing a Scud missile which the Patriot missile intercepts—and so on and so forth—until the other person runs out of missiles. Who will win? When will it stop? With kids becoming more sophisticated nowadays and the issuance of their "don't-have-to detectors" at an earlier age than ever, our frustration will continue as long as we use external controls such as threats, punishment and rewards to control our children.

Letting go

Part of a parent's role is to prepare for, not insulate, his kids from life. There is a point in a child's life when they want to assert themselves and let their parents know that they have the ability to think, act and feel as they choose, and not as parents or others want. This is where parents and other authority figures have usually either verbally or nonverbally informed the kids that the choice is not theirs to make.

As parents, we want our kids to be responsible, but kids have been telling me for years that we don't allow them to be. Parents want their kids to make good decisions, but the kids complain that we don't let them make their own decisions. This is a perfect opportunity for a parent to allow a child to suffer the consequences of his poor choices or allow him to earn more privileges. The choice is the child's to make. Allow a child the choice to earn either positive or negative consequences early in life, and he will become responsible and capable of making good decisions. Ninety-eight percent of the choices that a child will make in life will not be detrimental to his health. The choices they make may result in their suffering consequences but will not kill them. If they choose not to do their homework, not to go to school, choose to go to bed late, to talk back to us, to disobey our expectations, to use alcohol or other drugs and so on, they will pay a price.

During the elementary years, children can make many "poor choices," and the majority of them will not hurt them either physically or psychologically. During the adolescent years, though, many of the poor choices they may make can be deadly: choosing to drive drunk, choosing to ride with a drinking driver, becoming sexually involved without protection, or using alcohol or other drugs are just a few. Other poor choices that will definitely "influence" their life are becoming pregnant, failing in school or getting involved with the law. What kind of control do you have over these concerns? What kind of influence do you have? What areas do you have no control over?

Our kids want us to let go, to lighten up, but our instinct tells us to tighten up, hence the CONTROLLING on our part. Below are some questions for you to answer related to controlling. See how you do.

- ❑ Do you yell at your children repeatedly to get up in the morning?
- ❑ Do you bribe your kids to do what you want?
- ❑ Do you check on their every activity "just to be sure?"
- ❑ Do you use threats?
- ❑ Do you deliver empty ultimatums?
- ❑ Do you search their room?

WhMPA's choose these reactions on a regular basis in order to CONTROL their children's behavior. Sometimes they work, sometimes they don't. If there is no evidence to warrant overt control, then the parent is using excessive behavior to control his child. Seeking privacy and independence is part of a growing child's development.

One set of parents attempted to control their son's unruly behavior by removing his bedroom door and placing a mattress on the floor, providing only minimal food and refusing to talk to him. In response, the young man attempted to control his parents controlling him by choosing to turn up his stereo, sing loudly and prance around naked in his room. His parents viewed him as a nut! They wanted him locked up or fixed, as they put it. When I asked them to take an inventory of what they were doing, they became defensive and refused to believe they had any responsibility for his behavior. I see this quite often. The parents believe that it is all the kid's fault. When I ask the kids what they gain from these type of behaviors, they often say, *"It works."* According to the young man, *"It drove them nuts!"* He went on to say, *"My parents can't stand it when they don't see something affecting me the way they want it to. My way of controlling works better than theirs, I'm even having Fun!"*

Problem problem, who owns the problem?

Problems are the results of choices. Choices are in the hands of the person making them. Thus, the responsibility for the problem rests with the person making the poor choices. Not with the people around that person. **In thinking productively about life in this way, we can create a vision that our role as parents is to teach and model in frustrating situations; to show that all problems can be opportunities to grow and learn about life.** Becoming the teacher and model of "better choices," versus punishing with no teaching of better choices is the suggested method. **It puts us in a position to step back and rethink that when we are frustrated with our childs' choice(s), we have an opportunity to help our child evaluate his choice.** Instead of dwelling on the poor choices your child may have made, why not focus on helping them to evaluate those choices, identify the prices they may have paid, and brainstorm about better alternatives for the future?

Our daughter Holly provided a classic example of "problem problem, who owns the problem?" It was 8:30 on a Sunday evening and bedtime when Holly, who was then in the second grade, began to sigh, roll her eyes, and started saying, "she forgot."

In an anxious tone she said to my wife and myself, *"I need stickers, paste, glue, poster paper and scissors. My project is due tomorrow!"* To which my wife and I replied, *"You need to go to bed right now. Tomorrow, you need to let your teacher know that you forgot to do your project and that you are choosing to suffer the consequences."* Holly cried hysterically, pouting and attempting to guilt us into believing we were responsible for her getting into trouble with her teacher. We were being perceived by her as "the worst parents" for letting her get into trouble with the teacher. I could see the pouting lures, the temper tantrumming lures and the ever-popular crying lure. She used all her behavioral lures hoping for a bite. Both my wife and I felt tempted, particularly when she used the guilting lure that caught us many a time in the past, but we did not give in. We spit each lure out as it was cast our way. We **allowed** her to act the way she chose, but did not give in. It was the last time we can think of that Holly has been late for "**her** projects or homework." Problem problem, who owned the problem? Holly. Choices, choices, who made the choices? Holly. A WhMPA Mom would have run over to the all-night store, huffing and puffing up and down the aisles, swearing under her breath about how irresponsible her kid was. Suddenly, Mom, instead of the child owns the problem. Can you relate to getting sucked in by your kids like this? Can you think of other situations where you allowed your child to place responsibility for his or her poor choices on you or someone else? What can you do the next time your children try to "hook" you with one of their behaviors?

Anne was in high school. She was a young lady with a temper that would rival any tough kid you could think of. Her mother was frustrated with her because she was irresponsible. On top of that, the mother stated that Anne was always swearing at her, telling her she hated her, threatening to run away, as well as throwing fits of anger that resulted in her possessions being damaged or destroyed. Mother described Anne as a master of manipulation and control. Anne did not want to get up and go to school on many mornings. She would wait until her mother's screams would break glass. Getting up in a grouchy mood was a regular routine for her. She treated Mom like dirt while she was getting ready, accusing her of getting her up late, not having her clothes cleaned or her breakfast ready. Anne was a master at pushing Mom to the brink of insanity by calling her names and swearing at her until she gave in. The morning was capped off by Anne's insistence that Mom bring her to school because she did not want to ride "that farmer bus" to school. Mother pleaded with me to help her deal with her daughter and make her **responsible.** What I did was not make Anne responsible, but make Mother take responsibility for herself and herself only. What had gone on for many years was Mom had been taking on Anne's responsibility in many areas of her life. In elementary school she began doing her homework with her at the table every evening. This may not seem too bad, but in talking with Anne, she said that everytime they did this, she started whining and crying to get Mom to do the work for her. Eventually Anne said that Mom was doing the homework and she was just sitting at the table listening to her complain. In addition, Mom did her laundry every day, and folded her clothes and put them away for her. Anne told me that she was able to get her Mom to call into the school and say she was sick when she had not studied for a test or had not finished her homework. She did not want to fail. Anne said she would get into arguments with her mom about this and always hear Mom say, *"This is the last time I will do this for you,"* knowing full well that Mom would do it again if she wanted. Mom made her lunch for school, and drove her to school everyday and picked her up.

What happened to Anne after Mom and I visited together was fascinating. Mom explained to Anne that she was done taking on her problems and her responsibilities. The homework was up to her as well as the laundry, the rides to school, the making of lunch and getting up in the morning. Mom was handing over the responsibility. What occurred was a tremendous amount of whining, angrying, pouting, threatening and downright nastiness. It started with the morning wake-up routine. Anne got up late because she turned the alarm off. She came down the stairs and yelled at Mom for allowing this to happen. Mom remained calm and let Anne know that this was her problem. Just then the school called and asked if Anne was home sick. Mom handed the phone to Anne and said, *"It's the school calling about why you are not there."* Anne whispered to Mom frantically and said, *"Tell them I'm sick or I'll get a Saturday school."* Mom refused to do this and told Anne to get on the phone with the school. Anne refused to. Mom informed the school that Anne was at home without her permission. Anne went nuclear. She told her Mom that

she was not going to school anymore because of this. Mom came back with, *"You will suffer the consequences."* Anne threatened to run away. Mom let her know that she would do what she needed to do to get her back and that the expectations wouldn't change. Anne was upset. She stormed into her room and slammed the door. She came out in an hour and told Mom that she was not going to any Saturday school and that she couldn't make her. Mom agreed with her, and said that it will be between the school and her to deal with the consequences. Mom went on to say that the school had choices too. Anne was more upset and stormed back to her room. What eventually happened was that Anne accepted that her mother was not going to give in and that her Mom was not just talking the talk but walking the walk. The ball was now in her court. Anne continued to complain and pout in her attempts to change Mom, but Mom continued to practice what I taught her and remained calm, directed the conversation to the concepts of control, influence and no control, and used the word choices in all that she discussed with Anne. Within time, mother noticed a significant change in Anne's choices and her attitude. Not because Anne changed, but because Mom changed.

Some kids actually want to be punished by their parents! For some kids, this allows them to "hook" Mom and Dad into a verbal argument over the punishment and the reason for it; then Mom or Dad takes on the responsibility not only for the problem, but also for the solution. Remember, the key words in this scenario are **whose problem is it and and who makes the choices?** Many kids today have become experts at hooking Mom and Dad. That's why I believe many kids have convinced their parents that their middle name is "Get me, buy me, take me, give me."

When we attempt to control situations or people that we really have no business controlling in the first place, we will find that our controlling efforts backfire and often we will feel controlled ourselves.

You will find tremendous power in your own life as you begin to understand and accept that you cannot change people. After you have accepted this, you will see that others are in control of their own lives. Their choices, thoughts, actions and ultimately their feelings are their own. The choices they make can be either good or poor, but they are theirs. **Allow others to control their lives and you will be amazed at the control you will feel in your-**

self. The guilt placed upon you with statements like, *"It's your fault,"* or *"Thanks a lot for ruining my life"* will diminish along with the physical and emotional stress related to trying to control a situation you cannot control. In a very real sense you will be kicking the baby out of the nest and allowing him to take responsibility for himself, giving him the opportunity to develop good decision making skills.

The stubborn child

What about the child who is stubborn? By definition a "difficult" child is one who won't do what you want him to do—even after you have used your best skills to try to influence him to change his behavior. You tell him to do something and he doesn't do it. He continues to do what he wants.

The challenge to all of us is to step back and view the situation not as negative or stressful, but as an opportunity to build productive new thinking skills and learn more. You can begin by understanding that WhMPA thinking connects your **Worth** as a parent to the behavior of your child. WhMPA's believe a "good" parent should be able to change his child's behavior. As a productive thinker, however, you realize you only have influence over your child's behavior and little, if any, control.

I do not mean to suggest that we are not going to be affected by our children's choices or feelings. What I do mean is that we must detach. This is the mental, emotional and sometimes physical withdrawal from an unhealthy relationship. If you understand my concept of individual responsibility, you will allow others to own their own choices and their own outcomes **Allowing** is the key. We have a difficult time allowing our children to own the responsibility for their thoughts, actions and feelings.

A woman once approached me after one of my presentations and said that her father fit my description exactly. Her father always let her know what his expectations were, what her choices were and what she could expect as a result of her choices. He never argued with her. He was consistent with both the earned negative and the earned positive outcomes, and allowed her the opportunity to choose positive or negative consequences. The woman said that she now understands that what her father did was to allow her the necessary freedom of choice and structure. This gave her freedom along with responsibility. The problem, according to the woman, was that this approach never allowed her to argue with her father because he chose not to argue with her. *"I do jokes, I do windows, but I don't do arguments!"* he would tell her. The expectations in that home were clear, unshakable and unbreakable. What a great attitude to adopt.

Clear expectations allow us as parents to have freedom from guilt over our kids' choices, problems and consequences. Understanding that we have little or no control over other people frees us from taking responsibility for the outcome. Allow others to take control of their own lives, instead of manipulating or controlling them or the events in which they are involved.

This does not mean you should just give up when problems arise. But it does mean that we should base our decision to allow our children to have control over their own lives on reality and fact. We can do what we have control over to help our kids out and to influence them, but we must understand our limits.

By accepting and practicing this method of detachment, we will begin to notice that our children actually feel relief from our controlling, and ultimately feel more in control of their choices and their responsibility. You will see and hear fewer arguments.

How will you know when you are not allowing your children to take control of their own lives?

You will know you're taking on too much responsibility for your children's choices when you:

- ❏ Get excessively angry over your child's choices.
- ❏ Exert physical force in an attempt to control your child's behavior.
- ❏ Restrict your child's choices so much that they feel as though they are in prison and you are the warden.
- ❏ Hear them say, *"Leave me alone." "You treat me like a kid." "It's not your problem." "I can't wait until I'm eighteen."*

If you can relate to any one of these, then take a minute to rethink and allow your child to take responsibility for his own life. You will soon be amazed at the results. Remember that ninety-eight percent of the choices children make will not kill them. They may be frustrating, but with productive thinking skills you will save your sanity.

Along with setting clear expectations, we need to surrender at this stage, give up the defenses and accept without self-pity what we need to do. We have to give up our excuses, the rationalizing and the blaming of *"The world I live in." "My parents." "My job."* These are all the excuses we don't think we are guilty of. We need to eliminate the denial that has fogged up our glasses for so long and accept the natural consequences of our behavior, be they good or be they bad.

It is crucial to your child's growth that you accept the responsibility for problems that you, yourself, encounter. If you are overweight or depressed, accept that it's your weight or your depression and your responsibility to do something about it. If you model self-control whenever problems arise, good for you. If you don't, it is time for you to start. In the final analysis it is up to you to do something about your problems.

Turning over responsibility for life

Have you heard any of these statements?
"You make me angry."
"You made me lose my temper."
"You are making me unhappy."
"You are the one who will be responsible for my failing."
"You are making my life miserable."
"You never let me do anything on my own."

When are children able to take care of themselves? Children are dependent on us the second they are born, dependent on us to satisfy all of their wants and their needs. From that point on, we take responsibility for them to prevent them from dying among other things. But ultimately the child reaches a point when the parent needs to give him the power of choice to teach that he has the control, the power and the capability to take effective control of his own life. Doing this significantly reduces the child's risk of involvement in future destructive and high risk behaviors.

On the lecture circuit I often mention that when my kids started third grade their early morning routine was to get themselves up with their own alarm clocks, make their own lunches, pick out their own clothes, clean up their own rooms, pick up their own messes, make their own breakfast and do their own homework. Some people in the audience have questioned me about this and wondered if it is okay to allow children to do so much for themselves. It sure beats shaking them in bed, yelling up the stairs for the "last" time, bribing them to do their chores, threatening them with empty ultimatums, fixing the "wrong food" for their breakfast or lunch, picking out the clothes "I" like and they hate, and so on and so forth. **It naturally became a source of relief for us as parents, but also a tremendous source of pride and power for our children. The earlier you start handing over responsibility the better.** The more your children realize that you will do what they want if they whine, pout, complain or temper tantrum and say, *"I can't do it,"* the more they believe the responsibility for life's tasks rests with you. It becomes more difficult to "change" your childrens' "learned helplessness" the older they get. Not impossible, but more difficult. They will become like the fisherman, using their best pouting, whining, complaining and angrying lures in order to "catch" you, and manipulate you into doing what they want.

Becoming a mature and responsible person means learning how to associate the positive and negative outcomes with each choice that we make. Maturity and responsibility come from within and are not "given" to a child. **A child needs to be taught by our example as parents that *he earns* responsibility and maturity based upon his choices.**

If your child chooses to clean up his bedroom and you express too much love or positive regard to him for doing this, he will learn to associate doing certain tasks with being given love or positive regard. He will learn to give in order to get what he wants or needs. Pleasing others in order to get a reward is a set-up because it is based on another person having control of providing or not providing rewards or reinforcements. The child will become dependent on love, affection and positive regard "from" others. This does not mean that we say nothing to them, but we do not have to get all gooey and bring out the marching band every time they complete a chore.

We are raising a generation of lazy children who rely on others to **"get them, buy them, take them, give them."** Get me what I want. Buy me what I want. Take me where I want to go. Give me whatever I want. And if you don't, I will make life Hell on earth for you! They are often unwilling to work for anything unless they are forced to do so. How unfortunate. What we need to do in order to break this cycle is to allow the kids to understand that with an attitude like that, they will not be provided all that they want. This may take a long time to change, depending on how long it takes the child to change his attitude and behavior. Otherwise we will be allowing the child to control our choices.

Consider the story of a mother with two sons who always get what they want from Mom. Mom puts up a good fight, threatening to ground them, but never follows through. She threatens not to drive them to where they want to go, but always gives in. She threatens to let them be late for school, but then drives them anyway and hands them an excuse. She threatens to pull privileges from them, but gives in when they scream, pout, whine or threaten to run away. What the kids learned at a young age was how to control Mom, just as the baby in the crib learned how to control the parents by rapping the bottle on the bars screaming at the top of his lungs until they came in. What infants learn in the early years later comes in handy, wouldn't you say? Whatever internal source of control and responsibility they had was overshadowed by their mother's desire to be "in control" and not let them suffer any consequences.

By a certain age, children should be able to take on responsibility for themselves. In fact, you can groom them as early as they are able to comprehend what is going on around them. In doing so you teach independence and responsibility, making them unable to jump up and down screaming, "You made me late." "It will be your fault if I get a bad grade." "How come my jeans are not clean?" "You should have reminded me about the test." These are great excuses for kids not to accept responsibility themselves. **Independence, responsibility** and **accountability** are the cornerstones of what all parents want for their kids. The thousands of parents I have come in contact with have identified these as top on their list. The problem seems to be how we suddenly force our children to be independent and responsible for themselves. The parents and the kids who enjoy the most success in this area are the ones who started, at an early age, teaching and modeling these same behaviors to their children.

Teaching responsibility begins in the home. The age at which it begins seems to vary from child to child. An infant relies completely on his parents to take responsibility for everything he does. As time progresses, however, it is important to turn some responsibility over to the child. Teaching responsibility begins with short periods of time focused on one particular aspect of their lives where they are in charge, such as cleaning their room, completing their assigned chores, doing their homework, going to bed or waking up on time.

It is important to remember that we want to teach and model responsibility, not irresponsibility. Responsibility takes work and effort from us as well as from our kids. If we teach responsibility and accountability for one's choices early in life, a child will more naturally grow up recognizing that he controls his own destiny. Avoid solving problems "for" your kids giving them the impression that every time something goes wrong, someone else will step in and "fix" it. This results in postponing accountability for who owns the problem. This doesn't mean, of course, that you can't do things for your kids. It only means that the sooner you allow your child to accept responsibility for his actions, thoughts and feelings, the sooner you will have a child who acts responsibly. When you think of it, irresponsibility takes little or no effort on our part or our kid's part. That is why it is easier to be the kind of parent we all don't want to be—the irresponsible parent. But you are not that parent. Sure, you've made poor choices up to this point. Haven't we all? Are the choices you are making ones in which you will not be paying any prices—short term or long term? Are your choices the best choices you can make? Do you model productive thinking to your kids, including the choices they have and the steps to solve problems or do you blame other people for your choices and your problems?

What amazes me is the number of kids who

"control" their parents with issues that should be theirs to begin with. How many parents yell up the stairs once, twice, three times, begin to scream at the top of their lungs, threaten their kids with bodily harm—all in the name of getting them up for school? What this teaches the child is that he is not responsible for getting up for school and it also sets the parent up for blame for being such a "nag." The better option is to turn over responsibility to the child by getting him an alarm clock so he can set it and get up on his own. If he doesn't, there are usually consequences for getting to school late such as detention, Saturday school or in-school suspension. If your child is typical, he will blame you for these consequences, but remember where the responsibility lies. The child who refuses to follow through with responsibilities at school (attendance, being on time to class, following classroom and building expectations, completing homework) should understand that he will suffer the loss of additional privileges at home such as going out after school, playing with Nintendo or other games, visiting with friends or going to bed early as a result of his refusal to follow through with responsibilities.

It is my belief that if we don't teach our kids this kind of responsibility at an early age, the result will be young adults who tell us that their boss is a jerk for reprimanding them for being late, the cop is a jerk for picking them up for speeding and the teacher is responsible for their poor grades.

Choices choices, whose choice is it?

A telephone answering machine is an example of something mechanically dead. It has no choice but to answer the phone. Its actions are controlled by the outside ring and its sole purpose is to respond to that ring. If we believe that people, like machines, are controlled by outside forces, then we give up the idea that we have choices (limited as they may be at times) and we embrace slavery. We give control over to anyone out there. Yuck!

Humans are not machines. When we experience frustration, we can choose to be rigid or flexible. We all desire good treatment from everyone, we can choose to feel miserable if we don't get what we want. Nobody else can force us to think the way we think or do the things that we do. We are in control of these areas of our lives. WhMPA's will argue with this. They believe that their lives are

controlled, not just influenced, by "out there." Again, to refute our old friend "common sense," you can no more make me miserable than you can make me answer the telephone if I choose not to. As productive thinkers, we all need to challenge the common sense beliefs that we have stored up over the years. These beliefs have been provided for us by our parents, by their parents, by the media and by the world around us. WhMPA's hate to challenge. They like and desire comfort.

Picture yourself driving your car down the main street of the town where you live. As you come to an intersection the traffic light turns red, so you slow the car down to a stop. I lean over and ask you why you did this. You point at the the red light and say, *"It turned red and I always stop at red lights."* Picture another scene where you are at home and the doorbell rings, and I ask you why you go to the door. *"To see who it is,"* you reply. In another scene, you pick up the phone after it rings and I ask you why you did that. Your answer would probably be *"Because it rang."* Because I asked you these questions, you begin to question my sanity and planet of origin. Am I really as strange as you think? But stop for a minute and think, has there ever been a time in your life that you have rolled right on through a stop light or ignored it? Have you ever made a choice not to answer the doorbell or the telephone?

My point is, that **nothing we do is caused by what happens outside of us.** If we believe that outside forces cause us to make the choices we make, then we are essentially acting like machines and not as living people. We give up our choices and our control to others around us. Look around you and you will see what I am talking about. What do you do when you become stuck in traffic or get a spot on your shirt? How do you act or react if you want to play golf and it starts raining, or go to a movie and find it sold out, or discover that you failed a test, or that your boyfriend or girlfriend broke up with you? These factors influence your frustration, but they do not cause you to choose unhappy thoughts, actions or feelings. You do that for yourself. And so do the people you live with and work with.

The bottom line is that we are not a stimulus-response system that answers the phone simply because it rings, answers the door because the doorbell rings or stops at the traffic light because it turns red. We choose to respond that way.

As long as either you or your children hold onto the belief that the feelings you have are a result of what the "world" presents to you, you won't be willing to take **responsibility** for your own thoughts, feelings or actions.

Until we allow our children to let go of this way of thinking, they cannot take on the responsibility for their day. And until that happens, they cannot perceive themselves as being in control of their lives. Kids are just like adults in that they need to accept the results of their choices. They must understand the connection between choices and earned outcomes. By doing so, they will learn that life does not control them, but that they control life through the choices that they make. It takes effort and skill to create a good day. It takes productive thinking about ourselves and the world around us to take this step beyond WhMPA.

Setting the structure

Parents need to be the ones who set the structure in the home. Structure works best in the form of expectations. Notice I did not use the words rules, control or power. Structure implies parental expectations and offers children the choice to abide by or to not abide by those expectations. Rules, in a young person's mind, mean you "have to." Expectation means quite the opposite. You are expected to follow the guidelines. More importantly, though, you can choose to follow or not follow the expectations.

If you were to ask an adolescent what he wished for, at the top of the list would probably be his desire to be left alone, given more space and more independence. Adolescents believe that they would do just fine without controls. What we have learned from youth over the years is that **they want structure** because it gives them boundaries in which they can operate and a sense of security. Having to suddenly accept responsibility for their own lives is a hassle. The young girl who came up to me at one of my talks at a conference at Pepperdine University said, *"We are always telling young people to just say no; why don't we tell parents and adults to just say no to their kids?"* This young lady has the key to what I'm talking about here. She, like millions of other kids today, wants structure in her life, structure from loving, caring adults in their roles as parents, coaches, advisors and bosses.

A good form of structure to set up in your home might be as follows:

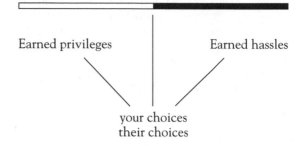

HOME EXPECTATIONS AGREEMENT

Earned privileges   Earned hassles

your choices
their choices

As the parent, you set the expectations in your family. These expectations may be in regard to your home, the school and the community. Expecting proper behavior from children in the areas of cleaning their bedrooms, brushing their teeth, going to bed on time, waking up on time, treating other family members with respect, abiding by curfew, not using tobacco, alcohol or other drugs, obtaining good grades, attending school and behaving at school is entirely reasonable. Sit down with your spouse and discuss what your expectations are in your home. Allow your kids to have input into the expectations. This gives them some ownership as opposed to a WhMPA's telling them, *"These are the rules in this house and that's the way it is—no discussion."* Allow your kids to come up with expectations they feel are reasonable and fair, and see what happens. You may be amazed at how reasonable their suggestions will be. Allow them to disagree with the expectations you come up with and let them express their feelings. You naturally have the final choice of what is expected. This will teach them that the real world is about expectations, opinions, choices and the outcome of those choices.

However, if your child is in jeopardy of hurting himself or others, or damaging property, he is not in a position to make choices. In this case you must do what you need to do in order to protect yourself, your child or your property. Stepping back and trying to figure out which needs your child is meeting at such critical moments is not suggested! Action instead of thinking is the answer here. Such behaviors as suicidal gestures, destroying the house, using a weapon, or being under the influence of drugs or alcohol are a few examples of situations where you need to step in and take control. Such people need to be stabilized, and allowed to rethink their problem and the choices available to them. Some people just need a little time to "chill out" and rethink about the alternatives. In the heat of the moment people sometimes choose to act insane, but as Dr. William Glasser, author of <u>Re-</u>

ality Therapy has stated in many of his lectures, "*We all have our islands of insanity, it's when your islands become continents that we should begin to worry.*"

Some people think all kids want their parents to take charge and set limits for them. And to a degree this is true. Kids need structure. What they hate is rigidity. Structure allows them to have control of their own lives.

Independence

Eric Hoffer stated a challenge to all of us when he said "*In times of change learners inherit the earth, while the learned find themselves beautifully equipped to deal with a world that no longer exists.*" One of the most unfortunate lessons that a child can learn in his journey through life is to give up and say "*I can't do it!*" Do you teach and model to your kids that they are able to make decisions by themselves? Are you perceived by them as someone who tries to control their thoughts, actions and/or feelings? In raising kids to be independent we must ALLOW them to make their own decisions and their own choices. Certainly some of the choices that kids have available to them today are potentially life threatening. In those cases, we do need to step in and take control of their choices or at least attempt to. But in the vast majority of situations, you will not be able to totally control your child's choices. A lot of people attempt to control their kids' choices by not allowing them to make decisions for themselves. The majority of people, though, have experienced times when they would like their kids to think, act or feel a certain way, but know they can't control those behaviors in someone else. In order to become independent and responsible, children need to learn that the choices they make will either lead to a positive outcome or to different degrees of discomfort. Allow your child to make his own mistakes and more importantly learn from those mistakes. Allow kids to affirm their worth to themselves and to others by allowing them to learn that they are in control of their choices and their lives.

The willingness to wear a flak jacket and helmet

In matters of style, swim with the current; in matters of principle, stand like a rock.
Thomas Jefferson

Pampering your kids allows them to avoid responsibility for the choices they make. Many parents keep dinner warm while calling their kids to the table repeatedly. After fifteen or more minutes of continuously reminding the child, he still sits down to a warm meal. If you really want to raise a responsible child, tell him only once that dinner is ready, and then go ahead and eat your own meal, while it is warm. If he chooses to not come to the table then **allow** him to eat his meal cold. This will require courage on your part. Your kids will not like it at first and may complain. Allow them to complain, but remind them that the structure has changed and if they want a warm meal they need to come to the table before the food becomes cold. Consequences and privileges are based on meeting expectations. You'll soon find that your kids will start coming in for dinner, getting up on time, not swearing, not fighting and getting their homework done. They are just like the baby in the crib who is confused over the parents' lack of response to his demanding behavior. The parent has set the structure and informed the child that he can choose or not choose to comply with the expectations. All the pouting, whining, crying and so forth will not help them get what they want. Teach them to be responsible instead of teaching them how to control the world around them in order to get what they want. When you try to change past behaviors, you can expect some resistance. Like the baby in the crib, they might cry harder, whine, pout or demand more dramatically, all in attempts to get you to not exert this kind of influence on them, but eventually they will learn that their choices no longer work. The most difficult part for parents is to be patient and allow enough time for the behavior to change. Allow them to choose their consequences or rewards. It is critical that you not jump in to rescue them. Do not lecture, criticize or preach to them. Put a sock in your mouth, twist one of those dog stakes in the back yard, and attach yourself to a leash and resist the temptation. Just hope you don't get tangled in the picnic table! The reward for you, and for them, will be worth it. You will be teaching and modeling for your kids that their choices will direct the outcome of their own lives.

As children get older, they usually ask for structure to be redefined and expanded upon. Make sure that you are clear about your expectations and values regarding what they can do, where they can go, who they can hang around with, what time they need to be home, the use of alcohol, tobacco or drugs, or maybe even at what age or under what circumstances you consider it to be okay to be involved in sex. These questions should open up the pearly gates of communication for you and your children to discuss your values and expectations, as well as find out more about where they are coming from. Allow your kids the opportunity to express their own opinions about these issues. You can agree to disagree on certain issues. You don't have to have an answer on the spot for every question about an expectation. You may need to discuss the question with your spouse or think it over for a while. Listen to what your child says and try to understand his feelings. But as a parent, you need to set the standards or expectations within your home. If your child does not agree with those standards or expectations, then he or she can choose to abide by or not abide by those expectations. **Remember, though, that expectations should be unshakeable, unbreakable and not negotiable!**

The following is a conversation between a mother who is having problems with her son. He was not following the expectations at home or at school regarding the use of tobacco, alcohol or other drugs:

Mother: *"My son said that he is going to use tobacco, alcohol and other drugs, and there is nothing that I can do about it. The athletic code at his school states that he cannot use these substances, but he said that everybody at school thinks the code is a joke, including him. There is nothing I can do to stop him."*

Dr. Thomson: *"Maybe you can't stop him, but there is something you can do to INFLUENCE him in his decision to use or not use tobacco, alcohol or other drugs. You have NO CONTROL over his ultimate choices, but you do have CONTROL over the choices you can make regarding consequences for his actions. You CONTROL the expectation that he is not to use tobacco, alcohol and other drugs if he chooses to be in athletics, and while he lives in your home and is under the legal age. The school CONTROLS the expectation that he not use these substances if he wishes to remain in athletics."*

Mother: *"But my son will not follow these rules. He has told me that he will do whatever he wants to. What do I do then?"*

Dr. Thomson: *"What do you supply him with around the house? Does he have use of a car or money to spend for things he likes?"*

Mother: *"He has a job after school and needs the car to get there. I can't take the car away from him or I will cause him to lose his job. I give him spending money each week and lunch money, and I provide the clothes that he needs for work or for school. He also has my permission to be involved with athletics. We both signed an athletic code of conduct which stated that he was* not to use tobacco, alcohol or other drugs, but he uses them anyway. What can I do?"

Dr. Thomson: "The expectation at home is that he not use tobacco, alcohol or other drugs. A consequence for that use could be that he not have use of the car and that he not receive extra money. It's his job and if he can't get there because of his choice to use, then his boss might reprimand him or fire him. His coach might take away his privilege to participate in athletics because of these choices. But it's not **your** problem unless you make it **your** problem. The expectations and the consequences are yours. The choice to use and the problems he encounters from it are his."

Mother: "But, what happens if he loses his job or if he doesn't get to play sports? What happens if he doesn't have new clothes or shoes?"

Dr. Thomson: "He will learn that poor choices on his part cost him the use of the car. He will learn to find other ways of getting where he wants to go. He could walk, ride the bus, catch a ride with a friend or co-worker or he could choose to not go to work at all. He will learn that poor choices on his part will cost him part or all of his sports season, depending on the school athletic code. He will learn that the food that is provided for him, the money and the clothes are all privileges he earns, and that by making good choices he will keep them coming and that by making poor choices he will put a stop to them."

Mother: "But he will blame me."

Dr. Thomson: "Maybe he will. If he's a WhMPA, he will blame you instead of himself. But help him understand that he is in control of whether or not he wants to be on the team. He is in control of whether he wants to use the car, or if he wants money in his pockets."

Mother: "He will go nuts if I follow through with this!"

Dr. Thomson: "He may become angry but it isn't likely that he'll go nuts. Have you followed through with other consequences he's earned in the past?"

Mother: "No. He usually talks me out of it. He usually screams at me until I can't take it anymore and I just give in to him. He has also threatened to run away or kill himself if I follow through."

Dr. Thomson: "He is good at the choices he makes in life. Unfortunately he has learned what choices push your buttons the most. He has learned to pout, whine, complain and even threaten to run away or commit suicide to get what he wants. The problem is that these behaviors have worked for him on numerous occasions. Changing his attitude and then his choices will take time and patience on your part. But the outcome will certainly be worth the effort. You will have a son who understands that problems are a part of life and that he has the ability to make the right choices in order to follow the expectations at home or not. If he chooses not to follow the expectations, then you will choose to not allow him the use of the car. You will not give him money and you will not give him rides to or from places. You need to let your son know that you expect him to inform the coach, the athletic director or another school official of his choice to not abide by the athletic code. Tell him that you will call the school at the end of the day to see if they have any questions of you."

Does any of this sound familiar? Can you see where the son is attempting to control his mother?

Can you see that the son really does not want to accept responsibility for his poor choices? If you are unwilling to be direct with your children, you will resort to using guilt and other behaviors to try to manipulate them into doing what you want them to do. If they are any good at controlling you, these attempts on your part will be useless. If you are indecisive, your children will react to your indecisiveness by ignoring you, talking back, making threats and acting disrespectful. It is your home and you set the expectations. You wear the helmet and the flak jacket. Don't take it off!

Accountability

Accountability means allowing your child to become independent and to make his own choices, tough as that may be. It also means allowing him to suffer the natural consequences that occur because of those choices. Parents should look at what they do "for" their kids that perhaps prevents them from learning responsibility. We often put much energy into protecting our children from making decisions on their own. Then we find out they made a poor choice and we hit the roof. The stimulus-response method punishes kids for not responding to situations the way you would like for them to respond (a WhMPA method of relating to others.) Accountability means allowing your kids to make their own decisions and earn the rewards or suffer the consequences. You can demonstrate caring with them when you explain your expectations in the first place. Allow them to disagree, but make sure they are aware of the consequences of making poor choices before they leave the house. In the beginning, expect your child to come home late and try to pull you into a fight, hoping you will once again accept responsibility for his poor choices. Be willing to receive a little heat from the kid as his way of ventilating frustration for his choices and consequences. Demonstrate caring, ask him questions about what went on and what choices he made. Make statements about your expectations and, if you want, your feelings concerning the problem. Be a teacher of better choices to consider next time the same situation comes up. That will prevent him from making the same choice and suffering the same consequences the next time. When you understand that you have total control only over

yourself, you won't be as likely to become excessively frustrated when your kids do not respond as you would like.

As parents, we naturally attempt to protect our children from any harm that comes their way. The problem is that we sometimes take this too far! A good example is a family whose daughter was found to be in violation of the school athletic code of conduct. She was arrested for driving under the influence of alcohol, which became the topic of conversation in the halls. During a conference with the athletic director, the girl admitted her guilt. The athletic code had spelled out the consequences and she was removed from competition for a percentage of her season. The mother felt her daughter was being picked on by the school authorities and felt that they had "no business" deciding what her child could or could not do on her own time. As a result she hired an attorney and took the matter before the board. The attorney was able to find a discrepancy in the vocabulary between the student handbook and the athletic handbook regarding the term "possession" as it pertains to the use of alcoholic beverages. As a result the consequences were lifted. That child learned that her mother and her attorney had the power to remove the responsibility and accountability for her poor choices. The school authorities were portrayed as "out to get her," when in reality they were responding to her poor choice in an orderly fashion. We all remember the days when the school would call, the parent would answer and after finding out it was the school calling would say, *Don't you worry, I will take care of everything.* Click! Not so anymore. The parent has an attorney and the student hands his attorney's card out to anyone accusing him of poor choices. When we rescue our children from responsibility and accountability for their choices, we foster irresponsibility.

When we interfere with the natural consequences of a child's conduct, we tell them they are above the law, above the rules and above the expectations. Think of the prices the parent pay for these choices. They may gain praise from their child for stepping in and bailing her out of trouble, but by allowing her to suffer the natural consequences stated in the athletic code, they would have taught her to make a better choice the next time she found herself in a similar situation.

You can't take things away from kids—can you?

I do workshops for athletes, coaches and parents entitled, **"Clique 1-The Program For Drug Free Athletics."** These workshops involve parents, athletes and coaches in pre-season meetings where the theme is working together to promote tobacco, alcohol and other drug-free athletics. These workshops have been very popular because they are so effective. They leave an impactful message and plan of action for teams to combat a common problem. After one particular workshop I did at a local high school, my wife, Carol, came home from an evening with her woman's bowling league. She had been approached by a couple of women who indicated that they had been in the audience. They expressed concern that once you give children a privilege, you can't take it away from them. They felt that you would be asking for trouble if you did. During one segment of the program I use a student volunteer from the audience. I ask him if he would like to have more freedom in his life, to get his parents off his back, to have more privileges and to take control of his life. The kids always say that this is definitely what they want. What I demonstrate is that all kids want responsibility, control and choices. I use a fishing pole to demonstrate my point. I have the student hold onto the line while I ask if he would like the use of a phone, a stereo

and some money. I provide props to resemble those items. They are always eager to get these items. I place a set of shoes around their neck to represent the freedom they want and I give them a letter jacket which represents one of the rewards associated with athletics. Finally, I provide the student a replica of a car. The audience loves the presentation because they become involved. They can relate to the props and the subjects are ones parents and kids are concerned with daily. The student is asked if he wants to have his parents and other people on his back or off his back? All have replied, *"Off my back!"* The student then is told to walk farther away from me, still holding onto the fishing line. Before they get too far, I let them know that the word rules in the home will be changed to the word expectations because they now know that they don't *"have to"* do anything they don't want to. Remember those detectors on the top of their head? The word expectations allows them freedom to choose. I explain to them that one of the expectations, since I am the parent, is that they be in the house at a certain time called curfew. We discuss the time and I set the earliest time to begin with, always letting them know that I am open to increasing it based upon their behavior. I also explain that if they choose to be involved in athletics or any co-curricular activity, they need to abide by the athletic and co-curricular codes, as well as my expectation that they choose to be tobacco, alcohol and drug-free. I ask them if they understand these expectations so far and point out to them that they don't have to do what I say because they know that they have choices and can certainly go against them if they choose. I then let out more line and allow them to go farther away from me. I stop them and let them know that they have been making good choices and coming in on time, and that there is no evidence of their using tobacco, alcohol or other drugs. Because of this, they have now raised their curfew and they keep going farther away from me. I explain to them that another expectation of them is to not only go to school, but to go into school! It's called attendance. I expect them to be where they say they are going and to get themselves up for school on time. I also throw in that I expect them to be responsible for their homework and that they need to achieve certain grades. The kids always nod in agreement and I am quick to point out with the use of the detectors waving above my head that they don't have to. They go farther and farther away. At this point, I begin shaking with the fishing pole in hand. I tell that that the reason for this is that I can't see what they are doing all the time. I can't monitor their every move. This is where the trust comes in. I provide them the information regarding the expectations we have and hope they make the right choices. I ask them how they are feeling being farther and farther away from me, gaining more and more freedom and privileges, and they usually reply, "Great!" I then inform them that I received a call from the assistant principal saying they skipped the last half of the day after lunch. The fishing line release is stopped and with the hook set the student is reeled in. I also heard from the teacher via interim reports that they are not turning in their homework. More line is reeled in. They are not showing up on time for class and violating curfew time. I reel them in some more. I have evidence of chewing tobacco and alcohol use, the line is reeled in even closer. Their disrespect for Mom and a bad attitude results in the line once again being reeled in closer and closer to where they began. Once the student comes back to where I'm standing, the money, the phone, the letter jacket and the stereo are removed as a result of the poor choices they made. The shoes are thrown to the floor representing grounding, time out in the bedroom, Saturday school, detention and in-school suspension. The car is removed also. The kid is visibly bummed out as a result!

The women at the bowling alley with Carol demonstrated that they had gotten the message, but they said, *"The girls went out for coffee after Mike's talk. We talked about what he said and we all agreed that he was funny and entertaining and that we learned a lot, but we also said that Mike might not totally understand the kids today because you can't take things like cars, phones, letter jackets and money away from kids who are fourteen to eighteen nowadays."* I could have screamed! My wife said she almost fell over. She wanted to hit them over the head with the bowling ball she had in her hand! She politely said to them, *"Why do you think he titled the book Who's Raising Whom?"* No wonder eleventh graders are going to states and countries thousands of miles away during spring break, and all of us are well aware of the poor and irresponsible choices they are making. No wonder kids are renting motel rooms with their dates during high school and their parents say nothing. In fact some parents rent the rooms and make the reservation for them. A kid problem. No. Like the little girl at Pepperdine told me, "It's not *that we have so much of a kid problem*

today; we have a parent and adult problem." Amen. No wonder kids treat their parents like crap and get away with it. And not only get away with it, but demand that they get to use the car, have a few bucks in their pocket from us and complain at the drop of a hat. When is it going to stop? One parent in my home town audience made the comment at my talk that if I held my kids accountable to those expectations, I would be the loneliest parent in town. So be it! Pogo said, *"We have met the enemy, and they is us."* Until we act like leaders and responsible adults, our country is going to continue to deteriorate. My kids are going to try the same trick regarding spring break as others will. There will be two answers: *"No. What part of 'no' don't you understand?,"* and, *"When do we leave?"* If they go, I'm going with to provide the structure I'm talking about. There will be expectations down there just like up here. Along with adult supervision. Spring break used to mean that we got to go to the other side of the street. Wow! Is this what the other side looks like? We have control over privileges. My challenge is not only to the parents but to the kids. How bad do you want what you want? At my athletic talks, I use my hand on one side to illustrate the tobacco, alcohol and other drugs. On the other hand I use athletics and all of its rewards. What I show the audience visually is that the two do not go together. There is not one kid on the middle or high school level who does not know that tobacco, alcohol or other drugs and athletics do not go together. My challenge to them is, *"How bad do you want to be an athlete? How bad do you want what you want? How bad do you want trust? How bad do you want extra money? How bad do you want the use of a car? How bad do you want a ride somewhere? How bad do you want a sleepover? How bad do you want to stay out later?"* The question to the kids should be: *"Are you willing to change your attitude and change your behavior in order to get what you want? The privileges will still be here, when you are ready. It's your choice. Take as long as you like."* Dickie Noles, a good friend of mine on the lecture circuit knows the damaging effects of alcohol and other drugs on an athletic career. As a former pitcher for the Philadelphia Phillies, Dickies dreams were affected by his choices related to alcohol and other drugs. Dickie states "Dreams are not made from the dreams you dream. Dreams are made from the choices you make." Dickie wished he had heard my talk in his younger years. His choices today are more positive.

HOME EXPECTATIONS AGREEMENT

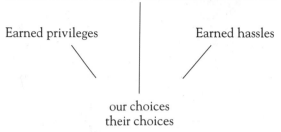

Earned privileges   Earned hassles

our choices
their choices

While up on stage with me, the young person looks at me quite confused at this point. They want us off their back, they want more responsibility, more decisions, more power, control and choices. What they have is a difference between what they want and what they have. What they have is less privileges than what they want. I ask them to make a gun out of their hand and point it at their parents, blaming them for their grounding, their teachers, blaming them for their poor grades, and their friends, blaming "peer pressure" as the reason for their choices. What I then say to them is that they have one finger on that hand pointing out and "blaming others" for their hassles when, in fact, they have three fingers on that hand pointing back to themselves. You can just imagine the look on their face. The sound that comes from their mouth sounds like a bunch of bucks snorting in the woods. I have them reach out their hand and I shake it, saying to them, "Welcome to life!" Now comes the moment they state that they can't wait until they are eighteen so they can do what they want. Do what they want! They are doing what they want, that is why they are in deep doo doo. Deep *earned doo doo*, I might add. Keep your helmet and flak jacket on and allow your kids to earn back their privileges. How long will that take for them to change their actions or their attitude? The length of time is in their hands, not yours. When they are ready to admit that they are the ones making the poor choices and they are ready to quit blaming you or others for their choices is when I suggest that we consider providing them with the earned privileges once again. Take another look at the structure of the expectations agreement form.

Allow your children to earn hassles such as sitting in their bedroom, going to bed early, being without their treasured toy, being without television, being without their stereo, being without the phone or being without the use of the car, their bike or a ride from you. **Allow them time to sit and rethink about whose problem it is.** Whose choice was it to earn the loss of the privilege? Provide them with questions to think about such as, *"What was the expectation or rule that you broke?" "What poor choices did you make to earn yourself the hassles you are getting?" "What better choices could you make next time?"* Let them know that they can earn the privileges back when they are ready to discuss these questions with you. Like many parents, you may "ground" them for a week. Keep a calm and direct tone of voice with them when doing so. Remember it is their problem not yours. When the week is up, allow them to come to you and ask for the privileges back. You will probably get various responses from various kids. One will come back and want to sit and rationally discuss with you the problem, their poor choices and their plan for better choices in the future. This might be what I call the "Eddy Haskel syndrome." It is when the child comes in like Eddy used to on the "Leave It To Beaver" show and schmoozes with Mrs. Cleaver, and says what she wanted to hear. You don't know whether it is the truth or just schmoozing in order to get back what they want. You might also have the child who comes back and demands back what they lost. In this case, they have not been taking their time without their privileges very serious. They have spent that time "blaming others" for what they themselves have earned. They have been pointing all five fingers at everyone else. How do we get them to take responsibility? To admit that it is them and not us or others? The only answer I can give you is time. Time without their privileges. Time will change a negative attitude. Time will change a person's thinking about their poor choices. Being without something they want will motivate them to change. How bad they want what they want will determine how much effort they put into changing their attitude or actions. A WhMPA has a hard time allowing time to go by. They want change in attitude or actions now. As a result there is yelling, threatening, demanding and powering behaviors used by the parent.

Remember the old days of sports programs? They asked you to come to the auditorium if you were interested in participating in some sporting activity. You went down there like cattle. The athletic director stood up front, and in a deep stern voice told you that participation would require dedication, commitment, hard work and loyalty. You might have to study on the bus with a flashlight. You might have to give up a boyfriend or girlfriend. (Oh no!) If they threw a letter jacket on the floor and told you that you had to crawl five miles to earn it, you would have done it. If they stopped you at the 2.5 mile mark and asked you to eat rocks to be a part of athletics, you would have done it! Being a part of the few and the proud was so important that if they said you had to wear pink socks throughout the school day you would have done it! Do you remember those old days? I say old because I find now with high school athletes an attitude of get-me, buy-me, take-me, give-me. When asked to abstain from tobacco, alcohol and other drugs they respond, *"What's the big problem with chewing tobacco, with wine coolers, with a few beers? ... They don't affect our performance ... We should be able to do what we want, when we want and the school should not be able to butt into our lives."*

Who's calling the shots here? Who's setting the expectations? Who's in control of issuing letter jackets? One coach stood up in a seminar and said, *"Dr. Thomson, if I went back to my school right now and confronted my team or activity with the expectation to be tobacco, alcohol and drug free, I would not have a team!"* So be it! Do you think that kids don't know that we are wimping out? Sure they do. And they will take every advantage that they can. If we have to go from the marching one-hundred down to the marching three, from the defending state title team to the team with some missing players, so be it. A group in one state told me that if they took this stand, they would be out of a job because the parents would go to the school board and demand that they be fired! The parents want to win, regardless of what the cost might be.

We want responsible kids, yet we will not stand behind those who hold our kids responsible. We want kids to make good decisions, yet when they make poor decisions and are held accountable by others we won't back them. Where's that helmet and flak jacket? The coaches in these workshops have told me that when they have confronted their players on their teams regarding these issues, they have been challenged by the parents' attorney. If the kid is guilty as the day is long but the parent gets an attorney to get him back on the team, what are we teaching the kid? What the hell are we doing here? Obviously the lessons of this book need to be taught to all who come in contact with young people today.

If you go the opposite side of the pendulum, you might choose to become a rigid and demanding parent. To accomplish this, you will need to use anger, threats, and intimidation to get what you want. Remember what some kids do to battle these attempts at control? Silence. Refusal to do what the parent wants. Going along with the parents' wishes in front of them, but behind their backs doing what they want to. Resisting control with controlling behaviors of all types: weird dress, purposefully getting into trouble in school and the community, sexually acting out, running away, and so on and so forth. This reaction on the parents' part closes down the permission to talk discussed earlier. There is an "I-will-talk-and-you-will-listen-and-do-what-I-say-attitude." As a result, your kids will placate you, avoid you or be extra mean to you.

Natural consequences

Think of the word "natural" when you think of natural consequences. What comes naturally? If, for example, you go outside in the dead of winter in a short sleeve shirt and shorts, you'll get cold. If you cut yourself with a knife, you will bleed. If you drink too much alcohol, you will become impaired. The dialogue from a parent might be, *"Be sure you dress warm. If you keep that up, you will get hurt. You know better than that."* Skillful parents set expectations and allow natural consequences to take care of themselves. The parent who becomes aware that her child has lost her bike or has not studied for a test has many choices. No need for, *"You dummy, you're so stupid." "If you stay up all night, you'll be tired the next day." "How could you be so careless about your new bicycle?" "When are you ever going to learn?"* *"You are old enough to know better."* *"If you were more responsible, this would never have happened."* While Mom is losing it with her child, however, she continues to look for the bicycle while driving through the neighborhood. Within twenty-four hours, Mom, still lecturing the child about responsibility, purchases a new bike. What does this teach the child? *"Sure my parents will get on my back, but what else is new? They'll buy me another one because they can't stand me not having one."* The parent who is frustrated with her child not studying for the test allows her to stay home "sick" from school the next day. What does this teach the child? Think of all the natural consequences that can be related to the following:

- ❏ Forgetting your lunch.
- ❏ Forgetting your homework.
- ❏ Forgetting to set your alarm.
- ❏ Losing or forgetting a piece of sports equipment.
- ❏ Forgetting to bring a piece of required sports equipment to the game.
- ❏ Not showing up for practices but showing up for the games.
- ❏ Speeding.
- ❏ Drinking under age.
- ❏ Not calling in to work.
- ❏ Not coming home on time.

I'm sure you get the point. The consequences are "natural" and directly connected to the choice(s) made. Do you prevent your children from suffering the natural consequences of their choices? What prices do you pay? Who owns the problem? Who owns the choice(s)? What prices do your children pay?

You should not use natural consequences under the following circumstances:

- ❏ If a person is in jeopardy of hurting himself while in your presence. For example: someone attempting to take his life, a child running into oncoming traffic, or someone using drugs.
- ❏ When a child is in jeopardy of hurting another person. For example: wielding a knife at another person or perhaps breaking a window with his own hand. Of course you shouldn't stand by and watch someone trash a room.
- ❏ When a child is in jeopardy of damaging property. One young man I worked with attempted to remodel his parent's house with a hockey stick by breaking everything

in sight.
- ❏ When the child's health is in jeopardy: refusing to eat, to get appropriate vaccinations, or refusing medical attention when needed, are examples.
- ❏ When a child is too young to understand. A child under the age of four should not be expected to be responsible all the time. They can't be short adults because they have very little experience with responsibility.

Logical consequences

These are consequences that are set up by parents or other adults. They are not natural consequences as in the example used previously of a young person involved in middle-or-high-school athletic or co-curricular activities. Most schools expect that both the parent and the student sign a code of conduct that spells out specific rules and expectations for participation. The logical consequence for choosing to use drugs or alcohol could range from expulsion from that particular activity to suspension for a percentage of time. The consequence for the choice is logical instead of natural. Other examples of logical consequences are:

- ❏ Speeding = getting a ticket.
- ❏ Skipping school = detention, Saturday school or in-school suspension.
- ❏ Stealing = trouble with the law.
- ❏ Using marijuana = trouble with the law.

One evening, my family and I decided to go to a movie. While sitting in the seats, munching popcorn and waiting for the show to begin, it became apparent that the young kids in back of us were going to be a bit rowdy. They went beyond rowdy and became obnoxious. Their comments were sexual and vulgar, and they began to swear. I gave them the typical glance back over my shoulder, figuring that would give them a clue that we were hearing what they were saying, but they did not stop. One boy in particular became even more vulgar and obnoxious. I turned around and calmly asked them to settle down mentioning that my wife and kids were there. They then put their feet on the back of the seats my kids were in and began pushing them wildly. That was it! WhMPA alert! I was on fire. All I could see was two high school kids hanging from a tree! I stood up and turned around. My wife grabbed my arm. I paused and did a little productive thinking instead of reacting. I could have easily been sucked in by these kids, as I would have been in the past, but not this time. I went out to the lobby and asked to see the manager. As it turned out, he and a police officer on duty at the theater were just a few feet away. When I explained the situation and asked for their assistance, they came in and removed the kids instantly. That is a logical consequence for being rowdy in a theater.

Home versus house—is there a difference?

Over time, the family has been the base of support where children get their basic needs met in life. But when we look at the family of today and compare it to the family of yesterday, we see more divorce, neglect, teenage pregnancy, drug abuse, single parents, emotional and physical abuse than ever before. The family system is crumbling before our eyes and the definition of family is changing just as rapidly.

If a relationship isn't established as the base in a family, how can you expect that rules will be followed? Home should be a place where you can go without fear, where you know that you will always be taken in, no matter what. Home should be a place where you can learn about responsibility, control and choices, to see which choices give you more responsibility and control over your own life and which ones do not. Home should be a place where you learn to accept yourself for who you are and are given the space in which to do so. Home should be where you learn how to relate to others, and where you know that there will be a lot of extra hands and minds at your disposal to help. When you face a tough problem, home should allow you to make mistakes and encourage you to be a risk taker. Parents should put the Bandaids on, pat you on the rear, and send you out the door to try it again. It's a place where you learn values and rules. Where you learn to discipline yourself, and where you learn to give and accept love. Home is a place you want to go to, where fun and humor abound. Home is a place where your imagination can flow freely and potentials are constantly examined. Homes are places where the whole spectrum of human feeling is portrayed from grief over the loss of a loved one to the joys of graduation. Our emotional vocabulary is learned and practiced at home. Let's take a look at some ideas that you can try out with other family members in order to create a positive communications environment.

Four characteristics come into play whenever I work with healthy and unhealthy families.

THE ART OF COMMUNICATION

Communication comes in two forms: verbal and non-verbal. In a healthy home, there is communication in a tone of voice and in a manner that gives others permission to talk about anything they choose to talk about—sex, drugs or rock and roll. Respect your children by listening to them and they will give you that same respect when you want them to listen to you. In an unhealthy home, communication exists to control. There is a lot of negative talk such as *"shut up"* or *"not another word!"*

A young man that I worked with had a conflict with a principal that emphasized this point quite well. He was the type of young man who had behavior problems in school, who disliked school in general and went more for social than academic reasons. His teacher asked him to leave a class and told him to report to the assistant principal's office for being tardy. When he arrived at the assistant principal's office, he was met by one of the assistant principals who escorted him into his office and before he could even open his mouth, the assistant principal leveled him with, *"I hope you know what a loser you are. You are never going to learn, are you? You are one problem after another. You are nothing but a slug around here. Your mom must be real proud of you. She must be saying that it's great to have a son who is lazy and no good."* The young man sat and listened to this guy cut him down, criticize and berate him. When asked to respond to the assistant principal, he said, *"I bet your mom is really happy with you too. She probably likes having such a fat, overweight piece of crap as you for a son!"* Naturally, the assistant principal hit the roof and suspended him for three days for "insubordination." WhMPA's believe they can say whatever they want to say to someone, but they control for the response they want. If they don't get the response, as in this scenario, they believe the problem is "out there," in this case the student.

H. Stephen Glenn, author of several books on parenting, indicates that in the 1930's, a child spent on the average three to four hours a day in interaction, actively involved in relevant experiences with various members of his immediate family. Today,

Glenn states, families on the average spend fourteen and one-half minutes per day "talking" with their children. Of this fourteen and one-half minutes, twelve and a half are spent with parents issuing warnings or corrections. This leaves a whopping two minutes for real talk without criticism, put-downs or interruptions.

Critical points to follow are:

1. Listen, don't talk.

When your child comes to you with a problem, don't immediately tell him what to do. Let him tell you what his problem is and allow him permission to talk first. Let him try to solve it on his own first. Remember it's not by chance that God gave us two ears and one mouth! Make a plan to use the two ears more than the national average.

2. Talk with kids on their own time.

You don't have to have therapy sessions with your child at specific times each week. You also don't need to orchestrate "quality time" with them. The best way to talk with your child is to have conversations with them on their time—when you're doing the dishes together, riding in the car, lying on the bed, sitting in front of the fire or taking a walk. These are just a few of the possible times to talk. Allow them to talk and you might be amazed at how talkative they become. But if you lecture or preach to them, they will shut down quickly.

3. Allow them to teach to you.

Allow your kids to teach you something they have learned to do. Kids love to show off to their parents what they have learned in school, or what they have learned in a sport or a hobby they have taken up. Give them the opportunity to show you how they built the model, what they learned in their sport today, what they learned in school, what their opinions are about world problems, and so on. You will be amazed what this does for them. Put the shoe on the other foot. What if your boss allowed you permission to talk about what you liked and disliked about the company and what you would do if you were the boss. The sky is the limit in both cases, as long as permission and trust are provided.

THE ELEMENT OF TRUST

Trust in a healthy family is not based upon what is said, but on what is followed through with on everybody's part. When you say you are going to do something and you follow through with it, you build trust one brick at a time. An unhealthy family lacks trust. Trust is connected with the issue of talk and when there is lack of talk, there is lack of trust. *"Why should I trust you if you don't demonstrate it?"*

Earning trust is in the hands of the child and not the parent. It is something the child must do, not the parent. I often hear the children say to me, *"My parents don't trust me."* Many times I want to say back to them, *"No lie,"* after hearing the choices their parents inform me that the kids are making. Sneaking out of the house at night, telling lies, drinking, skipping school, getting into trouble, not being where they said they would be, and so on. With the choices that kids are making where they have total control, they have a lot of nerve saying we, as parents, don't trust them.

Trust is the building block of the relationship between parents and children. Parents want to trust their kids and kids want to trust their parents. Adolescents particularly want to feel trusted by their parents. The reality of adolescence is that there is usually a lot of sneaky behavior, talking behind parents backs, secrets and half-truths. Lying about where, when, with whom and how is a favorite pastime of adolescents who often say they lie because they already know what their parents will say to any request they might make. *"I wanted to go to the party and I knew you would say no, so that's why I told you I was going to the movie. It's your fault."*

"Just tell us the truth and everything will be fine." As a result the kid tells the truth. They tell their parents about the choices that other kids are making, what is going on out there, what the world of adolescence and kids is all about. The parent visualizes everything from wild parties to horrible accidents. The parents freak! We ask for the truth, they give it to us, and we hit the roof, yell at them and ground them. We indirectly teach them that if they want something, they will need to either lie to get it, hoping they don't get caught, or ask us and take their chances on our decision. If you want to open the pearly gates of communication, you must be prepared for information that you might not want to hear. With this information, you will keep the gates open or shut them down. Remember all that I have taught up to this point. Remember what frustration, control, influence, and no control are all about? Remember to ask questions, to use a proper tone of voice. Remember to teach and to model.

Mike: *"I'm going to Robbie's house to spend the night. There's gonna be two other guys spending the night also."*

Eileen: *"Are Robbie's parents gonna be there?"*

Mike: *"Sure they are."*
Eileen: *"Have fun."*
Mike: *"I will."*

Eileen calls later to see if Robbie's mother needs any help. June wonders what she is talking about. *"The boys are at your house, aren't they?"* Eileen is furious. Mike is in deep doo doo! He has just earned himself some serious consequences for his poor choice.

Mike: *"I tried telling you, but you never listen to me; you never let me do anything; you don't trust me."*

To which most parents want to say, *"No kidding!"* Get a clue Mike. What are we supposed to think? No wonder we don't trust you. Do you think we are idiots? Do you think we were born yesterday?

In order to get what they want, most adolescents will resort to a lie. What they hate is getting caught. If they are caught, they will often try to turn it around and blame you for "making" them choose as they did. The best thing to rethink at this time is control, influence and no control. Understand that you had control over your actions and they had control over their actions. It was their choice to lie, and now it is their choice to suffer the consequences, whatever they may be.

I use a bucket in my presentations to kids. I put a bucket on the stage and hand out a roll of pennies to a kid from the audience. I explain that the bucket starts out empty but with **good choices** made by the person, the bucket begins to fill up. When the person makes **poor choices,** the pennies come out and go on the floor. I explain that the parents hold the bucket and that the kids hold the pennies. With the pennies out of the bucket, I let the kids know that they now have no cents.

Children often complain about the structure set up by their parents as not being fair to them by comparison with their brother or sister or some other person. It starts out as fairness to younger kids. *"You're not being fair." "How come I can't stay up later than my brother?"* The problem can only be explained to your children by explaining that they, too, will be able to stay up later, stay out later or go certain places in due time. Unfortunately, the kids of today have convinced their parents, through guilting and threatening, to allow them to choose these things prematurely. As a result, very few "for-older-people-only" choices are left for kids when they become older. Some of the decisions we have to be involved in with our kids are attending a rock concert, going to certain movies, going to certain parts of the city, staying out later than usual, attending an unchaperoned party, or sleeping over at another kid's house. The bottom line is that parents are going to make decisions based upon what they are comfortable with at the time. Parents will make good decisions and poor decisions. They can't be always right.

When talking to your children about these requests:

- ❏ Listen to their points, ideas, and opinions
- ❏ Present your side and your opinions
- ❏ Make a decision that is final. Make your statement about the decision and don't argue with them.

SHARING FEELINGS

Healthy families allow others to share feelings, both positive and negative. In an unhealthy family, there is no permission to do so.

Tom and Suzy had a problem with their son Tony who was coming in late for curfew, not doing his homework, skipping school and treating his parents with disrespect. They attended a talk that I conducted at their church and felt I could help them. When they came to my office, I knew immediately that something was up. I noticed that the parents sat on one side of the waiting room while the young man sat on the other with his chair completely turned away from his parents. Tony was wearing about forty pounds of earrings on one ear, dressed all in black, with strategic tears in his jeans, hair shaved on one side with what looked like two feet of hair on the other, 666 tattooed on his knuckles along with "Hail Satan" scribbled with a pencil eraser on his notebook, which he proudly displayed. I ushered them all into my office and opened with the typical, *"Tell me, what brings you here today?"*

Tom proceeded to tell me in a very angry, controlling voice that his son was nothing but a *"dirtball and no good lazy bum."* He went on to list the various things that frustrated him about his son and how he was one problem after another. The list seemed never ending. In order to speed things along and to prevent Tom from foaming at the mouth, I decided to ask Sandy for her input. When asking her for her perception of the problem, she sat quietly and stated *"I think Tom has said it best."* I then leaned toward Tony and asked him for his perception of the problem. He refused to answer my question and proceeded to snap his gum loudly and just stare at his dad. Dad just about hit the roof.

He began yelling at Tony and telling him that "this is costing me money" to which Tony just shrugged his shoulders and smiled.

In order to avoid an argument in the office, the parents were escorted back to the waiting room with an encouragement to read through the Humpty Dumpty magazines. Back in the office with Tony, I began to try and sift through the situation. What I found out was that he was not talkative to begin with and, in fact, he just stared into space. I began calmly talking about the kids that I have worked with similar kinds of situations. I wrote on the board the four characteristics I keep seeing in families. When I asked him if he is given permission to talk in his family, he blurted out, *"What do you think?"* With that I said back to him, *"I'm going to take a wild guess and say you don't get a chance to talk, is that right?"* Tony said *"You're a real rocket scientist, aren't you?"* *"That's part of that psychology training they put me through."* I asked Tony if he could trust or be trusted, and he said, *"They don't trust me and I don't trust them. So what?"* When asked about his feelings, he was quick to point out that he had a lot of feelings about what was going on. He hated the control, he hated the criticism, the arguments, the threatening, and so on. I found out that in his house he was talked to, not with and not trusted. Now that I was talking with Tony about his problems and I was allowing him permission to ventilate without putting him down, I asked him the question I was dying to ask. I wanted to know about his choice of black clothing, the 666 on his knuckles, as well as the "Hail Satan" written on his notebook. I knew that these were related in part to satanic ritualism and the like. I asked Tony if he was into this, to which he replied, *"Heck no, I'm not into that crap."* *"Then why do you display this so much?"* *"Because it just bugs the hell out of my Dad!"* He was no more into the satanic belief system than the man in the moon, but from the comments that followed, he demonstrated that the more he was controlled by his father to think, act and feel the way his father wanted, the more he resisted. He stated that he couldn't talk, trust or share feelings but that he refused to give into his father's controlling, hence the choices in his behavior.

Think of the pent-up feelings Tony had. It is like having a dryer full of rocks inside your stomach. Put the rocks (or problems) in the dryer and you hear them clanging around in the steel drum. Some people are given permission to express their feelings. Others are unable to share their feelings,

and as a result, have developed what I believe to be a carpet-like padding on the inside of their drum. They get no permission to share their feelings and they keep them bottled up inside. It has been my experience that when this occurs, those feelings will come out through the skin and people will demonstrate their feelings in their actions. With the pressure Tony felt from his father, it was like two pieces of bread with jelly on them. Push them together too hard and the excess will ooze around the edges. Tony had a lot of ooze.

LOYALTY TO THE FAMILY

Loyalty is directly related to the verbal and non-verbal display in the family with permission to talk, trust and share feelings. I have been amazed at the accuracy of my prediction that the family that works on communication is the one that does not have major problems with following household expectations. There is a difference between a home and a house. A home is a place where there is structure, love, relationship and accountability for your choices. A house is where there is little structure, if any, a "do-your-own-thing" mentality, little relationship and no accountability for choices.

Many have asked, *"Why don't kids have respect for elders that was prominent in the old days?"* The kids had the choice detectors up back then, but the respect for their elders was there. You were told to be quiet and you did what you were told. The key, I believe, is in the survey results indicated earlier that in the "old days," a relationship was built first and discipline later. Today, unfortunately, we look for discipline first and relationship later.

Home versus House
a. Parent leads.
b. Anybody leads.

a. Expectations set by adults.
b. No expectations.

a. Investment, then return.
b. Returns, no investment.

a. Consistency and structure.
b. Inconsistency, rigidity.

a. Allows choices.
b. Directs choices.

a. Allows self-control.

b. Takes control.

a. Allows decision making.
b. Makes decisions for.

a. Encourages responsibility.
b. Takes responsibility.

a. Tone of voice is modulated.
b. Out of control tone.

a. Problems are opportunities.
b. Problems are awful.

Key points to remember

- ❏ Punishment does not teach a person what to do as much as it teaches a person what not to do.
- ❏ You can lead a horse to water, and even though it might not drink, you can salt the oats to increase it's interest.
- ❏ WhMPA's focus on controlling their kids' choices.
- ❏ Productive thinkers allow their kids to own their choices.
- ❏ Teach children that when they have a problem in their lives, they own the solution for that problem.
- ❏ Teach that choices in life are within each person's control.
- ❏ Remember not to argue with the stubborn or persistent child.
- ❏ Turn over the responsibility for choices to your kids.
- ❏ Pay attention to the "get-me, buy-me, take-me, give-me" child by not allowing his demanding to take over your rational thinking.
- ❏ Set the structure in a home by establishing clear expectations, and allowing your children to earn the privileges and the hassles for their choices.
- ❏ Allow kids to gain independence in their lives through the choices they make.
- ❏ Be willing to wear a flak jacket and a helmet in upholding your unshakeable and unbreakable expectations.
- ❏ Allow kids to suffer both natural and logical consequences for the choices they make.
- ❏ Work on building a positive home atmosphere by giving permission for everyone to talk, to demonstrate trust, to express their feelings and demonstrate their loyalty.

Helpful hints

- ❏ Provide opportunities for your children to demonstrate that they can make more choices.
- ❏ Provide opportunities for them to have input on expectations.
- ❏ Allow them the opportunity to discuss additional privileges, as well as negative consequences, for the choices they make.
- ❏ Provide your children the opportunity to openly discuss whatever they want with you.
- ❏ Be willing to hold your children accountable for their choices, even if it is need-reducing for yourself.
- ❏ Teach and model to your children that the world is filled with wonderful opportunities to make choices. These choices can be good choices or poor choices.
- ❏ Kids are not good or bad, they are only people making their best choices at the time.

Productive Thinking Skill 5
Thinking from Wants and Behaviors to Psychological Needs

In this chapter, I will reinforce a very important point for our productive thinking strategy: **"Everything we think and do is purposeful and are our best choices at the time to meet one or more of our internal psychological needs."**

Up to this point we have learned that pouting, whining, crying, drinking, drugging, depressing, paining, complaining and angering to name just a few, are all purposeful behaviors that meet one or more needs. We have also learned that refusing to talk, wearing weird clothes, running away, threatening suicide and various forms of rebelling are also purposeful in meeting needs. We found out that adults' choices were really reflections of kids' choices. Temper tantrumming turns into complaining. Pouting turns into depressing. The choices just become more sophisticated with age. The baby in the crib became very creative with his choices as did the man on the psychiatric unit. Both were successful in pulling people toward them and satisfying their needs. The longer people go on using these choices without intervention from parents or others, the more they will continue to use these behaviors. As stated before, if you are catching fish with these "lures" why change the lure? These are just a few of the choices that kids, and adults for that matter, make as a result of frustration. Frustration leads to motivation, which in turns leads to searching for the "best choice at the time" to close down that frustration. Hence these behavioral choices arise. Even though people may pay prices for these choices later on, they are effective in getting what they want at the time. We have also learned that these choices can be viewed as "lures" in getting what we want, which is to meet one or more of their frustrated needs. The behaviors noted above should be looked at as flares in the air or flags waving. They are saying, *"Notice me, I'm frustrated in one or more of my needs."* By stepping back and rethinking, you will go beyond WhMPA. You will

be on a productive thinking level that opens up a tremendous amount of alternative choices to deal effectively with any problem.

The young man I spoke of earlier who chose to prance around naked in front of his parents after they removed his bedroom door used his best choice to get his needs met. His need for Worth was being threatened through the powering behaviors of his parents so he chose to regain some of that Worth. And he found out it worked quite well. The boy who wore the 666 on his knuckles, wrote "Hail Satan" on his notebook, wore forty pounds of earrings on one ear and shaved one side of his head was also telling a story of where he was at. He was making his best choice at the time to deal with the controlling behavior of his father. A person who uses alcohol excessively is doing so because, at the moment, he is meeting one or more of his needs. The problem is that within a period of time, he will pay prices in other need areas also.

But now that you are thinking on a productive level, you are going to look at your thoughts regarding these situations differently. You will understand that children make these choices because of frustration over not having what they want at the time. You will be looking at the differences between what they want and what they have. You will be separating the problem into what you have control, influence and no control over, and you will be looking at the choices both you and your child have. Problems will be opportunities to view "old problems" in a productive way.

What follows is a description of each of the eight internal psychological needs, including ideas for you to teach and model to your children to help build their own skills in these areas. You will also find a great deal of information that will help you provide a need-fulfilling environment with your children. As a result, you will find that your children will be coming towards you more often, work-

ing with you more often and will be happy and productive more often.

I. Security

Security is "having efficient thinking and acting skills to take effective control of your own life."

PLEASE HEAR WHAT I'M NOT SAYING

Please-hear what I'm not saying: Don't be fooled by the face I wear, for I wear a thousand masks. And none of them are me. Don't be fooled, for God's sake don't be fooled. I give you the impression that I'm secure, that confidence is my name and cool-ness is my game. And that I need no one. But don't believe me. Beneath dwells the real me in confu-sion, in fear, in aloneness. That's why I create a mask to hide behind, to shield me from the glance that knows, but such a glance is precisely my sal-vation. That is, if it's followed by acceptance, if it's followed by love. It's the only thing that can liber-ate me from my own self-built prison walls. I'm afraid that deep down I'm nothing, that I'm just no good. And that you will see this and reject me. And so begins the parade of masks. I idly chatter to you. I tell you everything that's really nothing and nothing of what's everything, of what's crying inside of me. Please listen carefully and try to hear what I'm not saying. I'd really like to be genuine and spontaneous, and me. But you've got to help me. You've got to hold out your hand. Each time you're kind, and gentle, and encouraging, each time you try to understand because you really care, my hearts begins to grow wings, very feeble wings, but wings. With your sensitivity and sympathy and your power of understanding, you alone can release me from my shadow world of uncertainty, from my lonely prison. It will be easy for you. The nearer you approach me, the blinder I may strike back. But I am told that love is stronger than strong walls. And in this lies my hope, only hope. Please try to beat down these walls with firm hands. But gentle hands—for a child is very sensitive. Who am I, you may wonder? I am someone you know very well. For I am every man you meet, and I am every woman you meet, and I am you, also.

Anonymous

"Please Hear What I'm Not Saying" can rep-resent a young person wanting guidance from an older person. In this case, that is you. You become the teacher. You become the model. The teacher and the model of skills to deal with the daily prob-lems of living. The only real problem is not hav-ing enough efficient thinking and action skills to meet your needs. Eric Hoffer states, *"In times of change, learners inherit the earth, while the learned find themselves beautifully equipped to deal with a world that no longer exists."* If you stay in the past, you will live in the past. Instead, replace your old thoughts, actions and feelings with productive thinking skills, and take more effective control of yourself. Then teach and model these skills to those around you, including your kids. Parents who practice the con-cepts of productive thinking seek training, take classes and listen to others through both ears. They encourage curiosity and always ask questions. They develop new skills, new interests. They discover that the more they know, the more they realize they don't know; that as their circle of knowledge grows, so does the outside edge of ignorance as it pertains to what they don't know. If you have been reading this book with an open mind and if you have been planning to implement productive thinking skills into your life, you are already going beyond billions of WhMPA's. Teach your children that life is a se-ries of everyday lessons called problems. You either learn the lessons or repeat the problems.

A child who is dependent on his parents or others for need fulfillment has not learned that he has the resources within himself to deal with life's daily problems. He will come back to you for a way to solve his problems. Unfortunately, he will be-lieve that the "outside world" is in control of his life, which in turn will foster dependency on "out there." *"If out there is nice to me, I will feel good; if not, I will feel bad."* He has not learned that he is responsible for his feelings.

Teach your children that they can solve their own problems. They can learn from others and ac-quire information that will build their skills, but they alone are going to decide what to think, what to do and how to feel. When we have control over our lives, we feel secure. When we feel out of con-trol, we feel insecure.

Here's an exercise about security that I use with many workshop attendees. Write down on a sheet of paper or mentally list *what gives you a sense of se-curity*. If you are like the thousands of people I have talked with, you probably put down something like people who respect you, friends, family, a retirement fund, stocks, a job, a spouse, kids, love from others, people doing what you want, stability in your family, a home and money. What is potentially wrong is that these are great ways to actually put insecurity in your life, not security! You do not have total control over these areas. You may end up with a lot of material possessions in your life, but I have yet to see a U-Haul behind a hearse! You are not going to take things, people or possessions with you, and they can all be taken away in a heartbeat.

As a young go-getter from small-town Superior, Wisc. living and working in the big city (Los Angeles area), I met a wide variety of people. The lure of money and material possessions was everywhere, including in my head. I wanted what all WhMPA's want—lots of possessions. The experience I had in LA was great. I met many people who had everything that you and I would consider to be "great stuff." If somebody were to ask us if we would be secure if we had this stuff, we would surely say yes, but a woman I met taught me differently. She described her marriage to a very wealthy man. She had a chauffeur, many furs, fine jewelry and a very large home overlooking the valley. Her husband gave her a dress boutique on Rodeo Drive so she would have something to do because she was bored. But, what she also had was lots of frustration. She had two kids whom she spent no time with, and it showed in their acting-out behavior. She had a husband who paid little or no attention to her, because his first love was his work. She herself lacked skills to move beyond where she was in order to take control of her life. She had a lot of "stuff" but she was miserable. Henry Ford stated, *"If money is your hope for independence, you will never have it. The only real security that a man can have in this word is a reserve of knowledge, experience, and ability."*

Your child may give you a hug one day and call you a jerk the next day. Your spouse might be there one day and gone the next through separation, death or divorce. Your job may be going great one day and the next day you might be laid off. If you think security comes from things, you will try to get more things to help you feel secure. Because you can lose things and people, it is inefficient to base your sense of security on them. We are always looking to "have it made." The reason we won't is that the world and the people around us are changing. The closest you can get to "having it made" occurs when you have a multitude of skills to meet your needs in any environment.

But if you have efficient thinking and acting skills to meet all of your needs in all of your environments, you will be happy. If you don't, you will be frustrated. People can take away all your things, but nobody can ever take away your skills. Effective parents focus on building skills within their own lives first, and then focus on being able to teach and model those skills to people around them, especially their children.

Teach and model a strategy to save your sanity to everyone you come in contact with. Teach a productive thinking model and practice using this model over and over until you put it into practice in all of your daily affairs.

PRODUCTIVE THINKING MODEL

1. **Evaluating:** Evaluate the problems you experience. Ask questions such as: What is the problem? What do I want? What do I presently have? Is there a difference? To what degree? What have you thought up to this point to solve the problem? How have you acted to solve the problem? Are your thoughts or actions effective in solving the problem? What prices or consequences do your choices carry with them? Are you willing to look at the problem differently in order to lessen the degree of stress you experience?

2. **Productive thinking:** On two levels: What you take in, and what you are going to do differently. To think effectively, remember that:
   - ❑ Your thoughts direct your actions and your feelings.
   - ❑ Your problems are differences between what you want and what you have.
   - ❑ You can go from out-of-control to in-control.
   - ❑ You can go from no choice to choice.
   - ❑ Your wants are pathways to meet your needs.
   - ❑ You can break outcomes into process steps.
   - ❑ Your problems can be opportunities.

3. **Achieving:** Make a decision to move beyond where most people are and apply the productive thinking model to your daily life.

4. **Acknowledging:** Acknowledge that problems are a part of life and that you can make good and poor choices to deal with them.

5. **Accepting:** Accept that people, and the world around you, are always changing and that you have limited control over others or situations. Acceptance will eliminate the confusion and frustration of trying to control what you can't control.

6. **Allowing:** Allow others to make their own decisions and choices. Understand that their choices are neither good nor bad. Allow them to suffer the natural consequences of those choices in order to provide opportunities for growth.

7. **Adjusting:** As a result of applying the concepts of evaluating, productive thinking, acknowledging, accepting, and allowing to problems, you can choose to adjust your thoughts, actions and feelings.

8. **Practicing:** Continue to use this model in all of your daily affairs and you will increase your skills.

You can apply this strategy to your life each day. Security comes from having the productive thinking skills to take control of your life and knowing that no matter what happens you will continue in the process of building new skills on a daily basis.

WhMPA: *I will feel secure if my children do what I want them to do. The more things and/or people I control, the more secure I will be.*

Productive thinker: *At best, I can influence my children and I will build skills to increase my influence. Those skills will influence my child's perception of me as need fulfilling. I will do this not to control my kids, but to feel good about myself. My security comes from knowing I have the skills to meet my own needs.*

WHAT YOU CAN DO TO CREATE A SENSE OF SECURITY

❑ Teach and model that security is based upon having the efficient thinking and action skills to take control of our lives, and knowing that we will continue building new skills on a daily basis.

❑ Teach and model that security is not in having material possessions or a gift from other people.

❑ Teach and model that we do not have to depend on other people for need-fulfillment.

❑ Teach and model that we can change our thinking from, "*I can't always get my wants met*" to "*I can always get my needs met.*"

❑ Teach and model that in frustrating situations, we must recognize what we have control, influence and no control over.

❑ Teach and model that frustrations are really differences between what we want and what we have.

❑ Teach and model that our thinking about problems will direct what we are going to do and how we are going to feel.

❑ Teach and model that we have choices to think, act and feel positive, negative or neutral when frustrated.

❑ Teach and model that life is an opportunity to rethink about stress as an opportunity for growth.

❑ Teach and model that we have control over the choices we make.

❑ Teach and model that power originates in our ability to think and act differently.

❑ Allow your children to make decisions on their own as often as possible.

❑ Allow your children to demonstrate responsibility for taking care of their own life.

❑ Provide your children opportunities to solve their own problems without your assistance.

II. Faith

Teach your children that **Faith is a belief in ourselves, a belief that we have the power to take effective control of our life and a belief in a power greater than ourself.** Productive-thinking parents work effectively with their children to help them understand that Faith is an opportunity to look at the negative times in their life as opportunities. Positive results can come out of negative situations if we believe they can. We can model and teach our children through verbal and non-verbal methods that problems are a chance for them to rethink what they want and what they can do in order to get what they want. Ask questions such as, "*Is getting upset about your problem helping you right now? If you continue crying (or whatever behavior you are choosing), is that going to help solve your problem?*" Are you giving them the impression that they are capable of solving their own problems?

Unfortunately, what you wear, where you live, what you drive and how you look are connected with who you are today. We need to help our kids understand that Security and Faith have nothing to do with what they wear, own, drive, and so on.

"*How I look is who I am.*"
"*I believe in myself if I look good.*"
"*What you think of me is what I am.*"
"*If I don't look good, I don't believe in myself.*"

Many young people confuse how they feel inside with how they appear outside. If they have pimples, they think their life is ruined and nobody can tell them differently. If you have ever had a pimple, you know what I mean.

"I'm not going to school."

"Why?"

"I've got a sore throat."

"You don't sound bad."

"I feel terrible, and besides, I'm not going with this big pimple on my forehead."

"You can't even see it, honey."

"Oh yeah, the thing is like a mountain! Everybody will notice."

Children's stories depicting these concerns are everywhere. In the story of "The Ugly Duckling," the little bird was rejected by better looking ducks. Later he found out he had a beautiful swan inside. "Rudolph The Red Nosed Reindeer" was rejected by others. Later he was accepted by others when he was the hero on Christmas eve. "Dumbo The Elephant" was ridiculed for his big floppy ears until they learned he could fly. "Cinderella" was a typical person—came into her beauty, was hated by her wicked stepsisters, had an enchanting moment at the ball, changed back after midnight and later, on her own, was accepted by the prince for who she was.

Just as important as our belief or faith in ourselves is our faith or belief in a power greater than us. In the Stone Age, people worshipped the power of the stars, rocks and animals. Druids worshipped the trees, Greeks worshipped a pantheon of Gods. The Romans worshipped the mystery of the universe along with numerous other Gods, while the Buddhists worship Buddha. Moslems worship Allah. Today people still believe in a power greater than themselves. But as I mentioned before, some people have taken this concept too far and paid prices for their Faith. They have turned their thoughts, actions and feelings over to a power greater than themselves. *"God will do it for us."* *"My life is miserable; I'm alcoholic and depressed because it's my higher power's plan for me."* We have numerous examples of people who have turned their entire life savings over to other people only to find an empty well of promises. Some people are masters at the power of motivation and understand how to appeal to people's basic needs. Cults motivate people primarily with the need for Belonging, not through sacrificing animals or others.

The problem with cults is that the people sucked into those beliefs are saying that they have no control over their choices. They surrender power and control to their higher power, or to someone else and relinquish responsibility. But nobody takes your power away; you give it away.

What about the kids who question the origin of Jesus, for example? The origin of religion? If there is a God? Where the Bible came from? Why we have to go to church? Is this okay? We already learned that children will question everything. They want evidence or proof to support their beliefs, even if their question is about religion. They want proof. Here's a suggestion. Ask them who the first president was? Who was the fifth president? How about the tenth president? Maybe they will know the first but probably not the fifth or the tenth, but eventually they will tell you the answer. Ask them, *"Why do you believe what's in the book?"* They will probably answer, *"Because it is written in the book and it is based on truth."* *"Truth from whom,"* you reply? *"The author,"* they state. Why do they believe the information contained in that book? Why don't they believe in a power greater than themselves? For many people, the area of religion stirs up some interesting questions and debates. My suggestion is to allow your kids to question each and every area they are concerned about. Encourage them to stay in contact with the church and find a group of people who can help them through their questions if necessary. Church youth groups are excellent at doing this. Many kids stay in contact with the church through youth groups not only because they can get answers to these questions, but also because they are able to meet all of their needs. The longer our youth stay in contact with religious activities, whatever their belief system, the lower their risk of negative behavior.

If your kids have been involved with church and suddenly decide to stop attending church functions, that should be a signal to you that something is wrong, either with people at the church or with them. Sit down with them and discuss it. If you are like millions of parents, you might express your own desires regarding church. If you believe that it is important to be involved with church, you will probably push your message very strongly. You could find yourself fighting with your child emotionally or even physically. The real problem for them is that you are trying to control their actions or thoughts. Allow them to ask questions. Acknowledge frustration and disagreement. Accept that they are exercising their freedom to think or act as they choose. Be open and calm in discussing the positive and the negative outcomes regarding their thoughts or actions. Be willing to adjust your thinking and your actions to their experience. Perhaps they would prefer another church or another day and time. Perhaps they just need to talk with another person about the difficulties or questions that concern them.

Develop faith in yourself and in others. At least once a day find the positive in what your kids do and what they say. Give them affection and let them know about their good choices. It's a great way to end the day. You don't have to make a big deal out of it, but letting them know that they have the ability to control their life is very important. Provide them with opportunities to demonstrate their ability so they will understand that they have the skills to control their own lives. They will quickly learn that relying on others to solve their problems or to choose for them puts them in a weak position and gives away control. Good choices on their part result in positive outcomes. Poor choices on their part result in negative outcomes.

Helping your children to believe in themselves is critical in becoming healthy, capable, responsible young adults. By believing in themselves, they will overcome their fear of failure. Belief in oneself comes from within, not from without. *"One pat on the back is worth two kicks in the pants"* is a phrase we often hear. There is nothing wrong with pats, hugs, kisses, high fives, awards, handshakes, stickers or trophies, but be careful. Some people get sticker crazy. Everybody gets them "regardless of effort." This is unfortunate, because it sets up a pattern of need fulfillment connected to "out there" and puts you in a position of giving your kids something for everything they do, which encourages them to believe that *"If I receive something from out there, I will feel good; if not, I won't."* I sometimes feel like we have to get a rubber arm with a suction cup that you can attach to the back of your child's head and every time they move, it automatically pats them on the back!

WhMPA: *I will put my faith in people and things outside of myself. My destiny is in the hands of some other force.*

Productive thinker: *With time, patience and work on my part, I can turn a problem into an opportunity for growth and learning.*

Faith is a belief first, then an action on my part. I believe that if I am responsible and choose efficient behaviors, things will turn out for the good.

WHAT YOU CAN DO TO CREATE AN ENVIRONMENT OF FAITH

- ❑ Teach and model that life is a series of opportunities for growth.
- ❑ Teach and model that faith is a power greater than yourself.
- ❑ Teach and model that a higher power provides guidance and advice for dealing with frustrations.
- ❑ Teach and model that you can celebrate the positive in yourself, others, situations and things.
- ❑ Teach and model that you can share the positive about yourself with others by being open.
- ❑ Teach and model that it isn't necessary to be critical of yourself, of others or of the world around you.
- ❑ Teach and model accepting and letting go, even if there is no reason.
- ❑ Teach and model a love for nature and the universe.
- ❑ Teach and model an awareness of things that people did not create.
- ❑ Teach and model what is positive in a person's physical, intellectual and emotional makeup.

III. Worth

Worth is the belief that you can go beyond where you are today, that you can take risks and that you have the ability to achieve and succeed in life on your own. Self-worth or self-image are all thoughts and opinions that you have of yourself. These thoughts and opinions will direct your actions, which in turn, will direct your feelings. The better you feel about yourself, the more positively you will view yourself and the world around you, and the more risks you will take. Worth is power. You believe that you have the ability to change your thoughts and your actions and, as a result, your feelings. This belief, which comes from a belief in your skills (Security) and a belief in yourself (Faith), will allow you to believe that you have the power to take effective control of your life, regardless of the problems you encounter. When you perceive yourself as having these skills, the power to believe in the positive along with the ability to go beyond where you are today, your Worth or power will increase. Worth does not come from outside an individual, but from within. The one and only person who can threaten your Worth is yourself. Your sense of Worth can decrease only if you choose to put yourself down, beginning with negative thinking about yourself and the world around you. Use problems as opportunities to teach and model Worth to your kids each and everyday. Remember to put these changes about thoughts, actions and feelings into your own life first. Your kids will notice the difference and, as a result, you will be teaching, through modeling that Worth comes from within.

Boys often measure worth by strength and power. Many times you will see boys demonstrate "tough" behavior in front of others, fighting to prove "worth." I used to play "King of the mountain" with my friends, standing on the top of a hill, which was really just a mound of dirt, with others trying to dethrone us. We felt like we were really the king of the mountain until someone came along and threw us down. The rise to power was as quick as the fall, with a lot of bumps and bruises. Boys continue to fight into adolescence to show strength and Worth.

In high school, Worth is often associated with toughness and drinking or other drug use. Unfortunately the more you drink or drug, the more power you accumulate. Your status is connected to how much you can consume. Drinking becomes drunking. The prices in other need areas can be significant, as many of us have seen over the years. Many students look up to a physically larger student as one who has Worth. The bigger the muscles the more Worth they are assumed to have. Look at the increase in the number of boys who are now working out with weights, indicating reward or Worth fulfillment. To aid in their muscle growth, some young people unfortunately use steroids. The problems with steroids are numerous, but the outcome of large muscle can be obtained in a relatively short period of time. But what you find under all of that muscle is a kid who has a lot of WhMPA thoughts, actions and feelings.

Girls, on the other hand, often have a difficult time with Worth because over the ages, women have been told not to be assertive with males. Women have been told in many direct and indirect ways they need to be seen and not heard. Male

domination over women still continues to this day. Look at the many sexual harassment charges that have been filed over the last few years, however, and you will see that many women are beginning to speak up for themselves.

Unfortunately many girls have been taught that Worth comes from what they have—nice clothes, nice hair or a nice figure. As with boys, perception of their Worth is based upon the outside, not the inside.

If you talk to kids nowadays and then talk to adults about when they were growing up, you will find that both want to have power, control, choices and responsibility, and both talk about not being allowed to have it. Parents tell their kids that if they work hard, study, stay drug free, don't become sexually active, stay out of trouble and mind their manners, good things will come to them. The problem occurs when you expect your child to wait for the good things. Children are not good at waiting for anything.

Trouble occurs when we do not allow kids to have control, power, decisions, choices and responsibility for their own life. Without allowing control, kids' lives becomes directed, not influenced by their parents. When other people direct your thinking, your choices or your feelings, your Worth is in their hands, not yours. When that happens, Worth becomes an external source or pathway to meet needs.

Excessive yelling, physical force, threatening, criticizing and manipulating are all ways in which WhMPA's control their kids. These behaviors work in the short run for some people. The louder I yell, the more control I might have over you. If I threaten you with something you think I will follow through with, I might get you to do what I want. But what are the prices? There are consequences with these choices. Controlling your child diminishes his Worth and teaches him that other people have control over his life.

Instead of controlling their every move, we need to influence our children and structure their lives so that they have the opportunity to develop skills to take more control. ALLOW them to make choices and to make decisions. ALLOW them to take on the responsibility for their problems. ALLOW them to have power and control over their own lives. This is difficult for parents, particularly WhMPA's. But the prices for not doing so are great indeed.

Mass media commercials, our political process,

our educational systems and our addiction to sports all imply subtly or overtly that true success means being young, physically attractive, getting good grades, being a great athlete, and having more money and status than others. Just watch commercials. The man or woman with good looks, money and lots of possessions wins. Barbie dolls indirectly teach kids right from the start that beauty is what you must have, along with the clothes, a Corvette, the "Malibu" series, and so on. You never see Barbi with imperfections, pimples, bony knees, flat hair and so on. She's airbrushed perfect! Ken is the same. A hunk. The man of the hour. Barbi's dream.

As parents, our drive for control and power, and our own need for Worth comes into direct conflict with raising our children productively. As children develop more skills in taking control of their own lives, they engage in a power struggle with their parents, often tearing the relationship apart. *"You can't think like that." "You can't feel that way." "You are not going to do that." "Over my dead body!" "You are not old enough to take charge of your life."* These all indicate our unwillingness to give up control of our kids. But the more you demand that your child do what you want him to do, the harder you will find it to behave in loving ways towards him. Many parents view negotiation and compromise as giving in, but the reality is that compromise and negotiation are necessary. Negotiation does not mean loss or failure. Many kids have sat in my office with rational and practical solutions to problems, but many parents are too stubborn to change their own thinking for fear of being seen as giving in. If you are only interested in winning, you'll eventually set yourself up to lose.

Self-worth must ultimately come from within, so we can best serve our children by teaching and modeling for them the skills that will enable them to take effective control of themselves. Teach them internal skills, productive thinking and better action skills, and they will have them for life.

Children who do not have a healthy feeling of Worth can overreact to normal problems and become seriously unhappy. Without a feeling of Worth, children may not have the determination it takes to establish independence. This, in turn, can lead to depression, low self-esteem, and even suicidal thoughts and actions. Kids without a sense of Worth try to gain the attention they so desperately want from people around them through poor choices. Can you see how the world around us sets

us up for these feelings? Can you see the difference when you choose to rethink and use the productive thinking model?

Building self-esteem or self-worth in your children is, of course, not an overnight process. It requires time and patience, but the outcome is definitely worth it. Share something positive with your child each and every day. The best time to do this is often just before they go to bed. Review the positive aspects of the day by describing to your child the choices which he made that lead to self-control and Worth. It is so easy to catch your child being bad, but catch them being good as well. Sit and talk productively with them about problems that occurred as a result of poor choices. Ask what they wanted and what they had. What poor choices did they make? Did these choices solve problems or create new ones? Ask them to think about what they could do differently in the future. Ask them to think about the areas where they have control, influence and no control. By using the productive thinking model, you become a teacher of better alternatives. **Remember, your tone of voice is critical.** Keep it calm and productive. Understand that you do not have control over what happened in the past. An effective teacher identifies talents that your child has demonstrated in school or around the house. **Catch 'em being good!**

Children are motivated to learn and do things from birth and usually perceive themselves as capable at a very young age. Invisible is miserable. Children don't want to be seen and not heard; they want to be involved. They want to be a part of the family and not just spectators. Teach, model and allow your children to take risks. Difficult problems will come up. Understand that solving them will take time, patience and productive thinking. Think about what the WhMPA would do. Would they rethink or react? How long would they choose to be upset over a problem?

Ever hear? *"Let me try." "Let me do it." "I can do it, if you let me try." "I wanna help."* If you have ever said to your child, *"You're too little to help, go out and play,"* you created a perception, without realizing it, that your child is incapable of helping out. Good luck later when you ask this kid to help out with the dishes or with setting the table. They have already learned that they're incapable.

Of course, there are a lot of things that children can't do, but look around and see what they can do. Allowing your child to help out with chores will give them a sense of achievement. They are capable of folding clothes, taking out the garbage, doing the dishes, getting themselves up, helping with dinner, making their own lunches and choosing their own clothes. Allow them to have a voice about homework times, bedtime, curfew, and so on.

Many parents have just about fallen off their chairs when I've said this in my lectures. They believe that if you ALLOW your child to own these areas of their lives, you are giving "control" over to the child. We are worried about "giving the control away" for fear of what kids will do with it. What's the worst they can do? If we believe that ninety-eight percent of life's problems will not kill us, then we can rethink. If we believe as a WhMPA does, that most of life's problems will kill us, then we react. But we can give this control over to our children, many of whom are dying to get it in the first place. The feeling of power and self esteem is the single most important way to increase Worth.

If you work at developing a relationship with your child first, discipline will follow. This can start at any age if you can rethink and begin to view yourself as a teacher as well as a parent. Children love to feel that they are a part of the family and of your life. You can build on your relationship by allowing them to help out with a project you are working on, washing the car, doing the laundry, painting, cleaning the house or the garage, and doing yard work. Probably, it would be much quicker and easier to do it yourself, but the benefits of including your children outweigh the extra time. For every return there must be an investment and the return on your investment is a loving relationship with your children.

To illustrate this, Carol and I attended an invention convention at our kids' elementary school where students were given the opportunity to become inventors as a part of their second grade class project. They were given the Freedom to choose their own invention, which they had to write about first and then build a model of. They then had the chance to stand next to their invention, dressed like scientists in Dad's white shirt, while their parents strolled through the halls asking questions about their inventions. I will never forget the look on Michelle's face. She was in tears as she told us, "My Mom did not like what I made, so she made this for me instead." Her mother had successfully stepped on her needs for Security, Faith, Worth, Freedom and every other need as well. The other kids we talked to were very excited about their inventions. I remember asking one student about his project. It

apparently was a sweeper system that could clean up the entire house. And according to the inventor, it could sweep things under beds and chairs so they couldn't be seen. He boldly stated, "I don't know if it could work in real life, but I made it myself and it's good enough for me." His pride and Worth were evident from his smile and demeanor. I wish we could say that about Michelle. Is a school project's purpose to meet the parent's needs? Or the child's needs? No one benefits when school projects are made by parents. But how much school work is really done by the parents and who really benefits? Who really loses?

Teach your children to believe in themselves. Teach them to use the statements, "I can. I'll try. I will do it. Attitude is everything. Anything is possible. The sky is the limit." Notice that these words indicate hope and involvement. We live in a social world, which involves risk-taking and it is important for us, as parents, to teach our children to experiment with life. Help your child affirm his own personal power. Help him accept others for who they are instead of what they are not. Help them enjoy life, with the challenges of meeting new people and being involved in exciting new things. Help them understand that it is human to make mistakes and to learn from them if they choose to. Teach them to look forward to each day as an opportunity to improve themselves, and increase their understanding of others and the world around them.

The idea behind affirmations such as these is to educate your children to the myriad of choices that they have in terms of thinking, feeling and behaving. If they believe that they can make their lives what they want to be, they will grow up more able to make necessary changes rather than waiting for someone to come and save them.

Use yourself as a model for relating to others, so that your kids can learn from your behavior. Approximately eighty percent of all input for humans is first processed as visual stimuli. Our children certainly learn a lot from watching us and others. How parents perceive their kids determines how they choose to act and feel toward them. The reverse is also true for how our children perceive us as parents.

WhMPA: *I feel worthless as a parent because my kids are not listening to me. My Worth depends on things outside of myself (kids, spouse, friends, job, and so on).*

Productive thinker: *My power is from rethinking about what I have control over in problem situations, and teaching and modeling that to my children. Worth comes from my belief that I have the skills to take effective control of my own life and the problems I encounter. I alone am responsible for my Worth.*

WHAT YOU CAN DO TO CREATE AN ENVIRONMENT OF WORTH

- ❏ Teach and model that Worth comes from inside, not from other people or things.
- ❏ Teach and model that the power of productive thinking builds a sense of Worth.
- ❏ Teach and model that external sources of Worth may feel good in the short run, but with time will fade.
- ❏ Allow kids to demonstrate responsibility for their own lives by making their own decisions.
- ❏ Teach and model what responsible decisions and choices are all about.
- ❏ Teach and model that your children have control over the choices they make.
- ❏ If problems arise, give your children time and guidance to work their way out of the problem by using the productive thinking strategy, but do not take on the responsibility for what they must do.
- ❏ Share the positive with them regarding what they do; catch them being good.
- ❏ Encourage your children to take risks and look for opportunities to achieve and go beyond where they now are.
- ❏ Allow your children to learn about responsibility and achievement through becoming involved in adult jobs around the house.

IV. Freedom

Freedom is a state of mind, not a condition of the environment. It comes from knowing that you have choices. It is believing that you are never stuck unless you choose to think, act or feel stuck. Freedom is having the internal belief that you have choices regardless of the environment you are in or the problems that you have. People who choose responsible behavior indicate a tremen-dous amount of freedom in their lives. Those who make irresponsible choices indicate that they have a lot of people on their back and are greatly restricted.

Being human, we naturally want the freedom to choose how to live our own lives, to express ourselves, to associate with whom we choose, and to worship, or not worship, as we believe. We want the freedom to choose how we will think, act or feel. So does everyone else, including our children. Responsible choice making is doing what you want to do without preventing others from doing what they want to do.

Ask yourself some questions like, *"Would I want a parent like me if I were a kid? Do I share with my children my expectations concerning their behavior? In school? At home? In the community? In other environments? Do I allow my child freedom of choice? Do I allow him to think the way he chooses? Do I allow him to act the way he wants? Do I allow him to choose his own feelings? Do I choose to not fight with him about the choices he makes? Do I choose to allow him to either earn the positive privileges of good choices or to earn the negative consequences? Do I let my children know that they have earned the negative choices? Do I model efficient choices in my own life? How well do I communicate with members of my family? Do I spend time with my kids alone in order to better find out who they are? Do I work on a relationship with my family?"*

Approximately fifty percent of the time you spend communicating with others is spent in listening to what they have to say. Put a boot in your mouth if you have to. Listen with both ears or have your mouth stapled shut.

Productive thinkers are people who understand that the only two things you have to do in your life are be born and die. Everything else is a choice. Nobody can force you to do something you don't want to do. Teach and model to your kids that everything they do is a choice. Teach them that people will provide them with expectations until the day they die, but they alone can choose to follow those expectations or not. You can set the expectations. Expectations such as letting them know you expect them to avoid tobacco, alcohol and other drugs. They can choose to go by these expectations or not. The power is with them, not you. Nobody can force them to behave in a positive or negative way. If they end up grounded or without certain privileges, you should choose not to argue with them. Allow them to go without a privilege until they decide to make better choices and abide by the set expectations. How long they choose to sit without certain privileges is determined by their attitude and their actions, not yours. This truly is the best way to teach them about the connection between making poor choices and negative consequences.

Teach your children that they are not bad kids because they make poor choices, but kids making poor choices at the time. It is not the end of the world for you, or for them. Ninety-eight percent of the choices they will make are not going to kill them though they might frustrate them. Consequences for making poor choices might be time-out in their bedroom, losing the car, losing out on the use of a toy, not going out with a friend, and so on. Choosing to have a negative attitude and actions around the house is not your problem, and is a natural or logical consequence of their choices. What they need to focus on is not the past so much as what choices they will make in the future. Simply giving the child time-out or taking away a privilege is not recommended. Instead give them an assignment to figure out what expectation they violated at home, in the community, or at school and what other choices they could have made. Will they do differently in the future? Ask them to tell you what they have learned from their experience. How long they stay grounded or without a privilege is up to them, not you.

As productive-thinking parents, we must allow our children to make their own choices much of the time. It will be hard at first to step back and let them decide. WhMPA's will tell us that this is disastrous. They believe that parents should be the ones with the control, power and choices. They do not want to give these responsibilities to kids. Productive-thinking parents, however, will only step in and make choices for their children when they are jeopardizing their own life, or someone else's life or property. Taking control of an out-of-control child is not being a WhMPA, it is just a good idea. When they calm down, you can talk productively with them about expectations and choices.

Allowing kids to be who they want to be is tough for parents because so many are living vicariously through their kids. In the area of children's sports, for example, whose needs are being met? Who's playing? One parent forces the child to play the piano. Why? Because she believes learning the piano builds character and self-esteem, but he wants to be playing with his friends. The fight begins and the parent wins by threatening punishment if the child doesn't play the piano. Sure, we would like our kids to be exposed to the arts and sports but "forcing" them is another story. How much we push our kids will be reflected back to us in their pleading to let them do their own thing. Pick your battles, but don't pick your child's activities to the point you're fighting with them over their participation. This holds true for their choice of career in life. What if they chose to go to a technical school versus a university? To not go to school at all? To become a singer in a rock band? To take a year off college and travel? None of these will kill them, but will they kill you? If they do, you're not **ALLOWING** them the choice to think, act or feel the way they want to. Whose life is it anyway? You can point out the pros and the cons of each choice, but you pay a significant price for forcing others to do what you want them to do.

The blamers and the "it's-not-my-fault" kids need to sit with themselves a little bit longer than other kids. They are usually stuck in a thinking pattern that enables them to choose to think in only one way. But time has a wonderful effect on the blamers. Time without Freedom and privileges can bring even the toughest kid to his knees and his senses regarding his control and choices. The old saying, *"I'm going to huff, and puff, and blow your house down,"* needs to be implemented here. Simply huffing and puffing does not always work. Sometimes you have to blow the house down. Allowing them to sit for as long as they choose requires patience, but it's merely tough, not impossible. The end result will be excellent for you and for your child.

A parent who wants to instill a home environment that promotes Freedom will substitute expectations for rules. By doing so you, will present a structure that allows your children to earn privileges or negative consequences. The choice is theirs to make, not yours. You will also turn over the responsibility, decisions and choices to your child, and give him power and control.

It isn't always necessary to respond to the negative choices your child makes. In order to save your sanity, you could choose to ignore some behaviors because it is impossible to respond to all the choices your child makes. And let's face it, when you find poor choices, what are you gonna do? A better option might be to give them some slack and look the other way as long as their choices don't hurt anyone.

Avoid power struggles since they are almost always over things that have already occurred and seldom lead to anything being accomplished.

Some kids may want to debate issues, expectations or consequences. Remember to listen, but don't let their problem become your problem. It may be tempting to argue with your child, but keep in mind that your child is attempting to gain control of the situation. Keep humming, *"I do jokes, I do windows, but I don't do arguments."*

WhMPA: *My kids are responsible for my negative feelings, actions and thoughts. They control my positive and negative emotions. My Freedom is controlled by other people or situations outside of my control.*

Productive thinker: *I am responsible for the choices that I make and my children are responsible for the choices they make. I may not be able to control other people, but I can control what I choose to think and do.*

WHAT YOU CAN DO TO CREATE AN ENVIRONMENT OF FREEDOM

- ❏ Teach and model to your children that they are responsible for all their choices in all situations.
- ❏ Teach and model to your children that the environment and other people influence them, but do not control their thoughts, actions or feelings.
- ❏ Allow your child to develop responsibility, power and control by letting him make his own choices.
- ❏ Establish unshakable and unbreakable expectations in your home with the assistance of your children.
- ❏ Allow your kids to help set these expectations. Reach a decision regarding the unshakable-unbreakable expectations.
- ❏ Challenge your children whenever you hear them attempting to place blame on others for their choices.
- ❏ Teach and model to your children that how they choose to think directs how they choose to act and feel.
- ❏ Teach and model to your children the benefit of changing things or situations they have control over instead of spending energy on people, things, or situations where they have little or no control.

- ❏ Teach and model to your children that the use of negative language such as "have to," "must," "can't," "should," "if only out there would change," "forced," "addicted," and so on constricts their choices.
- ❏ Teach and model the concept of Freedom using words such as "try," "want to," "will do," "will achieve," "want to know," "going to," "choose to," and so on.

V. Belonging

Belonging is the sense of love and caring you feel inside. Caring for others and being liked is a need we all have. Most of us tend to accept the common sense idea that survival is a basic need. But if the need to survive were primary, there would be no suicide. It would be impossible to kill yourself or even to risk your life for fun, as many skydivers and other thrill seekers do. The survival instinct is strong, but for a person who attempts suicide or jumps from an airplane for fun, other impulses or instincts must be equally strong.

Most people who commit or attempt suicide have described incredible loneliness and said that being dead seemed a better choice than continuing to live with such pain.

We need to have people in our lives who care about us and people in our lives we care about. Certainly we all have different levels of needing other people in our lives, but except for the person who chooses to live alone on a mountain top, we all have some need for Belonging.

The need for friends, family and love, best described as the need for Belonging, is as strong as our need to survive. It may not seem as strong a need as thirst or hunger, but, if over a long period of time, we did not have special relationships with family and friends that we often take for granted, the idea that life is hardly worth living would occasionally come to our minds.

Along with family and friends, many of us also enjoy a sense of Belonging with pets and sometimes even with inanimate objects such as a "beloved" automobile or a stuffed animal, boat or computer. If automobiles were purchased only to transport us from one place to another, the automobile industry would only need to manufacture one single, efficient model. Many of us, however, want an automobile that is special. New car owners often demonstrate that cars provide us with Security, Worth,

Belonging, Fun, and so on. We make many purchases for need fulfillment instead of necessity. Think about your latest purchase and which needs you were able to meet.

Our need for Belonging is most satisfied when our relationships are more or less reciprocal. Relationships that are lopsided result in feelings of misery and pain.

You don't need to empirically measure the Belonging in your life. If you have it, you know it and it feels good. If it is absent, as occasionally happens, you feel the pain we call loneliness.

There are three primary reasons or causes for increased loneliness in our society:

1. Today's society provides us without a great deal of free time. We are a society that by and large looks for other people and/or things to provide us with enjoyment. If you listen to your kids, you will probably hear a lot of, *"I'm bored."*

2. Many people do not know how to make and maintain good friendships. There are specific qualities or skills involved with being friendly. You do not just suddenly become a friendly, outgoing person. You learn from others around you which skills make a person friendly and which skills make a person unfriendly, but many people would prefer to wait for someone to approach them first, instead of being in control themselves and approaching others.

3. Our personal expectations are higher now than they've ever been before. Some of these expectations tend to be in the form of "outcomes." The difficulty is that outcomes are very rarely achieved unless goals are broken down into a process of achievable steps.

Everyone experiences some sadness and depression as a result of loneliness. The secret to avoiding loneliness is in knowing how to get rid of unwanted feelings of sadness and depression as quickly as possible. Happiness comes from bouncing back and becoming involved with your friends once more. Depressing behaviors are usually a way of letting the outside world know you are "on hold" and that you don't want to do anything. If you wish to avoid a lifetime of loneliness, you will need to re-evaluate your thinking or expectations instead of waiting for "out there" to change.

Like adults, many kids are lonely because they lack Belonging with parents who usually work, resulting in more latch key programs and day care facilities. Many kids arrive home from school while their parents are still at work, and less and less time is spent around the dinner table as a family. Add to this a lack of relatives in the same geographical area, and much Belonging is lost. **In my work with kids, this is almost always the need that is most frustrated.** Children want a relationship with their parents, but what they usually get is control which is the opposite of a relationship. They want friendly, caring parents and instead get criticism, yelling, demanding and threatening in a physical and psychological sense. As a result, these kids are frustrated over the difference between what they want and what they have, and often choose to hang out with anyone who offers Belonging to them in a way they want. The people they spend their time with may be making good or poor choices themselves. Sometimes kids make poor choices on purpose in order to draw attention to themselves, which is purposeful and usually works to bring people closer. Unfortunately, the price is high. Look, for example, at the drawing one young person I worked with at a leadership camp made describing his family.

The father in this drawing is busy with his "own thing" and thinks that the problem in the family is the young "trouble maker." If the young "trouble maker" would change, life would be better for everyone else. The mother, trying to be a peace keeper, is caught between the "trouble maker" and the father. What is really happening is that the young person is frustrated because his father gives so much Belonging to an inanimate object—the computer—and not much Belonging and attention to his son. Just like a good WhMPA, the father blames all problems on his son. He doesn't look at the bigger picture as it pertains to his son's frustration and the environment in the home. This young man was acting out in school, at home and in the community. As the young man said, *"Even negative attention from getting into trouble is better than nothing. It's my way of getting back at him for all the attention he gives to that damn computer!"*

Adolescents often deprive parents of their need for Belonging, viewing them as weird, square, out of it or old-fashioned. Parents often hear statements such as:

"Why do you wear those clothes?"
"That music you listen to is boring."
"You are so old fashioned."
"Your hair is really gross."
"Bell bottoms went out with the sixties, get with it."
"Just drop me off here, I'll walk the rest of the way."

If you are trying to meet your needs **through your kids**, good luck. At their age they care most about the fulfillment of their own needs. As a result, parents often become quite frustrated in the need areas of Security, Faith, Freedom, Worth, Belonging, Fun, Knowledge and Health. Adolescents prefer to satisfy needs through their friends. Accept this as a normal change children will go through. They may bless you with their presence at the dinner table, but otherwise will spend time in their room or with their friends. But the time they do spend around you is critical. If you can work on your relationship skills with them, the results will be to your advantage. If, however, you choose to be a WhMPA, your relationship will be poor. If they hear the broken record, *"Why don't you ever talk? Why don't you ever sit with us? Why don't you ever spend time with us?"* Your children will likely choose to move away from you instead moving toward you. What you choose to do or not do in the area of relationships will determine how they will act toward you.

No one wants to feel alone. Everyone needs to feel loved, accepted, cared for and appreciated. If children do not feel this, they will they turn to their friends, or in some cases, to gangs or the streets.

Hopefully you will be the base for your child's steady and reliable source of Belonging. But this need is often frustrated because we want our chil-dren to change and they want us to change. You will probably need to compromise, even when they demonstrate some real poor choices. It's important to remember that making poor choices does not make them bad kids. In fact our perception of them as being bad is what creates bad kids. Are you your child's best friend? Being best friends does not mean you allow them to do whatever they want to do, but that you **allow** them to be who they are and step in only when what they choose to do affects themselves or others in negative ways. In order to have a really good relationship with your child you need to look for the positive, to catch them being good and making good choices, to provide them with skills to deal effectively with life's problems, and with an environment that encourages the positive and allows them to achieve, to take risks, and to develop worth and power in their lives. Do you try to build a relationship with them by playing games or doing things together like taking walks, going on picnics, cookouts, camping or just doing chores? During these times, do you focus on a relationship instead of focusing on things they've done right or wrong, laughing like a kid, giggling like a kid and enjoying life like a kid? I'm not suggesting that you act childish, but childlike.

Put yourself in a child's shoes, then decide if any of the following would make you want to spend more time around yourself:

- ❏ Do you create an atmosphere of cooperation and mutual understanding?
- ❏ Do you practice open communication?
- ❏ Do you give permission to talk about all issues and problems, allowing opinions and alternatives to be expressed without criticism?
- ❏ Do you create an atmosphere where problems are viewed as opportunities for learning better alternatives?
- ❏ Do you create an atmosphere that allows your child to feel the power of choice to think and feel the way he wants?
- ❏ Do you create an atmosphere that is loving and caring, and models fun and pleasure?
- ❏ Do you create an atmosphere that allows your child to demonstrate trust through good choices, and encourages sharing information?
- ❏ Do you create an atmosphere where need fulfillment occurs "with" each other and not "through" each other?

Attempt to gain rapport with each of your children. Before you can be effective as a parent, you must first spend quality time with them. This will take time and effort on your part. I have had many parents come into my office asking for ways to gain control over their kids. **Children do not respond to control by parents or anyone else.** Neither do they respond to rigidity. They do respond to a relationship and to structure. Find out what your children enjoy and spend time with them doing it. Start when they are young and go from there. The more actively you interact with them the better your relationship will be. Going to a movie requires very little activity. You sit, you watch, you stay quiet. Playing catch in the back yard requires activity of which talking is usually a part. Observe your child over the next few days and note the things she likes to do. If she likes building blocks, get down on the floor. If she likes reading books, or playing dolls, get down to her level and stay there. If you want to build rapport, take time to commit yourself to doing the things with your kids that your kids like to do. This shouldn't stop when your child gets into school but should carry through for the rest of your life. It is like putting money in an investment account and the return will definitely be well worth it.

If you would like to try a modeling strategy for improving communication and social skills, you might try the following:

Get a paper bag and some magazines from around the house. Go through the magazines and cut out pictures, words or phrases that depict who you are as a person. You might choose a picture of someone watching television, a person smiling, a person scrubbing the floor, an outdoor man, a professional doing paperwork, or something else. Put these cutouts inside the bag. Then get your family involved by having your spouse, kids or significant other look through magazines and cut out pictures, words or phrases that depict who you are from their standpoint. Ask them to be perfectly honest in order to help you understand their feelings. Put those pictures, words, or phrases on the outside of the bag with tape or glue. You now have how others perceive you on the outside and how you perceive yourself on the inside. Do the images match up? Do you like what others see? How can this help you with your relationship with your kids or with others?

WhMPA: *If my children do not show caring toward me, I will feel awful. It is more important what others think of me than what I think of them. I expect something in return for what I give.*

Productive thinker: *I will demonstrate caring to my children without expecting caring in return. It is more important what I think of others than what they think of me. I can work toward having fulfilling relationships.*

WHAT YOU CAN DO TO CREATE AN ENVIRONMENT OF BELONGING

- ❑ Make sure you spend quality time with your kids.
- ❑ Watch your tone of voice, even when you are frustrated.
- ❑ Spend time with your children and let them know how much you love them. Tell them that you like the special qualities they have (sense of humor, quick wit, ability to take care of themselves, responsibility, good thinking skills).
- ❑ Demonstrate caring without demanding caring in return and giving without getting.
- ❑ Teach and model effective relationships by increasing your relationship skills with your partner.
- ❑ Teach and model that the most important step in beginning a friendship is your intent.
- ❑ Teach and model that saying "hello" first is within their control.
- ❑ Identify activities that you can both share and enjoy.
- ❑ Create a special time to spend alone with each child.
- ❑ Get into your child's world and find out what he likes to do.
- ❑ Remember that your child will not be with you forever, but that the thoughts about you and what you did will always be with him.
- ❑ Teach and model that friendship starts with giving to give with little or no intention of getting something in return.
- ❑ Teach and model that building relationships with others outside of the family increases relationship skills within the family.
- ❑ Listen, listen, listen and listen some more.

VI. Fun/Pleasure

Winning is not a sometime thing; it's an all-time thing. You don't win once in a while, you don't do things right once in a while, you do them right all the time. Winning is a habit. Unfortunately, so is losing.

Vince Lombardi

Fun/Pleasure is anything that makes you feel good. It is different for everyone, but is a strong need for everybody. If you can't have fun, it can become drudgery just to get out of bed each day. Abraham Lincoln once said, *"People are just about as happy as they make up their minds to be."* Notice that Lincoln also focused on the thinking aspect first. He, too, believed that it is your thoughts that direct your energy. How you think about fun is up to you, not the outside world. Kids have a big need for Fun and pleasure, and as parents we can teach and model appropriate ways of having fun. Teach your child to meet his need for fun in a way that does not conflict with his other needs and in a way that does not interfere with other people's needs. As a parent, you need to teach how to make the right choices.

I am reminded of a story about a group of kids participating in a traveling sports team. After the games, they returned to the motel where they were staying and where no one, including the coach, had set limits regarding behavior. As a result, the kids started testing the limits to see what they could get away with. First they ran up and down the halls. Then they started jumping on the beds, and throwing balls in the rooms and in the halls. Then the wrestling started. All the while they glanced over their shoulders to see if anyone was going to say anything. When no one did, they continued to see just how far they could go. One group of kids went to the lobby and purchased key chains that made vulgar statements when the button was pushed. The kids then ran around the motel pushing buttons at other hotel guests. They were being allowed to meet their need for Fun in a way that interfered with other people. Their parents did nothing, but shake their heads and said, *"What can you do? Kids will be kids."* With this type of parental attitude, it's no wonder that some kids never learn right from wrong.

"I'm bored." "Who is going to entertain me?" "Who's going to take me to the movies? Buy me a toy? Take me to the park? The zoo? Play a game with me?"

"I'll feel better if you do." Many parents take it on themselves to be the entertainment committee for their kids. We are all faced with the problem today that our kids want and demand instant stimulation from "out there." But what happens when out there is not available? Parents need to step back, walk away and give their child some spare time in which to be bored, or should I say, choose boring behaviors. You will be amazed at how creative children become when left by themselves. The key is not to step in when they pout, whine or complain because they don't have anything fun to do.

Can you remember the day that your parents bought a new refrigerator, stove, washer or dryer? You could hardly wait until the delivery truck arrived. The box was what you wanted, it was better than gold. It was the best toy you ever had. You used your creativity to build a house, a spaceship, a secret weapon or what have you out of a simple box. Modern technology has its downfalls.

It is very important to teach and model to our kids that it is better to be a fun maker than a fun receiver. Most Americans receive fun from a source outside themselves—television, video games, or other people, to name a few. The source, of course, is not always negative. It depends on how much we rely on "out there" to be the supplier of our stimulation and need fulfillment. But being a fun maker means you rely on yourself to create your own fun instead of waiting for someone to do it for you.

Fun often produces laughter, and laughter has been rightly called "the best medicine." Did you know that laughter can be, and is, used by psychologists to treat people who have various kinds of emotional disturbances? Norman Cousin's book, <u>Anatomy of an Illness</u>, documented his successful experiences with laughter therapy as a remedy for a degenerative spinal disease. Dr. William Fry of Stanford University describes laughter as a form of internal jogging. Muscles tense as we wait for the punch line or the ultimate incongruity. At the point that our laughter erupts, the muscles in the face, neck, chest, belly and diaphragm all get a good work-out. Laughter stimulates the cardiovascular system and exercises the lungs. As the laughter subsides, the muscles all relax profoundly until the tension level falls substantially below the pre-laugh level. Relaxation benefits may last up to 45 minutes. In general, the more intense the laughter, the more relaxing and the longer the effect.

Laughter can also act as a natural pain reliever

because it takes your attention away from pain and reduces tension. This in turn changes your perceptions or expectations, and actually creates physiological changes that reduce pain. Recent research indicates that laughter stimulates the production of endorphins—our body's own natural pain killers. Hysterical laughing is not necessary to trigger this kind of reaction; simple delight or amusement works just as well. Humor also allows us to relieve our overall stress level. WhMPA's quite literally do not see the humor in problems. To them, all problems should be viewed as negative, not fun. But the productive thinker believes otherwise. However, it allows us to look at life's paradoxes at a safe emotional distance and to separate ourselves from an annoying or uncomfortable incident, while reducing our subsequent stress level. Laughter is especially helpful for those times when our stress is of our own making. People naturally like to be around others who are having fun, but many adults give up their playfulness and sense of humor as they grow older. We become afraid of looking silly in front of others. Laughter and creativity, however, are linked. People who are not afraid to laugh at themselves generally allow themselves more latitude for taking risks and making mistakes. In order to be healthy in today's world, it is imperative to maintain a sense of humor.

> **WhMPA:** *I cannot have fun if I don't have things or people around me that are fun.*

> **Productive thinker:** *I can laugh at my troubles if I choose to. I am responsible for putting fun in my life. It is okay to be spontaneous and curious, or childlike. Laughter is a remedy for stress.*

WHAT YOU CAN DO TO CREATE A FUN ENVIRONMENT

- ❏ Take an inventory of the inexpensive fun activities you can do as a family.
- ❏ Plan to have fun each and every day.
- ❏ Look at the humorous side of problems.
- ❏ Identify what your kids like to do for fun and make plans to join them.
- ❏ Let yourself go and become childlike with your kids and with other adults.
- ❏ Model appropriate pathways to efficiently meet your need for fun.
- ❏ Play games for fun instead of for competition.

- ❏ Teach and model fun activities such as dancing, singing or playing music.
- ❏ Model that we can put fun into our lives and control how we think about fun activities.

VII. Knowledge

The more knowledge you have and the more information you have, the more choices you will have and the more secure you will feel. If, for example you choose to put the information from this book into your life, you will develop more skills and you will feel more secure. If you put the productive thinking skills stressed throughout this book into your life first, you will feel more secure and your kids will learn from you. There is nothing deadlier than boring information.

Remember that boring teacher you had? Was the information boring? Was it presented in a boring way? Was it need reducing? I bet it was. Remember that great teacher? The teacher who provided information that you really loved to hear? The teacher who made the subject come alive? Even the subject that you might not have liked? What made him different? What made him or her different is that they presented the information in a need-fulfilling way. It was Fun, it involved Belonging with others in a non-competitive way, it provided Worth because it required a risk on your part to ask questions or offer answers that might be wrong, knowing that you would not be put down or ridiculed by others. That met your needs for Security, Faith and Health, among others. Watch the movie "*Stand and Deliver*" and you will see actor Edward James Olmos deliver a great performance as a need-fulfilling teacher providing an environment that stimulated the need for Knowledge, as well as providing a safe and caring environment for the students in his classroom. Rent "*Dead Poets Society*" and you will again see this in action when Robin Williams, as a teacher in a private school for boys, brings poetry to life through his teaching—teaching which offers Fun, Faith and Belonging.

The Disney Company annually provides awards to the most distinguished teachers around the country. Not teachers with the highest academic degrees. Not teachers with the highest grade point average in the classroom. But teachers providing an environment where students can meet their needs through learning. All parents should watch these awards ceremonies to get ideas about need-fulfilling activities through teaching and modeling. Stimulating teaching is especially important for kids.

Role models are an important source of knowledge for our kids. Kids look to their role models for structure and self-identification, trying to become like that person. Role models can model efficient skills to deal with problems, teaching kids in unexpected ways. Of course there are models all around us. Among them are advertising, teachers, coaches, churches, even videos and television. All these have enormous impact on who we are at any particular moment. Because we learn both good and bad behavior from these models, it is quite important to learn how to discriminate between good and bad models and to teach the same to our children.

By acting as a positive coping model, you can teach your children new behavior and also reduce unwanted feelings such as anger, depression, fear and so on. As a parent you can use modeling in a positive, educational way that will meet your child's needs and your own.

You can present models in a variety of ways:

Live. Use yourself as a model. Is what you do consistent with what you say? If you want your child to lessen his risk of drinking, practice responsible drinking yourself. Teach your children to meet their Health need by exercising consistently, eating well, not smoking, treating other people with respect and modeling the productive thinking skills you have learned from this book.

Symbolic. Use television, audio tapes, videotapes, storybooks, posters or pictures of individuals to display positive behaviors and use these sources in your own life. Monitor the programs your children view and talk about them. Encourage your children to watch the people around them for positive messages.

Verbal. Describe to your children what behavior you expect. Speak about the positive things in life and encourage them to look at the positive even when they find themselves in negative situations. Start using the words control, influence and no control. Use the word "choice" to help your children understand that there are good and poor choices in all situations in life, and encourage them to build skills to meet all of their needs in all of their environments. Teach them that life is a process filled with opportunities for them to go beyond where they are.

As parents, you must take responsibility for providing models that you want your children to emulate. If you want to decrease the chances of your kids smoking, drinking, eating too much and exercising too little, you can influence that by providing models that emulate health, rather than self-defeating or self-destructive feelings and actions. Start with yourself. Continue asking yourself, *"Is what I'm choosing to do in my own life a good model for my kids?"*

Playing board games can help your kids increase their knowledge. Games such as "Wheel of Fortune," "Jeopardy," "Trivial Pursuit," and "Scattergories" encourage them to learn, but it's important to play the game to gain Knowledge, not to gain Worth through winning. Playing board games can also help your kids learn sportsmanship and how to relate more effectively with others. A number of board games are specifically designed to enhance communications within the family, and can be used to get into discussions about family issues and other matters that normally might not be talked about by providing permission to discuss some subjects and challenge values, and becoming a fun way to open up communication in a nonthreatening manner.

When my brother and I were growing up, we played "Uncle Wiggly" with a housekeeper. I loved it and hated it. I loved it when I was winning, I hated it when I was losing. Likewise, the house keeper and my brother loved and hated playing the game with me. When I was winning, the general atmosphere was good. When I was losing, the atmosphere was, to say the least, tense because I would throw the game pieces on the board. If I could see that the house keeper or my brother was going to win, I would pout, whine, throw game pieces and walk out of the room, and refuse to finish the game. What a WhMPA! The problem? My choices were the problem. The other problem was that my brother and the baby-sitter would continue to play the game with me, time after time. They did not refuse to play with me because of my pouting, whining, complaining and temper tantrumming. As a result, I secretly learned to gain control using pouting, giving-up, and whining, to name just a few.

WhMPA: *Some people are just born interesting. What others think of me is more important than what I think of myself. I can't let other people see what I don't know.*

Productive thinker: *I can choose to increase my knowledge in all areas of life. I can then choose to share this knowledge with all those I come in contact with. It is okay to be a learner. It is okay for other people to see that there are some things I don't know.*

WHAT YOU CAN DO TO CREATE AN ENVIRONMENT FOR KNOWLEDGE

❑ Play games to learn and not just to win.

❑ Open yourself up to learning and share what you have learned with others.

❑ Take an inventory of what makes you an interesting person.

❑ Evaluate each need area for your strengths and weaknesses.

❑ Plan to change what you don't like about yourself.

❑ Allow your children to share with you the things that interest them and the things that they learned.

❑ Look at the strange as familiar and the familiar as strange.

❑ Read the newspaper, watch the news, or listen to the radio and share something you learned with someone else.

❑ Evaluate your language to open up new alternatives for yourself and your family.

❑ Teach and model the importance of brainstorming alternatives when you become frustrated.

❑ Teach and model that knowledge is power only if you use it efficiently, and rethink in all of your need areas.

VIII. Health

Health is balance in both the physical and psychological areas of your life. People don't stop playing because they grow old; they grow old because they stop playing. Take an inventory in your need areas to see if you are choosing efficient pathways to meet your needs. Taking an inventory means that you need to ask yourself questions in each area to see if you are thinking the way you should be thinking in order to develop a healthy balance in your life. Psychologically, parents need to learn a strategy to save their sanity. You can do this by using the productive thinking strategy in all areas of your own life first. You will then teach and model that when you are frustrated, it is because you want something you do not have and

that the degree of the frustration is proportional to how badly you wanted what you wanted. The critical point that you will teach and model is that you choose to look at your problem differently than you did before and you identify the areas in which you have control, influence or no control, and that you can't always get what you want, but if you look at your problem differently, you can always get what you need. Finally, you will teach and model that life is a process, and the solution to problems needs to be viewed in the same way. Learn to make frustration your friend.

Health is, of course, also being in balance with the foods you eat and the exercise you get. The relationship between good physical health and positive mental health is very real. Have you ever become physically sick when you were stressed? Many people use headaching, for example, to deal with stress. Others choose overeating, overdrinking or overdrugging. The consequences for these choices are apparent, and the price you pay in other need areas is significant.

According to studies by the Department of Health and Human Services and the President's Council on Physical Fitness, less than half of the children in the United States today get adequate aerobic exercise. Children need to work out three times a week at an aerobic activity like running or cycling for twenty minutes without stopping. According to a 1986 Department of Health and Human Services study, eighty to ninety percent of all adults don't get enough exercise to boost their cardiovascular fitness levels. Forty percent of American boys ages six to twelve can't do more than one pull-up, twenty five percent can't do any. Only thirty percent of American girls ages six to seventeen can do more than one pull-up, fifty-five percent can't do any. Another study indicates that only thirty-six percent of American children have daily physical education in their schools. According to a Wall Street Journal/NBC News Poll in 1985, thirty-four percent of American men and forty-two percent of American women don't exercise at all. These statistics are sobering and disturbing. If indeed our mental and physical health are intimately connected, then we are in deep trouble, both as individuals and as families. We haven't been teaching and modeling these areas to our kids.

If you believe these statistics, then you can see why we are out of shape as a country. But there are many other advantages to exercise. What are they and why get yourself and other family members tied up into all this sweat and work? Take a look at the advantages, and then make your own choice as to whether or not exercise and eating better is a worthwhile investment of your time. First, exercise is an excellent stress reducer. It improves your overall strength and endurance and helps you sleep better and feel less muscular tension. Exercise helps you to improve your work performance by giving you more energy. Exercise promotes strong and healthy bone development and improves your appearance. Aerobic exercise can help to improve your problem solving, creativity and general intellectual ability. Furthermore, the family that exercises together will have more opportunities to communicate.

Regular exercise not only gets us in better shape, better able to manage stress, but improves mood and self-esteem, while decreasing depression. The more demanding your lifestyle, the more important aerobic exercise is to your continued good health.

Second, proper balance between nutrition and exercise will help you to reach and maintain your ideal weight. If you are overweight, begin a plan of action to deal more effectively with your weight problem. See your doctor if certain health conditions exist or if you are extremely overweight. Join a group or create a plan on your own. Evaluate other programs to see if they teach the skills you need to take care of your own weight. These skills should include productive thinking about food and sensible exercise to help you achieve what you want. Use a program that utilizes everyday food and encourages weight loss in reasonable ways. You will be teaching your children that foods are choices we make, choices we are in control of and choices that meet needs.

> **WhMPA:** *My health is dependent on something outside of my body. My food intake is controlled by what others eat. I need fast results in order to feel better.*

> **Productive thinker:** *Ill health is an opportunity to take an inventory of my life to see what I may be doing wrong. I am in control of my eating choices as well as my exercise choices. I am responsible for my health and can choose specific ways to improve it.*

WHAT YOU CAN DO TO CREATE AN ENVIRONMENT THAT MODELS HEALTHY CHOICES

- ❏ Take an inventory of each of your need areas and evaluate the choices you make to meet those needs.
- ❏ Rethink every health problem you have.

- ❏ Teach and model that learning about your body and how it works is efficient.
- ❏ Teach and model efficient eating habits.
- ❏ Teach and model non-smoking.
- ❏ Teach and model the appropriate use of alcohol.
- ❏ Teach and model a productive thinking strategy each time stress arises.
- ❏ Teach and model the benefits of physical fitness and provide opportunities for exercise as a family.
- ❏ Teach and model the ineffectiveness of relying on fad/crash dieting or other "quick change" schemes.

Key points to remember

- ❏ All behaviors are purposeful to meet one or more of your internal psychological needs.
- ❏ Begin to perceive negative behaviors as flares or flags that indicate a loss of need fulfillment in one or more areas.
- ❏ Frustration results not only from not getting what you want, but more importantly, from not getting your needs met.
- ❏ Behaviors or choices can be viewed as your best attempt at the time to meet one or more of your eight internal psychological needs.
- ❏ The real reason kids behave or misbehave is to meet one or more of their needs.
- ❏ Rethink that behaviors are like fishing lures. People use them to lure other people into meeting their needs.
- ❏ Psychological needs both motivate people and frustrate them.
- ❏ The choices you use to meet your needs may be either efficient or inefficient. The critical difference is that with efficient choices, you do not have any prices to pay in other need areas.

Helpful hints

- ❏ Needs can be viewed as the hub of a bicycle wheel with the spokes representing the pathways you choose to satisfy those needs.

- You may not always be able to get what you want, but if you rethink you can get what you need.
- When you become frustrated, practice productive thinking to open up alternative pathways to resolve your frustration.
- If your children have behavior problems, try to identify where they are frustrated.
- Look at what you do in your own life to meet your needs and what you model to those around you.
- Evaluate how you create a need-fulfilling environment in your home, workplace and other environments.
- Evaluate yourself to determine what draws people toward you and what motivates people to move away from you.
- Build skills in each of your need areas by deciding to add one new skill each week.
- Look at opportunities you have to build a relationship with your children.

CHAPTER 13

Productive Thinking Skill 6
Thinking from Outcome to Process

A DIFFERENCE

As the old man walked the beach at dawn, he noticed a young man ahead of him picking up starfish and throwing them back into the ocean. Finally catching up with the youth he asked him why he was doing this.

The youth responded by saying that *"the stranded starfish would die if left until the morning sun."*

"But the beach goes on for miles and there are thousands of starfish, how can your effort make any difference?"

The young man looked at the starfish in his hand and threw it back to the safety of the water.

"It makes a difference to this one," he said.

Author unknown

How long will this person continue to pick up starfish? As long as he sees value in doing so. Parents, too, will continue to hang in there with their kids through thick or thin, if they look at growing up as a process and not an outcome. You can't quit parenthood like you might a job you dislike. The benefits of parenthood are there. But where? Where are the benefits at the moment? That is the problem sometime for all of us. We want to see the results of our work immediately. We will most likely see the benefit of our parenting in the end. Our hard work will pay off. Your teaching and modeling will eventually take hold. Maybe not by noon tomorrow, but it will take hold. Just like the person picking up the starfish, patience becomes the word of the day for parents.

Many people want an "instant responsible kid, instant relationship, instant happiness or to become the instant parent of the year." Any program or technique that promises "quick, free, instant, and easy" results is probably not based on correct thinking. Virtually all programs promise some of these.

"How long is it going to take for my child to change his behavior?" If I had a dime for every time I was asked that question, I would have a boat load of dimes! Many of the people I see in my office ask how long it will take for change to be noticed in their family or in their child. They are naturally concerned about the cost of the sessions and are thinking of the bottom line outcome. I tell them it's $90 an hour. They come back with, *"Can you do it in a half hour?"* *"How about if I have a coupon from the paper?"* They are frustrated with a problem, which is why they came in and they want change now, not later. The problem is that the client actually holds the answer to this question. They are in the driver's seat. As a result, I go as quickly as they want to go—not as quickly as I might want to. They have the problem, but they are looking for help. I am there to provide them that help.

I used to become frustrated with parents who came to see me for professional advice. They would tell me how their life was going with their child and I would listen to them and quickly come up with "the answer" that would solve their problem. Even though I had been trained in using the skill development theory, I thought and acted otherwise. I was trying to wear the clothes of a productive thinker, but was thinking and acting like the king of WhMPA forest, and modeled to them that problems should be solved quickly and easily. Problems don't develop overnight and neither do solutions.

I now listen to problems with the same intent as before. I ask questions to help clarify points and find out from all parties their perception of the problem. If two people are involved, I often find two different problems. My next step is to identify what each person wants and what each actually has. From there, I can help them realize that the frustration they experience is due to the differences between what they have and what they want. Many times I use the chalk board in my office to point out these differences and to help them to see where they may be paying prices in other need areas. My goal is to help them widen their perception of their problem.

My role is different now. Before putting productive thinking to work in my own life, I thought of myself as a problem solver. Now I perceive myself as a teacher of productive thinking skills that can aid others in thinking productively about their problems. I listen to what they were thinking and doing prior to coming to see me. I then ask them to evaluate whether or not their prior thoughts and actions had worked for them. Most always I hear that they have not worked very well and that is when I start to teach them about productive thinking, so they can widen their view of their problem. We begin by redefining the problem in terms of differences. Redefining a problem helps them to evaluate their thinking and ultimately their feelings. I then help them begin to look at the areas where they have control, influence and no control. Next we look at the choices they have and the alternatives available to them. I then help them begin to look at their child's behaviors as possible flares or flags which represent frustrated need areas. By doing this, the parents can evaluate themselves in those same need areas to see if they need to change. Next we identify the process steps to a better relationship with their child, and the process steps for solving the problem. Finally I help them to understand that all problems can actually be opportunities for growth if they choose to look at them in a productive thinking fashion.

Many people have questioned this approach because it does not immediately solve problems, and takes time and patience. But this is a process approach that results in long term changes and it takes time to build a healthy relationship.

We, however, are a quick-fix society. We want results now. We do not want to wait. We want our eggs cooked now. Our meals zapped in an instant. Our patience is running thin. We live in a society that tells us that if we use a certain shampoo, a certain deodorant, toothpaste or soap, we will be happier, healthier, sexier, and of course, more popular. Such is the promise implied by the majority of television commercials. As a result, we have a "quick-fix" expectation that the use of these products will produce everything that we want in our lives—that relationships will get better and life in general will improve. If all of these implied promises were true, fights, arguments and divorce courts would be extinct by now. As a therapist, I could have just had

them use one of these "quick fix" methods. Brush your teeth with that certain product and, wow, you get what you want! Simple—right? Nope. That's Hollywood's perception. Reality is slower. Relationships take time. A healthy family takes time. A problem takes time to solve. Practicing thinking productively takes time.

The whole world of televised fantasy gives the impression that frustration can be settled quickly. Computers are in a race for the fastest processing time, microwaves strive to be the fastest, and if you have a headache, for God's sake don't take 400 milligrams, take 800 milligrams of extra strength, buffered, super-charged aspirin. The list goes on and on.

Most people want instant outcomes and are impatient with process. If they get the outcome, they feel good, but they don't want to have to work at making changes. They want to feel good now. They want something better than what they have now and they want their needs met. That is the thinking that is taught and modeled to them day after day. They can't wait for the weekend or to get that good job. They can't wait for the kids to graduate or to leave home, to win the lottery or to retire. Perhaps you can relate to these. The world is filled with messages that tell us everything will be better when certain changes take place.

How long will it take to build a relationship with your kids? It will take as long as it takes. What? It will take as long as it will take. WhMPA's do not want to hear this, but the productive thinker will understand it because relationships are always in process. A relationship grows from day to day without end. If a child refuses to talk to his parent, it may take quite some time. It takes awhile to regain trust once it has been lost. How long will it take for a child to be trusted after he has broken trust? How long will it take for a child to change his friends? To get better grades? It could take quite awhile. The CONTROL is with the child as are the CHOICES. If you choose to rethink in this fashion, then you are ALLOWING your children to own the responsibility and ALLOWING them to own the decision to change when they want to change. ALLOWING them to sit without their privileges for as long as it takes for them to come up with a better choice of behavior and a better future plan of action is ALLOWING them to be in control. A WhMPA would demand change immediately, because process takes too long. *"The heck with this process stuff. I want change now."* The

WhMPA wants everything instantaneously. Productive thinkers choose not to set themselves up for further frustration because of what they want. The productive thinker understands that he has influence, not control.

It isn't difficult to become a process-oriented person. By rethinking that each day is a new opportunity to meet your needs, you will begin to think in a process fashion. The idea is to put yourself in a position where you can meet as many of your needs in as many environments as possible. It is possible to meet your needs in every environment, but your choices are critical. You can choose to be miserable or you can choose to be happy. Teach your children that it is not the environment, but their choices that create happiness or unhappiness.

Think about how you can meet your needs in each of the following environments: bedroom, kitchen, work, recreation, school and car. You have a choice to create a peaceful atmosphere in the bedroom or the kitchen, to talk to people at work instead of waiting for them to initiate conversation, to listen to audio tapes in your car and so on. Can you choose to be miserable in these environments? Who is it up to? The environment? Yourself? Hopefully you can see that you are the person in control of your own need fulfillment. Teach and model these skills to your child.

Carpe Diem!

How many times have you heard your child waiting for an outcome to occur? Perhaps they couldn't wait until the weekend, to stay out later or to go to bed later. Maybe they wanted to be sixteen so they could drive. Or even to be eighteen so they could vote, twenty-one so they could drink, or get married. The list goes on and on. The problem is that most of these wants involve waiting for something to happen. Waiting for the outcome. Waiting for something they have no control over. Think about what happens during the wait. We need to teach and model to our kids that they need to live for now. *Carpe Diem. Seize the day!* Waiting for the outcome to occur is putting ourselves on hold for need fulfillment. Look for choices to be happy in all environments. Break each day down into choices to be made and you will see the process in each day.

It's okay to plan for the future and to make

goals. But break all outcome goals down into process steps that you and your kids have more control over. Look at the following list of problems:

- ❑ Getting better grades in school.
- ❑ Getting a job.
- ❑ Gaining trust back.
- ❑ Making new friends.
- ❑ Playing better in a sport.

Break each of those problems down into small steps that your kids have total control over. Deciding to study for one hour each evening, talking with the teacher, getting a student tutor, taking notes in class or working with a special study group will all help to get better grades. Take it one step at a time. If what they want is a better job, perhaps they could look over the want ads in the paper, talk with other people, look around for signs advertising job openings, prepare themselves for the interview or personally contact employers. In regaining trust, the productive thinker would evaluate how he lost his trust in the first place, evaluate his previous choices, identify better choices, and be willing to discuss future choices. In regards to making new friends, he would first want to look at his intent in approaching people, where and how he can meet people, what to say and what he can do. In becoming better in a sport, he can first evaluate his skills, identify areas of concern, ask others how to improve and practice what he learns. As you can see, the productive thinker views problems as opportunities for thinking productively. Goals are divided into choices that we are in total control of, which makes the outcome look less intimidating. The best live example I ever saw of a WhMPA teaching outcome and a productive coaching process occurred while I was working with The Center for Skill Development in Sherman Oaks, Calif. Next door was an amusement center that not only had video games and miniature golf but also a batting cage. Many days I went there for lunch to meet my need for Fun by playing some video games. I was able to observe two little league teams at the batting cage. One coach (a WhMPA) put his group of kids in the cage and pushed the start button. Balls started flying like rockets. Strike one, strike two, strike three, strike four, and so on. The kids were swinging with all of their energy, but kept getting strikes. The coach in his "coaching" way began to yell at the kids, *"What's wrong with you—you can't hit the broad side of a barn!" "That's not going to get us anywhere this season." "You swing like a little girl."* You could see the frustration and humiliation on their faces. About two cages down was another coach (a productive thinker) who taught his group of kids the steps involved in hitting a ball. He taught them how to choose the proper size bat. He showed them the correct hitting stance and swing, and where their eyes should focus. He then put the kids in front of the machine without a bat, and turned it on so they would become used to the speed of the ball and how to position their body. He taught them how to hit a ball (outcome) by teaching them all of the steps that go into hitting a ball (process). Next he allowed the other kids on the team to help, by letting them offer suggestions to each other on what they were doing right and what they needed to work on. The kids with the second coach were less frustrated and made more progress. What a great sight to behold. Jack Nicklaus is one of these great teachers. Jack states, *"I see the ball exactly where I want it to finish, then I see the ball going there, then I see the kind of swing that will get it there."*

Do you know some WhMPA coaches? Some productive thinking coaches? You can become a coach easily, often by being thrown in as a "volunteer." Coaches tend to rely on the skills that had been taught or modeled to them. They may have had a coach like a U-boat commander or productive thinking coach. They may have grown up in a family that felt that screaming, yelling, criticizing, threatening and the like were ways to "motivate" people. As coaches, they transfer these skills to the playing field with the title coach now behind their name. Even so, they can choose to become better coaches and people by practicing productive thinking.

Many times when we are confronted with a problem the solution can seem overwhelming but Dr. Applegate taught me the eight criteria to effective plan-making. By teaching your child the following eight criteria to good plan making, you will be teaching him a process to turn problems into opportunities. I use them to this day.

Simple	Keep your plan small and uncomplicated, not self defeating.
Specific	Outline what you will do, when, where and how you will do it, be specific.
Productive Thinking	Your plan should have some component to change the way you look at your problems and the way you look at the world around you.
Repetitive	Develop a plan that you can work on each day or repeat often.
Independent	Your plan should be contingent or dependent upon you alone and not upon others.
Immediate	Start your plan right away; the longer you delay, the less likely you will put it into action.
Written	Make your plan visible, put it in writing and refer to it daily.
Skill Building	Develop skills that will take you one step beyond where you are now.

When making plans to change a thought, action or feeling, keep those plans simple. Your plan should be designed to solve a specific problem in life. So many times WhMPA's make their plan so general that it is unachievable. To avoid that, make plans that encourage productive thinking about problems using the steps outlined in this book. Make plans repetitive which encourage lasting behavioral changes. Avoid the "one-shot deal," which might provide a quick fix, but does nothing to help avoid making the same mistake again. Make sure that the plan is not dependent on others for success. No, *I will change my attitude if you change yours.* Start a plan soon after you have decided to solve the problem. The more time that goes by, the less likely you will change. Write plans down so they will be visible not only to yourself, but to those around you. This includes telling others what you are going to do in order to solve problems. WhMPA's, of course, do not like this part of plan making. Being visible will allow others to ask questions about how their plan is going. Plans should take a person one step beyond where he was yesterday. WhMPA's make Z plans versus B plans. Like the alphabet, they jump from A to Z because they want a quick solution, not a plan that requires time or personal change. The recovery groups use the saying "One Day At A Time" as their way to bring these steps into focus. You may find that breaking this down to "One Choice At A Time" works best for you. The next time your kids have a problem, teach them to use these eight steps. Ask them questions using these criteria to see if they are at risk of setting themselves up for further frustration. Can you model these criteria to them using your own life problems as an example? Will learning to use these steps in your own life help you out with a weight problem, a drinking problem, a drug problem or a divorce?

One mother, Sue, chose to do something about her weight. She indicated that she had procrastinated about it for a long time. Her daughter was seeing me for her problems with her own weight and associated low self worth, and Sue felt that her daughter was getting permission to procrastinate because of her own example. In order to influence her daughter, Sue decided to start with herself and become a role model. She did her research and found a program that would teach her more than just a stop eating "Z plan" to solve her problem, and began by writing her plans down, posting it on the refrigerator for her family members to see. She was open to discussing with them what she was in the process of doing to solve her weight problem, and openly discussed potential problems and her choices to resist any temptation. She purposely used the words "control" and "choices" when it came to discussing her options and kept referring back to her daily slogan, "How bad do I want what I want?" Negative thoughts would creep in from time to time such as, "I don't have time to diet." She used her self talk of "I have time to eat, so I have time to choose what to eat" as her velvet hammer to alert her to the choices she has each and every time she puts something in her mouth. By doing so, she took more and more control of her own problem, and indirectly taught her daughter how she, too, could

solve her weight problem if she chose to. Sue was going beyond other weight reduction programs and looking at what needs she was meeting by choosing to overeat, and purposely making new choices to meet all of her needs in all of her environments. These choices were ones that she had either not used in the past, or learned by watching others who were at a weight she desired or by her own research. Her payoff was tremendous. She lost the weight that she wanted and accomplished her goal. Her daughter, on the other hand, kept procrastinating with her weight problem, but within time had made the same commitment to change that her mother did. Both credited the approach of productive thinking with their success. Controlling to be in control of themselves and not controlling for each other to change was a key component, according to both of them. Allowing the other to make her own choices at her own pace was also cited.

Key points to remember

- ❑ Life is a process, the only outcome is death.
- ❑ When creating goals, break them down into process steps that you have control over.
- ❑ Make your plans simple, specific, repetitive and immediate.
- ❑ Make your plans independent of other people or things.
- ❑ Write your plans down on paper and refer to them often.
- ❑ Make your plan skill-building by including the productive thinking areas.

Helpful hints

- ❑ Look for opportunities to teach process thinking and process acting to people you come in contact with.
- ❑ Observe others around you and look for frustrations they experience due to controlling for desired outcomes.
- ❑ Watch sporting events and observe the players, coaches and fans who choose to

think and act in an outcome fashion, and those who choose to think and act in a process fashion.

❑ Use the criteria listed earlier to develop a plan to change one area of your present parenting skills and implement it within the next twenty-four hours.

❑ Take the goals you have for your own life and break them down into process steps that meet the criteria for a good plan.

❑ Identify areas of your children's lives that frustrate them and teach them how to think productively about frustration in a process versus outcome fashion.

CHAPTER 14

PRODUCTIVE THINKING SKILL 7
THINKING FROM PROBLEMS TO OPPORTUNITIES

"The greatest discovery of my generation is that human beings can alter their attitudes of mind"
William James

Problems, stress, pain and anxiety are descriptions of frustrations that we all experience in our lives. A parent may experience frustration when his child's room is a mess, or when his child ignores curfew, doesn't do his homework or fights with other family members. WhMPA's think the problem is "out there," which puts the emphasis on out there as the "controlling" variable or cause of their distress. "Out there" influences you, but, of course, "out there" does not cause the problems or the thoughts, the actions or feelings that you choose in order to solve your problems. The problem is not just the child's behavior but your wanting something and not getting it. The degree of difference is determined by how much you want what you want and has nothing to do with the child. Many people, however, will identify the child as the problem. As a result a WhMPA tries to solve problems by focusing on the child or getting the child to change. To do so, a WhMPA may resort to threats of punishment, yelling or giving consequences. A productive-thinking parent, on the other hand, will focus on what she has control over and will utilize the productive thinking skills.

Mr. and Mrs. Franzen had multiple problems with their son: trouble in school (problems with grades, attendance, truancy and lack of motivation), he was difficult getting up in the morning (despite repeated yelling up the stairs by Mother and physical threats by Father), tardiness in delivering his morning papers (complaints by customers and supervisors along with having to deliver papers for him), constant fights about going to his Boy Scout meetings (yelling, pleading and threatening to take away privileges), as well as refusing to do any chores around the house (despite remind-ing him of his responsibility around the house repeatedly). These problems, together with the son's skipping school for a week without his parents' knowledge brought matters to a head. Because of these problems Mr. Franzen and his son were on the verge of physically fighting.

In working through this issue with the family, I listed all of the problems and asked them to identify who really had ownership of the problems. It was clear that the son did and that the problems in fact only influenced the parents. The son had total control over the problems and the choices that he was making. The parents had tried everything they knew of to "motivate" him, but to no avail. It was clear to me that the parents were making their best attempts to try to solve problems that literally were not their own. As a parent myself, I became aware that what we want for our children is not the problem, but how we try to "get them" to make the right choices often is. We all agreed that if the son were to be making the opposite choices in each situation, he would not have his parents and others on his back.

When we listed the material privileges that the son was receiving from the parents, we found out that he had received the use of a third car, as well as payment of gas, insurance and maintenance expenses for that car. He also received money from Mother for hot lunch at school, as well as for socializing with his girlfriend. Clothes were provided for him when he asked for them, as was weekly and sometimes daily laundry service. The parents had also purchased skis and a mountain bike for him because he "was bored and complained of nothing to do."

I hope you are getting the picture. Who has the problem? The parents were setting themselves up for frustration when they tried to exert control where they only had influence. The parents are working harder at trying to get the son to be responsible and make good decisions than he was. If anybody deserves the car, money skis or bike, it is the parents, not the child! They are motivated, but he is not. As a result, they are frustrated because "he just doesn't care" about what "they" believe is important in life. If he made money through the paper job, he would be able to go to college. The involvement in Boy Scouts would look good on his entrance application and so on. The problem is that this is their belief and not his.

My suggestion to all of them was to look at the list of problems and understand that if the son were not to follow through with any of their expectations, he would not die, nor would they. Not following through would not damage him in any way psychologically or physically. Not making the expected choices at home, in school or on the job would, on the other hand, create a great deal of frustration for him if he were "allowed" to suffer the natural consequences of his choices. I suggested that he be allowed to do what he wanted in each area. After all, it was "his problem." The parents were hesitant for fear that their son would not turn out the way they wanted: being responsible, making good decisions and understanding the connection between internal choices and the power and control over one's life. Asking them one question laid this fear to rest, *"How is he doing in these areas at the present time?"*

What I did stress to the parents was that they had a tremendous trump card to play. Not in controlling their son, but just in teaching him natural consequences. They had identified all of the privileges that they had control over providing or not providing for him. I suggested that, effective immediately, they discontinue rewarding him for his behavior. The use of the car would stop, the first National Bank of Mother would close, laundry services would cease, rides when needed would be stopped, as would be their yelling and demanding. You should have been in my office to see the son's reaction. He started to sit up in his chair, grumble and whine, complain and threaten to rebel. Up to this point, he had sat like a fat cat in the chair watching and listening to everybody in the room discussing and attempting to solve "his problem." Now he began to move when ownership of the problem rested with him. The only thing he liked was that his parents would stop yelling. But that wasn't enough. He was now frustrated because he was experiencing the loss of privileges that had, up to this point, always been constant in his life. In

response, he talked about quitting school. The parents indicated, with my assistance, that he could do this if he so chose, but to understand that living in their home would then include paying room and board. No arguments. He indicated he would quit Scouts and his paper route. The parents said that that was his choice not theirs. If he didn't feel he needed money to live, then more power to him.

One of the basic laws of physics states that a body at rest tends to stay at rest. It takes more energy and more power to start an engine than it does to keep it going. It also requires more force and energy to change direction than to keep moving in a straight line. The young man in this example was a body at rest. His engine was being cared for by his parents. He had no motivation to do anything differently. His frustration resulted only from his parents, school and supervisor at the paper being on his back, but the degree of frustration was not sufficient to motivate him to change his behavior because he was still getting what he wanted from his parents. He had become accustomed to using the car, getting a ride if he needed one, or money for social get-togethers with his girlfriend, for his lunch, for clothes when he wanted them, insurance payments, gas, and car maintenance, and to his parent making excuses when the school called. This kid had it made! He deserved a basket of flowers for his excellent manipulation and control of his parents. He had even managed to convince them that if they attempted to change things he might end it all. The parents discussed openly the story of a relative who committed suicide who had controlled everyone in the family for many many years. They were petrified over their son's possible suicide, and, as a result, he knew which button to push when they would put responsibility back on him. What a difficult situation to be in. Difficult, but not impossible.

It takes effort to turn problems into opportunities. Effort on the parents' part and effort on the child's part. But once you obtain the courage to start moving forward into thinking productively that problems can be opportunities, life will begin to change for you as well as for others around you. First, however, you need to throw the flag on the field, call time out, get the teams on the sidelines and discuss the expectations from that point onward. Not too many kids have sat up and stated, *"Oh this is really a great change of expectations,"* but I can tell you that in time, the results were what all of us as parents are looking for. Here's an interesting saying that relates to the difficulty we have in changing:

IT IS NOT EASY

To apologize,
To begin over,
To be unselfish,
To take advice,
To admit error,
To face a sneer,
To be charitable,
To keep trying,
To be considerate,
To avoid mistakes,
To endure success,
To profit by mistakes,
To forgive and forget,
To think and then act,
To keep out of a rut,
To make the best of little,
To subdue an unruly temper,
To shoulder a deserved blame,
To recognize the silver lining-
BUT IT ALWAYS PAYS.
Anonymous

One teacher who took a course from me explained what the seven steps of productive thinking meant to her. Here are her words: "As the course began to unfold, I became eager to hear more. Most of the material I had heard in bits and pieces from various places but never pulled together or laid out so well. I learned about choices—mine and other people's. I learned about control—and my lack of it. I learned about questions—to ask myself and to ask others. I learned about problems as opportunities. I learned about behaviors as 'lures' and needs as what motivates and frustrates people. I learned that all of these things fit together like a puzzle and if we just know where to put the pieces, we can get a real good start on putting it together."

"I was amazed to recognize how differently my behaviors were based on my role in a relationship. With my own son, I had all the right behaviors but the wrong motivations. I was giving him choices but all my efforts were based on controlling him. Since these behaviors were not successful, I was a basket case! I wrote down in my notes during class "My son is controlling my home." Only I can change that. At first I was confused. If my behaviors were the right ones, then what needed to be changed? It was not what I was doing that needed

changing but what I was thinking and consequently feeling. If I give him choices and he chooses behavior that is opposed to my choices, I should not get angry or uptight about it. I should remain calm, deal out the consequences and get on with my own life. Eventually, when the consequences begin to outweigh the benefits of the behavior, he will choose on his own to change that behavior. In the meantime, I will have saved myself a great deal of heartaches, headaches, and begin to work on building my relationship with my son. I will concentrate on helping him meet his needs that are frustrated in more productive ways by becoming a teacher and a model for him."

"I found out that in my role as a daughter in my family of origin, I was ALLOWING someone else's behavior to control me. I also let that control generate a great deal of anger and resentment. I think back on it now and wish I had taken this class sooner while there was still time to work on that relationship with my parents."

"In my role as a friend, I strive to have absolute control. I exhibit behaviors that border on temper tantrums and lay enormous guilt trips. I have come to think less of myself in these relationships and am anxious to make repairs by giving up trying to control the other person and concentrate on controlling what to think and feel. These changes will come closer to meeting my needs than my previous ones which have been completely unsuccessful and have led to many arguments and angry words."

"As a teacher, I have much the same difficulties that I have with my son. My behavior is good and appropriate, my thoughts and feelings are not. Again, I need to mete out the consequences and get on with teaching and not let the behavior of one or two students destroy the learning atmosphere of the classroom. I need to evaluate the environment that I am setting up with the students and my son to see if that environment is need fulfilling or need reducing. I need to focus on building a relationship with my students and my son first and worry about discipline later."

"I have been frustrated in many areas of my life for many years. I am pleased to have a starting point and the tools for dealing with those frustrations. "Choices, choices" and the wiggling fingers representing those "don't have to detectors" above my head are becoming common around my home and in the classroom. Now when something comes up, I know what to say. I begin with "What's the problem?" and we move from there to critical questions I learned, and the seven areas of thinking productively. In the meantime, I will work on controlling my thoughts, actions and feelings and oh yes, my tone of voice. Thanks for the class and the skills to practice for a lifetime."

Choosing to view problems differently

Let's take a look at the differences between what WhMPA's do when frustrated and what productive thinkers do:

WhMPA responses to frustration

- ❑ Thinks stress is something to be avoided.
- ❑ Believes that "out there" controls his thoughts, actions and feelings.
- ❑ Thinks, acts and feels out of control when stress arises.
- ❑ Gives to others with the intent of getting something in return.
- ❑ Thinks of self first, before others.
- ❑ Thinks that winning or being on top is the only goal.
- ❑ Meets needs through others.
- ❑ Blames "out there" for his frustrations.
- ❑ Looks at life as a series of outcomes to be conquered.
- ❑ Focuses on getting what he wants when he wants it.
- ❑ Thinks and acts in the areas of no control, or at best influence the majority of time.

These beliefs will automatically set you up for frustration. Notice the problems that arrive from choosing to think or act in these ways. Mr. and Mrs. Franzen followed these patterns by giving to their son with the intent on getting something in return, blaming him for their frustration, hoping that he would choose the lifestyle they wanted for him, and trying to meet their needs through him and his choices. But the price they paid for these choices was evident. Can you relate to making any of these choices? I would suspect you can, if you are like millions of other parents. Whether you have felt this way once or a thousand times before, you do not have to continue. You can choose to rethink about yourself and the world around you. You can choose to put the skills listed throughout this book

into your own life, and then teach and model them to your kids or anyone else you come in contact with. Can you see that your kids have made choices similar to these in their own lives? If you can relate to these or see others using them in their own lives, read over what you can teach them by using productive thinking.

Productive thinkers responses to frustration

- ❑ Thinking productively that stress, the difference between what they have and what they want, is not always to be feared; it can be an opportunity for growth.
- ❑ Discover that their thinking about a problem directs their actions and their feelings. They can choose how they want to think.
- ❑ Discover that what they can control, what they can influence and what they have no control over in problem situations frees them from the degree of frustration they are experiencing.
- ❑ Give up the notion that they are forced to think, act or feel a certain way and take control of choosing to think, act and feel the way they want to.
- ❑ Rethink that all behaviors are purposeful to meet one or more of their internal psychological needs. Disrupting or disruptive behaviors will be viewed as flags in the air indicating frustrated need areas.
- ❑ Rethink and enjoy life as a series of process steps toward an open outcome.
- ❑ Believe that giving to others is for the sake of giving and not controlling for something in return.
- ❑ Compete against self in order to grow.
- ❑ Think and act as a team player in relationships with others.
- ❑ Pursue happiness in all their environments.
- ❑ Meet needs through self or with others but never through others.

Do you notice the difference? Can you see that the productive thinker views stress as an opportunity and does not focus on "out there" as anything more than an influence? Sure "out there" influences our feelings, but productive thinkers do not stay stuck by blaming, arguing or pouting about those influences. They take control of what they have control over themselves and only themselves. They look at the choices they can make to solve their problems. Finding alternative pathways to meet their needs is important to them. They look at any problem as need-reducing so that they can understand that what they want may out of their control. By thinking on a need level, they understand that they might not always get what they want, but they will be able to meet their needs. A productive thinker will look for alternative choices to meet those needs. In order to do this, he will learn from others by asking questions, reading and observing. He will constantly look for new choices that will lead him to a happier, healthier life. With this strategy as his guide, he will choose to view his problems as a normal part of life. Again, you cannot always get what you want when you want it, but if you choose to rethink in a process way you will begin to close down the differences between what you want and what you have. Some problems cannot be solved immediately, and sometimes the solution takes a while, but the productive thinker will be able to reduce his level of frustration with each passing moment.

How WhMPA's React to Problems

- ❏ Work to change "haves."
- ❏ Want things they have no control over.
- ❏ Want needs met by others.
- ❏ Feel forced to behave.
- ❏ Gain happiness through outcomes.
- ❏ Believe stress is negative.
- ❏ Use poor choices to meet needs.
- ❏ Attempt to change "out there."
- ❏ Want problems solved now.
- ❏ Manipulate others to think, act the way he wants.

How Productive Thinkers Rethink

- ❏ Work to change "wants."
- ❏ Look for things or situations where they have control.
- ❏ Meet needs with others.
- ❏ See all behaviors as choices.
- ❏ Gain happiness through process.
- ❏ Believe stress is an opportunity to rethink.
- ❏ Use good choices to meet needs.
- ❏ Accept "out there" as only influence.
- ❏ See problems as opportunity to rethink

and build new skills.
- ❏ Allow others to choose and feel their thoughts, actions and feelings.

Contrasting the WhMPA approach and the productive thinking approach is important because it opens up new, more productive alternatives for handling problems.

Winners and losers

Successful people see opportunities in unlikely places. Ask a successful person what makes him successful, and he will tell you that he has learned how to take everyday situations and make them come alive if he chooses to look at the everyday situations in a whole new way. Unfamiliar situations become a challenge and not an obstacle by thinking of creative responses to every problem and enjoying a new way of thinking. Albert Einstein stated, "*A successful man is he who receives a great deal from his fellow man, usually incomparably more than corresponds to his service to them. The value of a man, however, should be seen in what he gives and not in what he is able to receive.*" Think of this verse and see if you can teach and model this to your children;

> The difference between winners and losers:
> The winner is always part of the answer;
> The loser is always part of the problem;
> The winner always has a program;
> The loser always has an excuse;
> The winner says, "let me do it for you;"
> The loser says, "that's not my job;"
> The winner sees an answer for every problem;
> The loser sees more problems with every problem;
> The winner sees a green near every sand trap;
> The loser see two or three sand traps near every green.
> The winner says "It may be difficult, but it is possible."
> The loser says, "It may be possible, but it is too difficult."
> BE A WINNER
> Author unknown

John P. Dudeck, a good friend of mine and an extremely successful financial services professional and entrepreneur, has some great information regarding winners and losers in his seminars for professional athletes, kids and business professionals. His information was nominated for the "Thousand Points of Light" award through the White House. His traits fit perfectly with the differences between WhMPA's and productive thinkers.

Traits of winners and losers

WINNERS
- ❏ Make it happen.
- ❏ Are great listeners.
- ❏ Strive to be part of the solution.
- ❏ Have specific plans.
- ❏ Say, *"Let me do it for you."*
- ❏ See a solution for every problem.
- ❏ Are curious and want to learn.
- ❏ Maximize their talents.
- ❏ Use and ally constructive criticism.
- ❏ Know what they stand for.
- ❏ Focus on optimizing their own potential.
- ❏ See the glass as half full.
- ❏ Plant flowers in their mind's garden.
- ❏ Love easily.
- ❏ Get rid of toxic people from their lives.
- ❏ Stay focused on their goals.
- ❏ Are consistent between words and actions.
- ❏ Anticipate.
- ❏ Are optimistic.
- ❏ Recognize others for doing well.
- ❏ Are team players.
- ❏ Look for the good in others.
- ❏ Have roots of integrity that stand.
- ❏ Speak up for themselves.
- ❏ Are loyal to others.
- ❏ Communicate openly and honestly.
- ❏ Turn pressure and stress into accomplishment.

LOSERS
- ❏ Watch it happen.
- ❏ Are great talkers.
- ❏ Are always part of the problem.
- ❏ Have excuses.
- ❏ Say, *"It may be possible but it's too difficult."*
- ❏ Say, *"That's not my job."*
- ❏ See a problem for every solution.
- ❏ Think they know it all.
- ❏ Waste their talents.
- ❏ Resist and resent constructive criticism.
- ❏ Don't know what they stand for.
- ❏ Focus on what's wrong with

everybody else.
- ❏ See the glass as half empty.
- ❏ Let weeds take over their mind's garden.
- ❏ Hate easily.
- ❏ Hang around with losers.
- ❏ Get lost on the process.
- ❏ Say one thing and do another.
- ❏ React.
- ❏ Are pessimistic.
- ❏ Try to take all the credit.
- ❏ Are lone wolves.
- ❏ Are quick to criticize.
- ❏ Blow away in a light firm breeze.
- ❏ Let others control their destinies.
- ❏ Are too selfish.
- ❏ Talk negatively behind people's backs.
- ❏ Let pressure and stress become an excuse for mediocrity.

Thomas Edison could find opportunities in mistakes. A newspaper reporter once asked him, *"How did you feel about your 10,000 failures before you finally invented the light bulb?"* Edison replied with, *"I didn't have any failures. I learned 10,000 things that didn't work. Each one of those discoveries gave me valuable information that eventually led to success."*

Creating controllable stress

If you are going to change your life as a parent, you will need to be motivated. When you have differences you have motivation. You want to create controllable stress for yourselves and your children because without stress there can be no motivation. Ask yourself these questions, *"What is it that you want that you do not have?" "How bad do you want what you want?" "Are you willing to work for getting what you want?" "How hard are you willing to work?"* These questions will motivate us to move in a direction to change or stay stuck. A productive thinker looks at the world as an opportunity to build skills as a parent and as a person by thinking productively in the following areas:

- ❏ YOUR THOUGHTS ABOUT YOUR PROBLEMS DIRECT YOUR ACTIONS AND YOUR FEELINGS.

- ❏ PROBLEMS ARE DEGREES OF DIFFERENCES BETWEEN WHAT YOU

WANT AND WHAT YOU HAVE.

❏   SEPARATE PROBLEMS INTO WHAT YOU
    HAVE CONTROL OVER, WHAT YOU
    HAVE INFLUENCE OVER, AND WHAT
    YOU HAVE NO CONTROL OVER. APPLY
    THE CONCEPT AREAS OF ACKNOWL-
    EDGMENT, ACCEPTANCE, ALLOWING
    AND ADJUSTMENT TO ALL PROBLEMS.

❏   LOOK FOR NEW THOUGHTS, ACTIONS
    AND FEELINGS THAT YOU CAN
    CHOOSE TO IMPLEMENT NOW IN
    AREAS YOU HAVE CONTROL OVER.

❏   IDENTIFY NEW CHOICES OR PATH
    WAYS THAT WILL FULFILL NEEDS
    THAT HAVE BEEN BLOCKED, OR ARE
    UNFULFILLED. WORK ON CREATING
    A PERCEPTION OF BEING A NEED-FUL
    FILLING PERSON TO THOSE AROUND
    YOU.

❏   IDENTIFY THE STEPS THAT WILL BE
    REQUIRED TO CLOSE DOWN THE
    DIFFERENCES BETWEEN WHAT YOU
    HAVE AND WHAT YOU WANT.

❏   UNDERSTAND THAT ALL PROBLEMS
    CAN BE OPPORTUNITIES FOR
    GROWTH IF YOU USE THE STEPS
    OUTLINED HERE.

Applying the productive thinking strategy

Acknowledge that problems are a normal part of life.

When people come to me for therapy, my job is to help them widen the lenses through which they have been looking at their problems. Your role in parenthood is the same.

In order to begin the productive thinking process, it is important to understand that problems are opportunities for growth. If you perceive yourself as successful instead of unsuccessful in problem solving, you will build confidence in your ability to take more effective control of your life. When you begin to think and act in this fashion you will then be able to teach and model this belief to your children as they experience their own problems.

Even though your past may influence you, you are in charge of your own life, your own thoughts, your own actions, and your own feelings. When you become aware of your power to make good choices, you can begin to build a new life for yourself based on what you want.

Step back and identify troublesome situations.

Gathering all the facts or information about a problem is an important place to begin. Be as objective and open-minded as you can be. Identify the problem by asking questions such as, *"What's the problem?"* Help others step back, widen their lenses and take a picture of the problem they are having. *"What would others say the problem is?"* This allows time to think about how others perceive the problem.

It is important to start here by stepping back and taking a *"camera check"* of what you believe the problem is. A camera check allows you the opportunity to rewind the tape, so to speak, and review in slow motion what was done or said. This will help you to look at the problem from different angles. Since other peoples' perception of the problem may be different from yours, asking them how they perceive it allows them to describe their perception and opens up communication in a constructive way. This will prevent you seeing only your side of the problem.

Different people obviously have different views of the same problem. Not only will they view the problem differently, but they may react differently.

Create internal motivation by identifying what you wanted.

Share with others what you want or expect from them. Share your reasons for wanting what you want because they will definitely ask. Remember your tone is critical. Remember to ask them what it is that they want. You might consider asking questions such as, *"What do you want?"* *"What do you think other people connected to your problem want?"* Get others to be specific about their wants. Help them understand that other people have wants also. Asking questions can demonstrate caring and will make others more willing to try to see the problem from your point of view.

Identify your present reality.

Share with others what you want. Let them know your frustration level and ask them if they are frustrated. Teach them that differences between what they want and what they have are what creates a problem for them as well as for others, and that those problems can range from minor to major for both parties involved. Teach your kids that it is normal to experience frustration if they have a difference between what they want and what they have. Teach them that frustration can be an opportunity to grow and learn if they so choose. Let them know that you, too, are frustrated, but that you choose to make your frustration an opportunity instead of another problem.

It is important to realize that a problem is simply the difference between what you want and what you have. The next step is to help them realize that the intensity of the problem is directly related to how much they wanted what they wanted.

Identify which thoughts, actions or feelings were used to solve the problem.

Determine what attempts have been made to solve the problem. It could be helpful to make a list of previous choices by asking questions such as, *"What have you been choosing to do to get people on your back?" "What have you been choosing to do to get people off your back?" "What thoughts have you had about the problem?"* You can share with others what you saw them doing and/or how you believe they might be choosing to think about their problem. It can also be helpful to ask others how they view a problem you are experiencing and how they believe you might be choosing to think or act. Open communication about what is going on is vital in establishing and maintaining relationships with your children, your spouse and others.

Identify whether the thoughts or actions were effective enough in solving the problem.

The following questions need to be answered, whether the problem is yours or your child's. *"Are your present thoughts and/or actions getting you enough of what you want?" "Are you paying any prices or consequences for how you choose to think or act?" "Is what you choose to think helping you enough to solve this problem?" "Is what you are choosing to do helping you enough to solve this problem?"* As with other questions, remember to consider what prices you or others see them as suffering. If you are helping your child solve a problem, it is critical to present these statements to them in a calm, cool and matter of fact tone. Avoid presenting ultimatums. Allow them to answer these questions, for these are motivating questions that will help a person decide if

they are to take ownership of a problem, as well as gain a direction they choose to go from that point forward.

Think productively that problems can be an opportunity for growth and learning.

You and your children could spend the rest of your lives focusing just on your problems, or you could choose to accept problems as facts of life and move into a mode of productive thinking to handle those problems more efficiently. A WhMPA would allow the problems to run his life while complaining that none of the problems were his fault.

Think productively and separate problems into areas of control, influence and no control.

This is the component of productive thinking that will help save your sanity. In your head or on paper make three columns. Title each column either "control," "influence" or "no control." Take a problem that you and your child are experiencing, and separate it into these three areas. Ask yourself and your kids, *"In this situation, what is it that we have control over?" "What is it that we have influence over?" "What is it that we have no control over?"* I believe you will find that if you are frustrated, it is probably because you are trying to control things, people or situations you have no control over. Eventually we all learn that we do not have control over many things. Teach and model the steps of acknowledgment, acceptance, allowing and adjustment to each problem. The results will be favorable as well as stress reducing for everyone.

Think productively and brainstorm choices that can be used to solve problems.

It is not easy to teach and model to your children that everything they think and do is a choice. They get confused with the connection between all of the choices they have and the words *"rules," "have to," "must"* and *"can't."* Seeing the world as a place where they can choose depressing, angering, pouting and complaining, all to meet one or more of their needs, will change how they react to the frustrations they encounter in daily living. Understanding that they can choose to be happy or miserable in all situations places the ownership where it belongs, on them.

Think productively and identify the process steps that are required to accomplish problem solving.

To live in the present, to believe that **"today**

is the first day of the rest of your life" is a positive way to think and act. But WhMPA's do not think-process. They believe outcomes bring them happiness. Rethinking that life is a process means meeting as many of your needs as possible in each of your environments without paying negative prices. It is important, therefore, to make plans that are efficient. The eight steps to efficient plan making are: simple, specific, productive thinking, repetitive, independent, immediate, written and skill building. Teach and model to your children that making plans and practicing these eight steps is critical in order for them to get what they want.

Think productively and identify the psychological needs that will be unfulfilled or unresolved, and create a plan to meet those needs.

Teach and model that wants are the habits and the pathways that we all learn in order to meet our internal psychological needs, and that there are usually a number of ways for each of us to meet our needs. You may not always get what you want, but by practicing efficient thinking and action skills, you can always be in a process of meeting your needs. Help your kids get off a problem they may be experiencing and get down to the needs that may be frustrated. They will eventually understand that they may want things that they have little, if any, control over. If that is the case, they will also understand that they have alternative choices if they choose to rethink in the area of needs versus wants.

In Bill Glasser's words, I can choose to *"fulfill my needs in a way that does not deprive others of their ability to fulfill their needs. I accept the consequences of my chosen behavior. I have found that responsible behavior tends to create happiness, but unhappiness does not cause me to behave in an irresponsible way."*

Key points to remember

❏ Stress can be viewed as either positive or negative. It is your choice.

❏ Choosing to view problems as opportunities for growth will change how you approach problems.

❏ Rethinking that problems are inevitable frees you up to begin to rethink in a new way about the problems in your life.

❏ Acknowledging that your thinking directs your actions will motivate you to think in either a neutral or positive way.

❏ Understanding that you control only yourself and the choices that you make will give you a sense of power.

❏ Thinking productively that happiness is your choice will motivate you to think differently.

❏ Thinking productively from a want level to a need level opens up alternative choices for you when you are frustrated.

❏ Enjoying life as a process and not an outcome provides you with a guide for life.

Helpful hints

❏ Look for situations that can be turned into opportunities to practice the productive thinking skills listed in this book.

❏ By observing the choices others make when they are frustrated, you can learn new choices for your own frustrations.

❏ Plan to use at least one productive thinking skill every day.

❏ Teach and model at least one productive thinking skill to at least one person each day.

❏ Learn to apply the productive thinking strategy to each area of your life—at work, at home and at play.

❏ Continue to practice this productive thinking strategy in all of your daily affairs.

CHAPTER 15

WHAT'S THIS PERSONALITY STUFF ANYWAY?

Personality as we well know is a part of all of us. Whether we like it or not, personality preferences are what make us draw close to each other and also what create frustrations in our relationships with others. Who and what we like and dislike is determined by our personality. My fascination for the use of the Myers Briggs Type Indicator (MBTI) grew out of my relationship with Joseph J. Quaranta Jr., Ph.D. Dr. Quaranta was my advisor during my doctoral program at The Ohio State University and became my mentor. No disk is adequate to hold all the information Dr. Quaranta has in his brain about the MBTI. His insight and wisdom is not only practical, but insightful.

There are sixteen personality types outlined in the theories of Carl Jung and Isabell Briggs Myers. These personality types develop in childhood and continue to develop throughout our lives. The use of typology in this chapter will provide a framework for understanding the development of these various personalities as well as provide a better understanding of our reactions to specific behaviors of our children. The MBTI is useful in parenthood. This personality inventory, developed by Isabel Briggs Myers and Katherine Briggs, identifies the sixteen psychological types and is not only useful for understanding parenting but also for understanding your children and their preferences. The issues outlined in this chapter are designed to demonstrate how Jungian typology theory, as developed in the MBTI, can be useful in parenthood. **You will understand the way a child *prefers* to learn or to process information, and how he makes decisions and communicates with others.**

The theory behind the MBTI assumes that preferences are inborn and can be falsified by family and other environmental pressures. The first step is to identify true preferences.

Try the following exercise. Write down your full name, home address, zip code and telephone number:

Now complete the same task, but this time use your other hand:

Did you find any differences in your ability to do this? If you are like most people, you probably discovered quite a bit of difference in your ability to write and experienced some level of frustration with this task. Was it small? Medium? Large? Extra-large? Can you see how this little exercise actually creates frustration? We want to be in control all the time. The second task, however, created a difference between what you wanted and what you had, and you experienced frustration. What does this exercise teach you? You can see that everyone has a preference for everything they do, including writing. Because my brother is left-handed, I could never understand how he could write, hit, throw, or do anything else and he felt the same way about me.

Parents can be assured that finding out about your own preference type, and that of your children, is a releasing experience. Learning about personality type frees us to recognize our own natural qualities, as well as recognize qualities others possess. Your personality type indicates your preferences in life regarding your energy source, the ways you take in information, the way you reach a decision and your lifestyle preference. Not only will you learn about yourself, but you will also be able to understand others you live and work with. Understanding the way different personality preferences interact can improve parent-child relationships and other relationships in your life. Since building a strong relationship with your children is your primary goal in reading this book, take some time to read through this section. See if it identifies you the way you are the majority of the time. In order to assess your own preferences, do not consider how you would like to be or how you would like to be perceived by others. Keep in mind that there are no right or wrong characteristics, just different personality types.

Read through the vocabulary used with the MBTI and read the descriptions for your personality type, and see if you agree with what is said about your type. See if what you read is true for your own childhood and your parenting style. Next, read the description for the opposite personality type. Understand the differences in preferences for each type. This is critical if we are to go beyond WhMPA.

Orientation of energy—extroversion or introversion attitude

Direction of Focus of Energy

EXTROVERT
- ❏ Energized by outer world.
- ❏ Focuses on people and things.
- ❏ Active; needs to do things.
- ❏ Expressive.
- ❏ Wide breadth of interests.
- ❏ Experience life, live it, then try to understand it (maybe).
- ❏ Interaction with others.
- ❏ Outgoing and enthusiastic.
- ❏ Genuine, or what they appear to be.
- ❏ Trial and error.

Approximately 75% of us are extroverted. The extrovert's energy is on the outer world. Extroverts focus on people and they enjoy material things. Having material possessions to show off to other people is important to extraverts. They enjoy feedback from others regarding their possessions and are more active in their day to day lifestyle. They dislike inactivity, preferring to be busy whenever they can be. They may touch things first and then later think about asking permission to do so. They like variety and action, and have a breadth of interests. They enjoy several different interests instead of focusing on one area at a time. They have a difficult time doing homework with others, in front of the television or while listening to music because they are easily distracted. They will look for a quiet place to study and will probably become upset with others for disturbing their peace. This seems odd because they are so talkative most of the time.

For this reason if you are going to have an important talk with an extroverted child, you should select an environment free from any distractions. Talking with them about something "heavy" in a video arcade, a crowded room, a restaurant or while they are playing Nintendo will not be the best option. The distractions around them will pull them away from your message. Extroverts are often impatient with long, slow jobs unless the job provides them an opportunity to talk while they work. They are sociable and enjoy interaction with others. If you send the extrovert to his bedroom for time out, he will hate it because it becomes boring very quickly. If you put them in an in-school suspension room where they cannot talk, the true punishment is not being able to talk. If they happen to be feeling oriented as well as extroverted, going to an in-school suspension room will be a total embarrassment as well as a miserable experience because of the no-talking rule. The fact that other people know they are in trouble is motivation enough for them. At home, as well as in school, they will understand information if they can discuss its applicability with others around them. Again their need is to talk and interact.

They will meet their needs more through other people than with them. The more that people like them, the more need fulfillment they feel. If people dislike them for any reason, the extrovert feels down. Their emotional status goes up and down according to the environment and the people around them and they will be hurt more often and more deeply if a relationship goes sour, especially in the area of boyfriend-girlfriend relationships and related breakups. Their energy level is up when the relationship is going well, but falls if the relationship starts to go bad. They love being around people—the more the better. They are often very conscious of what others might be thinking about them and dislike being alone for long periods of time. They interact well with others and are good at socializing. They will talk, and talk and talk. Do not cut them off or they may pout. When people mention that God gave them two ears and one mouth, they question it.

Many extroverts will talk without listening to others. Sometimes they will talk without thinking about what they are saying and will put their hands up in class while thinking about how they will respond. Telling an extroverted child to *"settle down"* or *"sit still"* when something exciting is about to happen or is happening, is like attempting to control diarrhea by thinking positively. Good luck! If you tell them *"not one more word,"* you can expect either one more word or a sigh, or a roll of the eyes. You would do better telling them to *"stop and think about what they had done"* or *"stop and think about what they had said"* or *"stop and think about what they are going to do or say in the future."* Give them some time to cool off, settle down, and regroup.

Extroverts are what they seem to be. They wear their emotions on their sleeves. When around an extroverted person, you probably had little trouble figuring out what was going on with them. If you keep your mouth shut, they will let you know how they feel. In fact, if you sit quietly with an extrovert, they will talk first. They dislike silence and if given a chance, they will talk.

The environment around the extrovert affects them more than others. When the weather is depressing, they are more depressing. When the weather is sunny, they are sunny. My Dad loves to cut a willow branch and show people that it is a barometer of the weather to come. He nails the branch to the outside of the house, and sure enough it will point upwards when the weather is going to be better and downwards when the weather is to be worse. We could accomplish the same thing by nailing an extrovert to the side of the house. When the weather is good they look upward and smile and when the weather is lousy they will droop and depress.

Extroverts are experiential people. When they experience something, they live it, and then they understand it. The Nike slogan of "Just Do It"

might be taped to their heads. When thinking of the extravert I'm often reminded of the scene in "Bambi," where she went flying down a hill and onto the ice. If Bambi could have talked, she might have said, *"What the heck am I doing out here!"* Extroverts relate to this. Many times extraverts do something really dumb and moments later will say, *"What the heck did I do that for?"* They just do it first and think later. They learn by trial and error. Often they make repeated mistakes. We need to teach the extrovert to slow down and consider their choices beforehand. We need to teach them that what's inside of them is what counts. Many times parents want an extroverted child not to interrupt with questions or comments. The reality is that an extroverted child will probably interrupt with questions and comments because that is what they prefer. Parents want their extroverts to listen more and talk less. The extrovert prefers the opposite.

INTROVERT

- ❏ Energized in inner world.
- ❏ Focus on thoughts or concepts.
- ❏ Intimate and quiet.
- ❏ Reflective; needs to think.
- ❏ Depth of interests.
- ❏ Needs to understand something before putting it into practice.
- ❏ Concentration by self.
- ❏ Inwardly directed, not too concerned with what others think.
- ❏ Not really what they seem to be.
- ❏ Consider deeply.

Approximately 25% of us are introverted. Introverts are energized in their inner world. They prefer to focus on their thoughts and ideas. They are the thinkers instead of the actors. They think and think and think, driving the "Just Do It" people wacky. They prefer quiet for concentration. They do not mind spending a long time on one project without interruption. They are reflective and need time to think things through. Their motto is "let me watch first." At social gatherings they are more likely to stand back and quietly observe others, and when ready, approach people. Introverts like for you to talk with them instead of asking them questions. They prefer for you to allow them time to participate in a conversation, and will look for an opening if an extrovert will allow them time to pause and reflect. I usually find them to be very quiet and need to give them time to think things over. Sometimes I have had to hold another meeting just for the introverts hours later to see if they were ready to discuss what was presented. If they choose to tell you what's on their mind, they will usually say that they were taking in information but, *"Those damn extroverts were blabbing so much they could not have got a word in edgewise anyway!"*

In school, introverted kids will wait to raise their hands while they think through a question. The introvert is inwardly directed, and attempts to understand what he sees or hears in the world around him. They require time to digest and dissect information before they are ready to talk about it. If a son or daughter is introverted and the parent is extroverted, the parent will often become very impatient when the child does not immediately answer a question. An answer may require some thought on the part of the introvert and to blurt out an answer would be out of character. When a child arrives home from school, the parent may ask, *"How was school?"* The introverted child may say either *"okay"* or nothing at all with maybe a shrug of his shoulders. This drives the extroverted parent to the moon. *"Speak to me!"* The introverted child needs time to reflect on the parent's question.

If you place an introvert in his room for time-out, be sure that you give him an assignment to think about. They may need to think about, *"What expectations they chose to break," "What poor choices they made," "What they will do differently next time."* Overall the introvert is quiet; they will talk when they want to talk and they will let you know who

they are when they are ready to let you know. Some might perceive them as being snobbish or stubborn. This may drive the extrovert crazy, particularly in the presence of people he would like the introvert to meet. When the extroverted parent introduces the introverted child to friends and the child responds with just a look, a smile, or a quiet "Hi," the extroverted parent might become frustrated. The extrovert child, on the other hand, would respond with a resounding, "Hi," eye contact, a smile and probably more interaction. The extrovert parent will feel great when this happens. They feed off people who are active and involved with others.

The introvert has a depth of interest. He will learn about something that interests him and take it to a deeper level of understanding. In learning a computer, for example, the extrovert will learn to use it in a "quick down and dirty fashion" while the introvert will want to understand the use of the computer, and may first spend a long time going through the manual and books associated with the computer. This is true in many other activities as well. The introvert first needs to understand, while the extrovert learns by doing. Introverts need to study and reflect on what they are taking in. They are like Thumper in "Bambi," standing on the ridge watching Bambi sliding down the hill and on to the ice, and thinking, *"Bambi, Bambi, why don't you think about what you are doing?"* The problem comes in that the introvert may think and think and think about doing something, and then may not follow through with actually doing it. The introvert will meet his needs more often with a person than through him. In fact, introverts will meet many of their needs by themselves and not need other people. My brother, Brent, for example, is introverted and can spend hours on end in the house watching football. Brent would spend the first hours of our arrival at the campground kicking the fire and staying close to the campsite. Being the extrovert that I am, I was over to the next campsite seeing if they had kids. On the day that we were going back home, I was sad to leave my new-found friends. Brent was now ready to meet them. My mom had no trouble asking me to socialize, because that was my type preference. Brent, on the other hand, would socialize but disliked being pushed into it. He, like other introverts, needed to do it on his time. You will find more extroverts trying to change introverts in this way than introverts trying to change extraverts. Controlling to be like others want them to be is disliked by introverts, as well as other people. Allow them to be who they are. Being the extravert that I am, I would be meeting others, interacting and playing football rather than watching it. We need to teach the introvert to take risks and open up more with people. Sharing what is on their minds with others should be emphasized. But parents who expect an outgoing, talkative, interactive child will become frustrated with an introverted child. You will hear them saying things like, *"Say what's on your mind,"* or *"Don't be shy, say it."* The introvert is quietly hoping that you will shut up and leave him alone to think about what he is experiencing.

Perceptive function— sensing or intuition

Ways of Taking In Information

SENSING
- ❑ Data.
- ❑ Concrete facts.
- ❑ Likes precise directions.
- ❑ Details/micro-thinking.
- ❑ Reality-based.
- ❑ Focuses on the present.
- ❑ Actuality, Doable, Experiential.
- ❑ Here and now.
- ❑ Utility.
- ❑ Linear thinking.

Approximately 75% of us are sensors. Sensors tend to pay special attention to the information they perceive through their five senses. Let them taste, touch, see, hear or smell what you have presented to them and they will be in heaven. In school and in life they will learn if they can touch, pull, taste, or do. They will not do well with sitting, writing, listening or reciting. Hands-on, multi-sensory activities will make learning anything fun for them. When taking in information, the sensing person is interested in the facts, the data, the detail. Do not bore them with theory. They want you to get to the point quickly. Sergeant Friday in the television show "Dragnet" would love the sensing person. "Just the facts" was his motto. The sensing person is reality-based. He likes an established way of doing things and enjoys using old skills more than learning new skills. When he receives information, he wants to be able to apply it. He sees things as they exist in front of him.

If you ask him to read a chapter in a book, he will do it one paragraph at a time. You will not find him skimming paragraphs and getting the general theme. Often he will literally see what is right in front of his nose at the time. The sensing person responds to actuality and sees things in the present tense. Ask him what he wants to know, and he will tell you that what he needs to know is for right now. The future to him is important, but using information for the moment is what interests him.

The sensing person is utilitarian and linear-thinking. He needs to have all the pieces laid out in front of him and to be able to go from one piece to another as it is presented. If he is learning math, he needs to learn one concept at a time. When teaching fractions, for example, you might ask him to use everyday items like ice from cube trays. Ask him what percentage of the ice cubes remain after removing two of them. Ask him to determine what percentage of oranges were eaten from the bag brought home from the market. He needs to be taken from step 1 to step 2 to step 3. Do not attempt to go from step 1 to step 4 or he will not understand. The Arthur Murray dance steps are necessary for these folks.

This also means that a sensing person will go on and on about a topic that he is discussing. You may begin to get bored, and wonder when he is going to get to the point. He does not leave out any details which may drive you nuts if you lack patience, but he needs an appreciative audience.

If given a project with a deadline, the sensing

child will set his own pace to accomplish the task. He needs to have all the pieces of the project laid out in front of him in a sequential way to make sense of it. When he does this, he may ask lots of questions. He sees things in a detailed micro-thinking sort of way. If you put a rose in front of him and ask him what he sees, he will see a rose. No more, no less. Give the sensor a pile of horse manure and he will see it as horse manure. Yuck. He will not be the creative person on a team, but instead will be the worker bee looking for someone else to be creative and take the lead. If a teacher gives him a vague assignment such as writing a story about life, he will probably become upset because he will not be sure what is being asked of him. The best thing to do is to have him either talk it out or ask the teacher for clarification.

Use the funnel approach in asking questions of sensing people. This occurs when you ask vague questions initially and work toward more specific questions as though you were working your way to the spout on the funnel.

The sensor needs to learn to step back and look at the bigger picture when problems arise. He may indeed have a problem in his life, but his difficulty is looking at future consequences for his present choices. It would be to his advantage to learn how to widen his lenses when taking in information from others. Asking him questions in order to expand his thinking about an issue will be helpful. If he is fighting with other siblings, don't just tell him to *"stop fighting!"* because he will look at you with vague eyes. Be more specific and let him know what actual behavior you are talking about. Be specific with him about what you expect and what the specific consequences will be if he chooses to disobey. I advise asking this type of child to repeat back to you what he believes you said so that you will know if he heard it the way you wanted it heard.

INTUITION
- ❏ Meaning of facts.
- ❏ Theoretical.
- ❏ Associations/macro thinking.
- ❏ Hunches, speculations.
- ❏ Possibilities, potential.
- ❏ Future.
- ❏ Fantasy.
- ❏ Global thinking.

Approximately 25% of us are intuitive. Intuitive people use their senses when taking in information, but will quickly look for the meaning behind the sense and behind what others say. They are interested in possibilities. They will take the information and look at the possibilities. If you give them information about a computer, they will not just think about it, but about how they can apply it to different situations in their life. Give the sensor information about intricate details of a car's engine and he will get bored easily. They just want to start the engine and let it hum. An intuitive person might be fascinated with information about a car's engine and would want to know how each action leads to another action, from turning the key to the engine starting. They look for associations in the information they obtain.

They are macro-thinkers. The lenses through which they view the world are at a wide angle setting. They not only take in information, but wonder about it. This can present a problem while the sensor will just take in the information, nothing more, nothing less. The intuitive person will take it in and think about it and think about it some more. The problem comes when their thoughts turn irrational or worrisome or lead to unwarranted conclusions. They sometimes worry to the point of becoming paranoid. Their thoughts can be helpful or hurtful to them.

The intuitive and the sensor differ in taking in information and coming to a conclusion in a timely manner. Being a sensor, I was asked by the teacher to read chapter one and answer the 10 questions in the back of the book. The sensor in me would go immediately to the 10 questions, look up question 1 and go back in the chapter to find the answer! Intuitive children usually skip reading the directions given to them in a project, look at the example given and figure out on their own what to do. Given a reading assignment, the intuitive child reads through the chapter and looks at other related material to find the answer and may even research the background for the answer. They connect new thoughts with old thoughts.

During the oral examination for my doctoral degree, the committee members stated that my associations with William Glasser, Gary Applegate and Albert Ellis were definitely a part of my academic orientation. The committee members wanted to know where these people came from. As a sensor, I informed them that Glasser was from Los Angeles, Applegate from Beverly Hills and Ellis from New York. Being the intuitive group they were, they just about fell off their seats. What they really wanted to know was, where did these three get their ideas from. I thought to myself, *"Ask me questions about their theories and I will tell you what the answer is."* I also thought, *"Who cares where they came from as long as I know the answer to the question at hand."* The intuitive person follows hunches and speculations. When looking at a rose, he will see not just a rose, but a particular type or variety. Intuitive people use theory and consider the future when putting information together, which can be both positive and negative. Since the future is so open to interpretation, the possibilities are endless. The sensor wants to "Just Do It" and the intuitive person wants to "Just Experience It." Intuitive people are global thinkers. When you present information in a step 1, step 2 fashion, they do not mind if you jump around. They will have fun with all of the possibilities, crazy or not.

Intuitive people are what I like to think of as the Legos people. Like my son Christopher. If you give him some Legos, he will take them and make things that will amaze you. Your limit is in your brain. Give the intuitive person a pile of horse manure and he will dig and dig and dig. When you ask him why he is digging, he will tell you that *"There's got to be a pony in here some place!"* We need to teach the intuitive people that when they receive information from others, sometimes it's just information and nothing more. They need to learn how to not over-interpret. They need to go from wide to smaller lenses sometimes, since this will help them to focus their energy on one thing at a time.

Judging function— thinking or feeling

Ways of coming to conclusions

THINKING
- ❑ Analysis.
- ❑ Objective view of others.
- ❑ Logic, firm.
- ❑ Impersonal.
- ❑ Critique.
- ❑ Reason.
- ❑ Criteria consistent.

Approximately 50% of us are thinkers. Thinkers reach conclusions by analyzing what they see and hear and are objective, logical and firm, like Dr. Spock on "Star Trek." They need to think things through, but when they reach a decision, they will stick to it and it is unlikely that they will be swayed by other peoples' opinions. In decision making, they are not opposed to hurting other peoples' feelings. They are often rigid and authoritarian. They are opinionated and let their views be known, even if it offends other people. Feelers are often hurt by thinkers' decisions.

The thinker is often considered rude and outspoken, and reaches conclusions through careful reasoning and criteria, which may be in the form of laws and/or policies. The feeling person has a hard time with decisions. Ask the thinker where he wants to go to eat and he will let you know. Ask the thinker to make a decision to lay off or fire people, and he will look at the reasons for this action and consider it to be right and logical. When a thinker is involved in a relationship, it is more difficult for him to show and express his feelings. He lives in his head. Not that he does not have a heart, he just does not express it as much as the feeler does. When you discipline a thinker, he will need time to reflect on what has happened and he will not show much emotion. The thinker who is sent to his room or not allowed to go out will keep his emotions in check. The thinker needs to learn to consider the feelings of others when making decisions and reaching conclusions.

FEELING

- ❏ Sympathy.
- ❏ Subjective view of others.
- ❏ Humane, harmony.
- ❏ Personal.
- ❏ Appreciative.
- ❏ Value oriented.
- ❏ Criteria based on circumstances.

Approximately 50% of us are feelers. These are the "warm fuzzy" people of the world. They love it when you give them compliments and pay attention to them. They tend to wear their feelings on their sleeves and are sympathetic with others. They meet many of their needs through people instead of with them and, as a result, are hurt more often. They appreciate frequent reassurance. If they are put in a position where they are being disciplined for something, they will "feel" it more than the thinker. They will wonder if they are "bad" more often than the thinker. If they are extroverted and feeling, God help them. They will lose their energy and feel miserable all at once. When they are "grounded" as kids, they suffer. The introverted thinker, on the other hand, may thank you. The feeler will let people know how they are feeling at the drop of a dime. They are open to wearing a Don Ho shirt, strumming a ukulele and singing "Feelings, whoa whoa feelings" over and over which will drive the thinker to the brink of insanity. They will be thinking, *"get to the point—get a clue—get a life."* When making a decision, the thinker has little time for the feeler. The thinker makes his decision and that is it, while the feeler makes his decision and wonders over and over if the decision is right. You will hear him say things like *"Are you sure this is okay with you?"*

The feeler is subjective in outlook and wants input from many sources. This can be good or it can be a problem. When they receive feedback from others, they may be overloaded. They seek decisions that are harmonious. Ask the feeler where he wants to go to eat and he will say, *"Wherever you want—that will be fine."* If he doesn't like where he eats or what he eats, he won't really say. Ask the feeler to make a decision to lay off or fire people, and he will be uncomfortable or even miserable. He considers other people's feelings as well as his own when making decisions. Thus, it becomes difficult for him to make a decision the more feeling he is. We need to teach feeling people how not to become so emotional when making decisions. It is important to teach them to use their heads in order to reach conclusions and decisions. They need help in analyzing and organizing information.

Orientation to outer life— judging or perceptive attitude

Attitude Toward the World

JUDGING

- ❑ Organized, deadlines.
- ❑ Settled, closure.
- ❑ Planned, systematic.
- ❑ Decisive.
- ❑ Control one's life events.
- ❑ Set goals/no surprises.
- ❑ Covert procrastination.
- ❑ Time is to be planned.
- ❑ Make things happen.

Approximately 50% of us are judgers. A judge is organized. They believe other people should be organized also. A place for everything and everything in its place is their motto. My son Christopher's room looks like it came from a "Better Homes and Gardens" magazine. His baseball card collection is arranged according to each team, with plastic pages neatly holding each card. His homework is done before it is due. Deadlines are the judger's stock in trade.

If you were to send a judger to bed before he finished his homework, he would lie awake worrying about it. The judger is always early for any event and impatient if he might be late because prior to the event, he perceives himself being on time. Being late is not in line with the picture he has created in his head. The judger's appearance is set according to the guidelines in GQ magazine—even though he's probably never read it. He definitely wants what he wants when he wants it. He wants it now. Not later, now! Get in his way and he may bowl you over. Watch out! The more judging a person is, the less tolerant he is of change in any routine. The less tolerant he is of other people's opinions.

As stated before, judgers are opinionated, much like thinkers. They believe that they have the right answers and decisions. If they are lost, you will find them too stubborn to ask for directions. The judging person lives by a planned and definitive schedule. The Daytimer system or daily planner is their Bible. A to-do list is someplace in their pocket. If there was such a place, they would shop at the ultimate office store, "Files-R-Us." Organization is critical. Desk organizers, file organizers (labeled neatly, of course) as well as labeled shelves are their loves. Their garage is clean as a whistle. The stronger your preference in this area, the more organized, controlled and controlling of others you are. Judgers have specific goals and objectives. They plan ahead for many things in life. Take a trip with a judger and he will have the trip planned with a scheduled departure time, potty breaks, tour time and arrival time. An airline's dream come true. They do not like detours or changes. Like the Blues Brothers, Jake and Elwood, they are on a "mission from God" and they will not stop until they get there. They are on a schedule and to interfere in any way spells trouble for whomever or whatever is the cause. Our job with the judger is to help him loosen up. The seven-step productive thinking strategy to save our sanity should be drilled into their heads if they want to live a longer life. We need to teach them that 98% of their problems will not kill them. Their thoughts will. Helping them identify their irrational thinking and inefficient actions will help them tremendously.

PERCEIVING

- ❑ Flexible, no deadlines, no closure.
- ❑ Pending, no closure.
- ❑ Spontaneous, open to change.
- ❑ Tentative.
- ❑ Let life events happen.
- ❑ Undaunted by surprise.

- ❏ Overt procrastination.
- ❏ Time is to be open.
- ❏ Let things happen.

Approximately 50% of us are perceptive. Perceptive people are flexible people with no deadlines. They change with the wind. They are spontaneous. If a change occurs in their plans, they will go with the change. If you take a trip with a perceiver, be prepared for "a ride" with no real destination. They stop when they become interested in something they see and stay as long as they like. They have no plans and no goals. They let life happen and are undaunted by surprises. When will they get it done? When they are done! They are the artists and done when the last brush stroke is put down—no sooner. They might not know what day of the week it is let alone what time it is. The judger, on the other hand, might know the lunar cycle! My daughter Holly's room is quite the opposite of Christopher's. We can look and wonder if she is in there under all that stuff. When we wonder how she lives in there, she states, *"just fine, thank you."* Ask her where something is and she will show you. Even though it looks disorganized there is order to her disorder. Look at a kid's locker in school. Or think back to your locker in school. The judger has a neat and organized locker. The perceiver opens up his locker very cautiously because he is concerned that what's crammed in there may fall out! In the "The Bank Dick" W.C. Fields plays a bank loan officer who is surrounded by "judgers" who have a place for everything and everything in its place. Their desks are spotless. On Fields' desk, however, there is a mound of paper four feet high and when the bank president asked where a certain clients' file is Fields looks at the pile, rolls his eyes, reaches in, and pulls out the file in question.

When it comes to clothing style, the perceiver may walk out of the house wearing one sock of each color and not be bothered. This would drive the judger wacky. When it comes to homework, remember when Holly almost fainted at 8:30 on a Sunday night? She had a project due the next day and bedtime was 8:30. Perceivers will wait until the last minute to get it done. Many times they prefer to work on projects at the last minute. They find that this works best for them which drives the judger nuts. How can you wait until the last minute? Many times they will get it done after the deadline. It's not a problem for them. I have taught courses at The Ohio State University and the judger will come up to me and ask how long the course paper will need to be, whether double or single spaced, how many references, before the course has even started. The perceiver thinks about asking me this question just before the paper is due. Many times they will do the paper the night before.

Many times perceivers think about going to college after the application deadline. This drives judging parents up the wall. If they do get to college, you will find perceivers out on the campus mall taking in the sun, watching people go by and loving every minute of it. They will be your "career college" kids with many years spent getting the degree. Judgers as we have learned are quite the opposite. They are highly organized and are probably able to tell you what quarter they will finish just after they begin. Ask the perceiver to clean his room and he will start the job, become easily distracted and finish it sometime down the road. While putting away clothes, he may make it into a basketball game of shooting the clothes into the drawers. The game may go on for a long time. They have "all the time in the world." The judger, on the other hand, will have a plan for cleaning the room. Because they know that they have something else to do later and want to stay on schedule, our job with perceivers is to teach them to tighten up their lifestyle and bring closure to the loose ends in their life. Let them know the benefits of doing so.

Verifying your type and your child's type

Are you the same type as your children? What are the differences and similarities? What are the positives with your type? What are the negatives with your type? Knowing what you now know about the above preferences, place your name next to the preference listed. Identify your children's preferences and place their name next to the preference listed. Do the same with your spouse.

Extravert
Energized by outer world.

Introvert
Energized by inner world.

Sensing
Work with known facts.

Intuition
Look for possibilities and relationships.

Thinking
Base decisions on impersonal analysis, and logic.

Feeling
Base decisions on personal values.

Judging
Prefer a planned decided, orderly way of life.

Perceiving
Prefer a flexible spontaneous way of life.

Here's a list of the productive thinking skills I have laid out in this book. Below each area you will notice the eight personality characteristics. Have some fun and decide for yourself the answer to the questions under each area. There are no right or wrong answers. These areas and questions are presented for your review as well as discussion purposes:

Your thoughts direct your actions and your feelings.
Which personality type will have the most problems with thinking in this area?

Extravert	Introvert
Sensing	Intuitive
Thinking	Feeling
Judging	Perceiving

Problems are degrees of differences between what you want and what you have.
Which personality type will have the most problems with thinking in this area?

Extravert	Introvert
Sensing	Intuitive

Thinking	Feeling
Judging	Perceiving

Separate problems into what you have control, influence and no control over. Apply the concepts of acknowledgment, acceptance, allowing and adjusting to all problem areas.
Which personality type will have the most problems with thinking in this area?

Extravert	Introvert
Sensing	Intuitive
Thinking	Feeling
Judging	Perceiving

Look at new thought, action and feeling areas where you have control which can be implemented immediately.
Which personality type will have the most problems with thinking in this area?

Extravert	Introvert
Sensing	Intuitive
Thinking	Feeling
Judging	Perceiving

Identify new choices or pathways to fulfill needs that have been blocked or unfulfilled. Work on creating a perception of being a need-fulfilling person to those around you.
Which personality type will have the most problems with thinking in this area?

Extravert	Introvert
Sensing	Intuitive
Thinking	Feeling
Judging	Perceiving

Identify the process steps that will be required to close down the differences between what you want and what you have.
Which personality type will have the most problems with thinking in this area?

Extravert	Introvert
Sensing	Intuitive
Thinking	Feeling
Judging	Perceiving

Understand that all problems can be opportunities for growth by using the above steps.
Which personality type will have the

most problems with thinking in this area?

Extravert	Introvert
Sensing	Intuitive
Thinking	Feeling
Judging	Perceiving

By using these guidelines, you can increase your self-awareness as well as confirm your own self-perception. You will learn how the preferences of each person differ and you will be able to step back and think productively about your strengths and gifts as a parent, and recognize the strengths and gifts of your kids. With an exercise such as this, you can look at how you can capitalize on your own strengths and the strengths of others you live and work with. You will understand that your preferences and your child's preferences may be different. With these differences in mind, I hope you can begin to understand more fully the significance of the productive thinking strategy focused on in this book. Parents do have an inherent position of power over their children. That is a fact that cannot be disputed. But without awareness of these differences in personality types, parents may project their preferences, impressions and perceptions on their children as being "the right way." There is no "right way." No type is better than another. There are positive traits and there are negatives traits with each of the types listed above. That is what makes life so interesting, if we choose to rethink in this way. I hope you will be able to apply this new thinking to your parenting skills, your interpersonal skills and your professional life. Where are you going to have your differences with others? Your similarities with others? What annoys you the most about preferences other than your own? What do you do that annoys others with different preferences? Can you identify problems you have had with your kids where it is evident that your preferences are clashing with their preferences? How could you have been more effective? Which type is going to want to control people, situations or things? Which type is going to have a tough time allowing others to think, act or feel the way they want to? Which type is less likely to accept the fact that they have no control over people, situations or things? Which type will be more apt to take on other people's problems? Which type will worry more about the choices that their children will make? Which type will be able to adjust their thoughts and actions more easily? Which type will meet their needs through people more often than with them? Which type will want what they want when they want it? Which type will have trouble with patience? Which type will look at problems as opportunities? Identifying and understanding different personality traits will go a long way toward promoting healthy relationships.

CHAPTER 16

YATS ESOOL

We found out early in this book that many people around the world are asking the same questions. What is going on with our kids today? What happened? Today's adults grew up on a different planet. The choices that kids are making today are light years away from the choices in the past. As a result, many parents are looking for that strategy to save their sanity—or what's left of it.

We also found out that nobody gave us a manual when our kids entered into the world. As stated before, you do get more instructions with a new microwave than you do with a child. Many problems crop up with too few solutions provided. Learning through experience becomes many people's best choices at the time. Because you have children, you will have problems. Hopefully the chapters in this book have provided you with a different set of lenses through which to view those problems.

We found out that the kids on this "new planet" say things like, *"So." "Whatever." "That's cool." "You can ground me for the rest of my life because I'm not going to change!"* With these changes came an attitude of demandingness in the form of a "me" attitude or the "I-don't-care-about-anyone-but-myself" attitude leading to the common middle name of "get me, buy me, take me, give me."

We have found out that what kids really want is more responsibility for their own lives and more independence from others. Along with this, they want to make their own decisions about friends, music, money, what to wear and when to study, to name just a few areas. Children want to take effective control of their own lives and take on that responsibility. Children want to have power in their own lives. And last but not least, we found out that children want to make their own choices and not be controlled by parents or other adults. They hate rigidity via rules and restrictions but want structure laid down from us in a caring, mat-

ter of fact, calm tone of voice. They don't want to be screamed at, they want to be talked with. They want to be allowed to demonstrate trust as well as express their feelings without being put down. In fact, these are not just wants for children but wants for adults as well.

We found out that adolescence was perhaps best described in the title of Phil Collins' song "Land of Confusion." It is the dressing room of life where kids try on not only new clothes, but new hairstyles, new friends and new choices. With structure as a guide, they are given permission to "spread their wings" and try to fly on their own.

We found out that Pogo the philosopher might have been right when he said, *"We have met the enemy and they is us."* By starting with ourselves, we can begin to put the skills outlined in this book to work in our own lives first, and then teach and model to our children the productive thinking skills outlined in this book.

We have learned that our thoughts about our kids, as well as ourselves, will direct our actions and our feelings. These thoughts can make or break our relationship with our kids. Problems can now be thought of as differences between what we want and what we have. These differences can be like shirt sizes: small, medium, large or extra-large. Once we learned that we all have differences, we became more comfortable with the next step, which was that we could separate our problems into three simple columns of what we have control, influence and no control over. By doing so we can reduce our level of frustration with any problem that arises in our life. With this new thinking skill we understood that the choices we make to deal with the problems we encounter are limited only by our thinking. Allowing our children to make decisions and take on the responsibility for those decisions means giving them the power, control and choices that they want. Tough as this concept may be to swallow, the outcome is really in our children's best interest. Next, we found out that the core of all human behavior is the satisfaction of internal psychological needs. We found out that all behaviors are purposeful to meet these needs, from the baby's first choices to the adults' more sophisticated choices. We found out that these needs motivate and frustrate all people. Along with this we understood that the behaviors exhibited by today's youth can be viewed as flares and flags in the air. Flags and flares that will help us understand which of their needs are frustrated. Flags that will allow us an opportunity to teach and model more efficient choices to satisfy those frustrated needs. We then found out that we can choose to think about the outcomes in our life or focus our thinking on what we have more control over—the process. By learning the eight steps to good plan making, we found out that we can put some clear focus and thoughts in our decisions to change our behaviors with ourselves and with others. Our final productive thinking skill taught us to view our problems in our own lives and our children's lives as opportunities to use the previous productive thinking skills. We found out that ninety-eight percent of the choices and problems that we are presented via our children will not kill us or them. Frustrate us, yes. Kill us, no. To top it off we found out that the personality characteristics of our children does impact on the choices that they will make in life, as well as the choices that we make in our lives. Allowing people to be who they are, accepting their characteristics as who they are, and adjusting our responses to them as a result, will save our sanity when coupled with the previous productive thinking skills.

My first professional colleague, Al Lehrke, taught me some interesting things during my years at the high school we worked at. Al had a saying on his desk top that read "Illegitimi non-carborundum." When asking Mr. Lehrke about these sayings, he indicated to me that Jimmy Hoffa had it on his desk and that it meant in effect, "don't let the little things get you down." On my way out the door for the day Al would lean around the corner and shout out "Yats Esool." For days I would just say good-bye and be on my way. One day I stopped and asked what this meant. Al said spell it backwards, and walked out the door. I sat in my office and wrote it on a paper. Sure enough, when you spell it backwards it spells out STAY LOOSE. To you the reader and purchaser of my book I say YATS ESOOL!

Michael M. Thomson Ph.D.

Suggested Purchase List

Below you will find a listing of books that I strongly recommend to you in your search for continued growth and knowledge. They are excellent resources for your personal and professional library.

Applegate, Gary. Happiness: It's Your Choice. Berringer Publishing. 1989.

Balter, Lawrence. Who's In Control? Poseidon Press. 1989.

Burns, David. Feeling Good: The new mood therapy. New York: William Morrow and Co., Inc. 1980.

Ellis, Albert and Harper, Robert. A New Guide To Rational Living. Wilshire Book Company. 1975.

Faber, Adele & Mazlish, Elaine. How To Talk So Kids Will Listen & Listen So Kids Will Talk. Avon Books, 1980.

Ford, Edward E. & Englund, Steven. For The Love Of Children. Anchor Press: Doubleday, 1977.

Ford, Edward E. (with Robert L. Zorn). Why Marriage? Niles, Illinois: Argus, 1975.
    Choosing To Love. Harper & Row, 1983.
    Permanent Love. Brandt Publishing, 1979.

Glasser, William. Reality Therapy. New York: Harper & Row, 1965.

Glasser, William. Take Effective Control Of Your Life. New York: Harper & Row, 1985.

Glasser, William. Control Theory In The Classroom. New York: Harper & Row, 1986.

Glenn, H. Stephen & Nelsen, Jane. Raising Children For Success. Sunrise Press. 1987

Helmstetter, Shad. Predictive Parenting. Pocket Books. 1989

Maultsby, Maxie. Help Yourself To Happiness. New York: Institute For Rational Living, Inc. 1975.

Nelsen, Jane. Positive Discipline. Sunrise Press. 1981.

Powers, W.T. Behavior: The Control Of Perception. Chicago: Aldine. 1973.

DID YOU BORROW THIS COPY?

ORDER FORM

Books are $14.95 each. Purchase orders will be accepted from recognized schools and institutions. Bulk order inquiries invited. Call for information.

Quantity : _____ Subtotal: _____ Shipping and handling: _$3.00 per book_ Total $: _____

Method of payment: ❏ Purchase order ❏ Money order ❏ Check ❏ **VISA** ❏ MasterCard

Card Number _____

Card's Expiration Date _____

Signature of Card Holder _____

2 CONVENIENT WAYS TO ORDER

Name of Card Holder (please print) _____

Productive Thinking Skills
Post Office Box 751
Dublin, OH 43017-0851

(800) 290-2482

SHIPPING INFORMATION

_____ _____
Name   Profession

_____
Street Address

_____ _____ _____
City   State   ZIP

(_____)_____
Telephone

About The Author

Dr. Thomson received his doctorate from The Ohio State University with a major in Education and a minor in Psychology. As a Psychology Intern, Dr. Thomson provides counseling services with The Center for Counseling, Planning and Development in Columbus, Ohio. He is awaiting the national licensing exam as a Psychologist. With his many years of experience in helping others Dr. Thomson is a Certified Chemical Dependency Counselor, Certified Reality Therapist, Certified Skill Development Counselor, Senior Faculty Member with The Center For Skill Development in Los Angeles and an adjunct associate professor with The Ohio State University. In addition to teaching and lecturing nationwide (his seminars have reached nearly a million people) Dr. Thomson has extensive professional experience, including Drug Education-Human Services Specialist for the Austin, Minn. public school system, Clinical Counselor and Supervisor of adolescent chemical dependency services in the Department of Psychology and Psychiatry at The Mayo Clinic, Director of the Center For Skill Development in Los Angeles, Program Director of adult and adolescent drug-alcohol in-patient centers in Minnesota and Ohio. He was also the Director of the first American-run drug-alcohol program located just outside Stockholm, Sweden in the village of Knivsta, and provides consulting and lifeskills for athletes seminars to Big Ten athletic programs around the country.

Dr. Thomson enjoys his life as a father of two productively-thinking children, Christopher and Holly, along with his marriage to his wife Carol.

YOU CAN ALWAYS WRITE TO DR. THOMSON

Dr. Thomson is always willing to help. Dr. Thomson's high energy message reaches thousands of people each year all over the world. His highly acclaimed presentations are both entertaining and educational. Whether it is a keynote address for your conference, a seminar for your group or any of his training programs for parents, educators, business and industry, athletes or student assemblies, Dr. Thomson leaves the audience with a message they are not soon to forget. His audience involved techniques are entertaining, fun, and most of all educational. Any message addressed to Dr. Thomson and sent to the address below shall be given prompt and full attention.

McLean Publishing Group
P.O. Box 751
Dublin, Ohio 43017-0851

INDEX

A

ABC framework 50
Abraham Lincoln 135
Abraham Maslow 31
Accepting 31, 81, 100, 122 123, 171
Accountability 102, 108, 117
Achieving 122
Acknowledging 71, 81, 82, 88, 122, 123, 156
Actions 5, 7, 14, 20, 25, 28, 30, 33, 34, 35, 37,
    40, 41, 42, 43, 45, 46, 47, 48, 50, 51, 52,
    54, 55, 56, 62, 63, 64, 65, 66, 67, 68, 72,
    75, 76, 80 81, 82, 83, 84, 85, 86, 87, 89, 90, 99,
    100, 102, 103, 104,105, 106, 111, 112, 116,
    117, 121, 122, 123, 124, 125, 126, 127, 130, 131, 137,
    149, 155, 160, 161, 162, 163, 164, 165
Adjusting 81, 123, 168
Adolescence 18, 19, 20, 21, 23, 52, 115, 126, 170
Adolf Hitler 96
Albert Einstein 152
Albert Ellis 50, 52, 164
Alcohol 23, 28, 29, 36, 37, 38, 46, 51, 63, 64,
    67, 71, 74, 79, 82, 83, 84, 86, 88, 93, 95,
    99, 106, 107, 108, 109, 110, 111, 112, 114, 115, 120,
    124, 129, 139, 174
Alcoholics Anonymous 37, 71
Alexander and the Terrible, Horrible, No Good, Very
    Bad Day 62
Allowing 16, 19, 26, 27, 41, 42, 43, 76, 81, 100,
    102, 105, 108, 112, 117, 118, 123, 126,
    127, 128, 130,133, 143, 146, 150, 154,
    155, 168, 169 170, 171
Andy Griffith Show 94
Angrying 14, 72, 75, 99, 101
Arguing 14, 35, 36, 48, 83, 151
Arnold Schwarzenegger 20
Asking questions 84, 154
Asking questions 20, 54, 84, 85, 90, 95, 96, 128,
    152, 154, 155, 163
Athletes 109, 112, 153, 174
Attendance 21, 80, 103, 109, 148
Awfulizing 59
Awfulizing 54
Awfuls 53, 54

B

Bambi 160, 161
Band-aid therapy 37
Barbie 127
Bart Simpson 19
Bartender therapy 37
Basic premise 24, 32
Begging 5, 68
Behavior modification 36
Being on time 80, 103, 166
Belonging 24, 25, 26, 27, 28, 29, 30, 32, 38,
    40, 58, 68, 70, 89, 124, 131, 132, 133,
    134, 136
Bible 94, 124, 166
Biting 14
Blamers 130
Blaming 15, 22, 44, 56, 63, 101, 111, 151
Blow fish syndrome 94
Blues Brothers 166
Board games 137
Bragging 27
Buckminster Fuller 14
Buddhists 124

C

Camera check 154
Captain Kirk 8
Carl Jung 158
Carpe Diem 144
Center for Skill Development 32, 144, 174
Charles Manson 19, 96
Cheating 27
Cheerleader therapy 37
Chevy Chase 21
Choices 3, 4, 5, 7, 12, 13, 14, 15, 16, 17, 18,
    20, 21, 22, 23, 24, 25, 26, 27, 28, 29, 31, 32, 33, 34,
    36, 38, 40, 41, 44, 45, 46, 49, 50, 53, 54, 55, 56,
    62, 63, 64, 66, 67, 69, 70, 71, 72, 75, 77, 78, 80, 81, 82,
    83, 84, 85, 87, 88, 89, 90, 93, 94, 95, 96,
    97, 98, 99, 100, 101, 102, 103, 104, 105, 106, 107,
    108, 109, 110, 111, 112, 113, 114, 115, 116, 117,
    118, 120, 122, 123, 124, 126, 127, 129, 130, 131,
    132,133, 135, 136, 137, 138, 139, 143, 144, 146,
    148, 150, 152, 155, 156, 160, 161, 168,
    169, 170, 171

Church 116, 124, 125, 137
Cinderella 124
Clayton Aldefer 31
Clique 1, 109
Closed-ended questions 85
Clothes 16, 18, 19, 20, 24, 27, 46, 47, 51,
　83, 89, 92, 98, 99, 101, 106, 107, 120, 126, 127,
　128, 133, 142, 148, 149, 167, 170
Co-curricular 109, 113
Coaches 52, 104, 109, 112, 137, 145, 146
Cognitively deficient kids 57
Comfortable 15, 32, 35, 45, 51, 67, 116,
　136, 165, 170
Communication 53, 86, 87, 106, 114, 115, 117,
　133, 134, 137, 154, 155
Comparison questions 71, 85, 86, 95
Complaining 45, 68, 70, 71, 72, 101, 120,
　137, 155
Consequences 4, 5, 15, 23, 25, 28, 33, 41, 49,
　51, 66, 67, 68, 72, 74, 75, 78, 86, 95, 96, 97, 98,
　9, 100, 101, 102, 103, 105, 106, 107, 108,
　112, 113, 116, 118, 122, 123, 126, 129, 131, 138,
　148, 149, 150, 155, 156, 163
Control 2, 3, 4, 5, 6, 7, 9, 10, 12, 13, 14, 15,
　16, 17, 18, 19, 20, 21, 22, 23, 24, 25, 26,
　27, 28, 30, 31, 32, 33, 35, 36, 37, 38, 40,
　41, 44, 46, 47, 48, 49, 52, 53, 55, 56, 59, 60, 62,
　63, 64, 65, 66, 67, 68, 69, 70, 71, 72,
　74, 76, 77, 78, 79, 80, 81, 82, 83, 84, 85, 86, 87, 88,
　89, 90, 92, 93, 94, 95, 96, 97, 98, 99, 100,
　101, 102, 103, 104, 105, 106, 107, 108, 109,
　110, 111, 112, 114, 115, 116, 117, 118, 120, 121,
　122, 123, 124, 125, 126, 127, 128, 129,
　130, 131, 132, 134, 136, 137, 138, 139, 143,
　146, 148, 149, 150, 151, 152, 153, 154, 155,
　156, 158, 160, 161, 166, 168, 169, 170, 171, 172,
Controllable stress 153
Controlling behavior
　12, 34, 35, 68, 69, 70, 75, 89, 112, 120
Could've 54, 59
Crazying 14, 25, 27
Criminal activity 26, 27
Criticism 75, 88, 115, 117, 132, 133, 153
Crying 10, 12, 14, 15, 69, 70, 71, 80, 86, 98, 99,
　105, 120, 121, 123

D

David McClellan 31
Daytimer system 166
Decision making 4, 20, 22, 74, 88, 118, 164
Demonstrating caring 77, 83, 84, 85, 90
Department of Health and Human Services 138
Depressing 14, 25, 26, 27, 30, 38, 50, 67, 68, 69,
　70, 71, 72, 75, 120, 132, 155, 160
Detachment 100
Detectors 21, 22, 92, 95, 97, 109, 117, 150
Detention 23, 103, 110, 113
Dickie Noles 110

Difference 4, 5, 13, 21, 25, 31, 33, 41, 47, 48,
　50, 51, 62, 63, 64, 65, 66, 67, 70, 72, 73, 74, 76, 80,
　81, 83, 84, 85, 86, 92, 96, 97, 111, 114, 117, 120,
　122, 123, 126, 127, 132, 139, 142, 143, 148, 151,
　152, 153, 154, 155, 158, 159, 167, 168, 169, 170
Disney 18, 21, 52, 136
Disputing 54, 56
Dragnet 162
Dress 80, 93
Dress 6, 16, 18, 19, 46, 89, 93, 112, 116, 122,
　128, 170
Dressing room 18, 19, 170
Drinking
　3, 6, 26, 33, 38, 67, 84, 97, 115, 120, 126, 137, 138, 146
Drugging 3, 6, 30, 33, 38, 46, 120, 138
Druids 124
Drunking 14, 26, 126
Dumbo The Elephant 124

E

Earl Nightingale 48
Earrings 19, 46
Earrings 19, 46, 51, 89, 92, 116, 120
Edward James Olmos 136
Efficient 25
Efficient 2, 3, 4, 25, 26, 27, 32, 33, 44, 57,
　64, 68, 69, 72, 77, 87, 89, 121, 122,
　123, 125, 129, 131, 136, 137, 138, 139, 155, 156, 171
Elementary school 16, 18, 19, 47, 99, 128
Emilio Estevez 52
Emotional problem solving 56, 57
Emotional problems 50
Emotional problems 50, 51
Epictetus 42
Eric Hoffer 105, 121
Evaluating 45, 47, 48, 49, 53, 56, 59, 75, 85, 87,
　122, 123
excuses 86, 92, 101, 102, 149, 153
Expectations 48, 76, 86, 87, 93, 97, 99, 100, 101,
　103, 104, 105, 106, 107, 108, 109, 110, 111,
　112, 113, 117, 118, 129, 130, 131, 132, 149, 161
Extravert 159, 160, 161, 162, 168, 169

F

Faith 24, 28, 29,
　30, 32, 38, 40, 75, 123, 124, 125, 128,
　133, 136
feelings 4, 5, 15, 20, 23, 25, 26, 28, 32, 33,
　35, 36, 37, 44, 45, 46, 47, 48, 49, 50, 51, 52, 53,
　54, 55, 56, 57, 59, 62, 63, 64, 66, 67, 68, 70, 71, 72,
　73, 75, 76, 77, 80, 81, 82, 83, 84, 85, 86,
　87, 93, 99, 100, 102, 103, 104, 105, 106, 108, 116,
　117, 118, 121, 122, 123, 124, 125, 126, 127,
　129, 131, 132, 134, 137, 143, 148, 150,
　151, 152, 154, 155, 164, 165, 168, 170
Flags 26, 28, 120, 139, 143, 151, 171
Flares 26, 28, 120, 139, 143, 171
Franklin D. Roosevelt 40

Freedom 6, 21, 23, 24, 25, 26, 27, 28, 29, 32, 38, 40, 75, 76, 85, 95, 100, 109, 110, 125, 128, 129, 130, 131, 133

Fun 20, 24, 27, 28, 29, 30, 32, 38, 40, 45, 52, 56, 58, 81, 85, 98, 114, 116, 131, 132, 133, 135, 136, 137, 144, 162, 164, 168, 174

G

Gary Applegate 31, 32, 82, 164
Get me, buy me, take me, give me 99
Get me, buy me, take me, give me 5, 170
Get them, buy them, take them, give them 102
Getting up 74, 78, 80, 98, 99, 103, 105, 123, 148
Good choices 3, 5, 22, 25, 36, 88, 95, 107, 109, 116, 118, 125, 129, 133, 152, 154
Greeks 124
Griffith Thomas Elementary School 47
Guilting 25, 27, 69, 70, 98, 116

H

H. Stephen Glenn 114
Hair 18, 19, 20, 27, 46, 47, 71, 80, 89, 116, 126, 127, 133, 170
Hairstyles 18, 27, 170
Health 2, 6, 7, 9, 13, 24, 27, 28, 29, 33, 34, 38, 40, 50, 53, 54, 75, 82, 97, 100, 113, 114, 115, 116, 125, 127, 133, 136, 137, 138, 139, 143, 169
Helmet and flak jacket 111, 112
Henry Ford 122
Higher power 24, 82, 124, 125
Hitting 14, 45, 63, 75, 86, 94, 145
Holiday Inn syndrome 35
Home 2, 4, 6, 7, 9, 10, 16, 19, 20, 27, 28, 30, 33, 34, 38, 41, 43, 44, 47, 48, 65, 71, 74, 75, 76, 77, 80, 82, 83, 86, 89, 92, 93, 99, 100, 102, 103, 104, 106, 107, 108, 109, 110, 113, 114, 117, 118, 122, 129, 130, 131, 132, 133, 140, 143, 149, 150, 156, 158, 159, 161, 162
Home environment 47, 48, 77, 130
Homework 2, 3, 18, 22, 33, 35, 47, 74, 77, 78, 80, 85, 87, 93, 97, 98, 99, 101, 102, 103, 105, 109, 110, 113, 116, 128, 148, 159, 166, 167
House 6, 7, 8, 9, 10, 16, 18, 23, 35, 49, 56, 74, 75, 89, 92, 93, 104, 106, 108, 109, 113, 114, 115, 116, 117, 127, 128, 129, 130, 134, 135, 148, 153, 160, 161, 167

I

Illegitimi non-carborundum 171
In-school suspension 23, 28, 103, 110, 113, 159
Interpretations 42, 43, 44, 46, 49, 53, 54, 59
Introvert 160, 161, 162, 165, 168, 169
Intuition 162, 163, 168
Invention convention 128
Irrational beliefs 51, 52, 53, 54, 55, 56, 57
Isabell Briggs Myers 158

J

Jack Benny 88
Jeffrey Dahmer 19
Jim Jones 96
Joseph J. Quaranta 158
Judging 164, 166, 167, 168, 169
Judith Viorst 62
Just think positively 34

K

Katherine Briggs 158
Kicking 14, 94, 100, 161
Kindergarten 17
Knot in the knickers 83, 84
Knowledge 7, 24, 29, 33, 38, 40, 71, 75, 121, 122, 133, 136, 137, 138, 148, 172

L

Lamaze classes 8
Latch key programs 132
Laundry 3, 99, 128, 148, 149
Leading the horse to water 95
Letter jacket 109, 110, 112
Linda Blair 8
Logical consequences 78, 113, 118
Loneliness 34, 49, 131, 132
Losers 152, 153
Loyalty 26, 112, 117, 118
Lures 13, 14, 15, 16, 24, 69, 70, 98, 101, 120, 139, 150
Lying 23, 27, 80, 115

M

Makeup 18, 19, 125
Making statements 77, 84, 87, 90
Mark Twain 4, 23
Mass media 126
Mick Jagger 28
Misery martyr 68
Miserying 69
Moslems 124
Motivation 48, 50, 64, 82, 120, 124, 148, 149, 150, 153, 154, 159
Mr. Lehrke 37, 171
Mr. Staffilino 47
Musterbizing 54, 59
Musts 52, 53, 54
Myers Briggs Type Indicator 158

N

Name calling 75
Natural consequences 74, 101, 108, 112, 113, 123, 149
Need fulfilling 26, 27, 28, 30, 31, 47, 74, 123, 150
Need reducing 26, 30, 47, 136, 150
Needs 13, 15, 16, 24, 25, 26, 27, 28, 29, 30, 31, 32, 33, 36, 37, 38, 40, 55, 64, 67,

69, 75, 82, 83, 86, 88, 89, 94, 95, 101, 102, 104, 106, 114, 116, 120, 121, 122, 123, 124, 126, 128, 130, 132, 133, 135, 136, 137, 138, 139, 140, 143, 144, 146, 150, 151, 152, 154,155, 156, 159, 160, 161, 162, 163, 165, 168, 169, 171

Negative feelings 50, 76

negative feelings 44, 45, 50, 53, 62, 76, 131

NIKE 45, 160

Nintendo 103, 159

Non-verbal 36, 87, 114, 117, 123

Norman Cousin 135

O

Old Woman in the Shoe 94

OPEN-ENDED QUESTIONS 84

Optical Rectitus 84, 87

Other drugs 23, 51, 64, 67, 76, 81, 89, 97, 104, 106, 109, 110, 112, 129

Oughts 52, 53, 54

Outcome 19, 56, 85, 100, 101, 104, 105, 106, 107, 122, 125, 126, 127, 132, 142, 143, 144, 145, 146, 147, 151, 152, 156, 171

P

Pampering 105

Paralanguage 86

Parent Burnout 83, 93

Parent burnout 5

Passive-aggressive 87

Pathways 25, 26, 28, 31, 33, 40, 73, 122, 136, 138, 139, 140, 152, 156, 168

Perceptions 54, 55, 56, 57, 75, 136, 169

Perceptive 47, 162, 166, 167

Permission 26, 47, 48, 99, 106, 112, 114, 115, 116, 117, 118, 133, 137, 146, 159, 170

Personality 158, 159, 161, 163, 165, 167, 168, 169, 171

Personality type 158, 159, 168, 169

Phil Collins 18, 170

Physical changes 20

Physical punishment 30, 75

Physical punishment 30, 75, 86

Physical reaction 83

Plan making 145, 146, 156, 171

Pogo 41, 110, 170

Poor choices 3, 5, 22, 36, 46, 49, 53, 56, 72, 87, 88, 95, 96, 97, 98, 102, 107, 108, 110, 111, 112, 116, 118, 122, 127, 130, 132, 133, 137, 152, 161

Positive feelings 45, 52, 75, 76

Pouting 14, 15, 16, 25, 26, 27, 30, 68, 69, 70, 71, 75, 80, 98, 99, 101, 105, 120, 137, 151, 155

Power 3, 4, 10, 13, 16, 20, 21, 22, 24, 26, 27, 32, 38, 41, 46, 53, 62, 66, 67, 68, 82, 88, 89, 94, 95, 96, 99, 101, 104, 108, 111, 121, 123, 124, 125, 126, 127, 128, 129, 130, 131, 133, 138, 149, 154, 156, 169, 170

Power of Positive Thinking 34

Practical problems 50

Practical problems 50

Practicing 4, 50, 71, 76, 100, 123, 143, 145, 156

Pregnant 8, 28, 29, 51, 63, 97

Prejudices 46

Privileges 6, 23, 33, 41, 78, 83, 87, 97, 102, 103, 104, 105, 107, 109, 110, 111, 118, 129, 130, 143, 148, 149

Process 8, 9, 10, 23, 50, 52, 54, 56, 58, 66, 68, 71, 76, 85, 88, 122, 123, 126, 127, 128, 132, 137, 138, 142, 143, 144, 145, 146, 147, 151, 152, 153, 154, 155, 156, 158, 168, 171

Productive Thinking 7, 13, 24, 25, 32, 34, 40, 41, 42, 43, 45, 47, 49, 51, 53, 55, 62, 63, 64, 74, 75, 81, 92, 93, 96, 97, 101, 102, 104, 114, 120, 122, 125, 136, 137, 138, 139, 140, 142, 145, 148, 149, 150, 151, 152, 154, 155, 156, 166, 168, 169, 170, 171

Providing alternative 77, 84, 87

Psychological changes 19

Psychological needs 15, 24, 25, 31, 32, 36, 67, 83, 89, 95, 120, 139, 151, 156, 171

Punishment 30, 33, 66, 75, 86, 94, 95, 96, 97, 99, 118, 130, 148, 159

Pure feelings 64, 70, 71

Q

Quick fix 34, 143, 145

R

Rambo 85

Rational beliefs 52

Rational Emotive Therapy 52, 54, 55, 57

Reality Therapy 37, 104, 172

Refusing to talk 27, 98, 120

Rejection 64

Responsibility 2, 4, 6, 13, 16, 20, 22, 26, 28, 47, 53, 54, 55, 56, 69, 74, 82, 88, 90, 98, 99, 100, 101, 102, 103, 104, 105, 108, 109, 111, 113, 114, 118, 123, 124, 126, 129, 130, 131, 134, 137, 143, 148, 149, 170

Rethinking 120, 129, 144, 156

Richard J. Gelles 92

Rides to school 99

Rigidity 105, 117, 134, 170

Robin Williams 136

Role models 88, 137

Romans 124

Rudolph The Red Nosed Reindeer 124

S

Sarcasm 75

Satanic ritualism 117

Saturday school 99, 103, 110

School daze 15
Security 23, 24, 27, 28, 29, 30, 32, 38, 40, 75, 77, 94, 104, 121, 122, 123, 125, 128, 131, 133, 136
Self talk 53, 59, 146
Self-esteem 92, 127, 130, 139
Sensing 162, 163, 168, 169
Serenity prayer 74, 81
Seven critical questions 66
Sexual harassment 126
Sexual promiscuity 3, 6
Shakespeare 45
Sherlock Homes 56
Shoulds 52, 53, 54
Should've 54, 59
Smoking 27, 30, 33, 92, 137, 139
Sports 12, 46, 74, 107, 112, 113, 127, 130, 135
Spring break 6, 93, 110
Starting with actions 34
Stepping back 43, 54, 59, 66, 82, 83, 104, 120, 154
Steroids 126
Stopping a bad habit 32, 73
Structure 6, 16, 18, 27, 46, 47, 69, 93, 100, 104, 105, 106, 110, 111, 116, 117, 118, 126, 130, 134, 137, 170
Successful people 152
Suicide 24, 68, 93, 107, 120, 131, 149
Suiciding 14, 38, 72
Swearing 27, 30, 33, 63, 64, 80, 98, 105
Sybil 9, 19

T

Tackle box 13, 24
Talk 2, 6, 8, 16, 17, 22, 23, 24, 26, 27, 30, 35, 38, 45, 47, 48, 49, 50, 53, 54, 55, 58, 59, 64, 65, 68, 74, 81, 85, 87, 88, 89, 95, 97, 98, 99, 110, 112, 114, 115, 116, 117, 118, 120, 125, 126, 127, 130, 133, 137, 143, 144, 146, 159, 160, 161, 163
Talking back 22, 27, 30, 108
Ted Bundy 19
Telephone answering machine 103
Temper tantrumming 14, 15, 16, 25, 26, 71, 75, 80, 98, 120, 137
Terrible two's 13, 15
The crib 14, 15, 24, 25, 68, 71, 102, 105, 106, 120
The good old days 21
The Ohio State University 6, 47, 158, 167, 174
Thomas Jefferson 105
THOUGHTS 40, 80, 153, 154
Thoughts
5, 16, 20, 23, 25, 30, 32, 33, 34, 35, 41, 42, 43, 45, 46, 47, 49, 50, 52, 53, 54, 55, 57, 59, 62, 63, 64, 65, 66, 67, 68, 72, 75, 80, 81, 83, 84, 85, 86, 87, 99, 100, 102, 103, 104, 105, 120, 121, 122, 123, 124, 125, 126, 127, 131, 134, 135, 143, 146, 148, 150, 151, 152, 154, 155, 160, 161, 163, 164, 166, 168, 169, 170, 171
Threatening 5, 14, 25, 30, 35, 45, 66, 67,

75, 83, 85, 86, 96, 98, 99, 101, 102, 105, 112, 116, 117, 120, 126, 130, 132, 137, 145, 148
Time out 33, 97, 110, 149, 159
Tobacco 23, 46, 51, 76, 80, 81, 104, 106, 107, 109, 110, 112, 129
Tone of voice
16, 47, 54, 77, 78, 84, 85, 86, 87, 90, 111, 114, 115, 127, 134, 151, 170
Top Gun 85
Trust 3, 6, 12, 16, 26, 30, 48, 51, 58, 75, 78, 110, 115, 116, 117, 118, 133, 143, 144, 170

U

U-Boat Commander 30, 145
Ugly Duckling 124
Unhappiness 55, 56, 62, 67, 68, 69, 70, 71, 144, 156
Unshakable and unbreakable 100, 131

V

Velvet hammer 53, 86, 146
Verbal 22, 36, 43, 74, 86, 87, 99, 114, 117, 123, 137
Vince Lombardi 135
Virginia Waters 55

W

W.C. Fields 167
Weight problem 139, 146
Where Most Parents Are 32, 33, 35, 37
Whining 10, 16, 68, 69, 71, 99, 101, 105, 120, 137
WhMPA 32, 33, 34, 35, 36, 40, 41, 43, 44, 45, 49, 50, 51, 52, 54, 59, 62, 63, 64, 65, 66, 67, 73, 81, 82, 83, 85, 86, 87, 93, 96, 97, 98, 100, 103, 104, 107, 108, 112, 113, 114, 118, 120, 121, 122, 123, 125, 126, 127, 128, 130, 131, 133, 134, 136, 137, 139, 142, 143, 144, 145, 146, 148, 151, 152, 153, 155, 156, 159
WhMPA belief system 51
William Fry 135
William Glasser 31, 48, 104, 164
William James 42, 148
Winners 152, 153
Wizard of Oz 89
Working to be comfortable 35
Worth 19, 24, 25, 26, 27, 28, 30, 32, 38, 40, 45, 46, 59, 100, 120, 125, 126, 127, 128, 129, 131, 133, 136, 137
Would've 54, 59

Y

Yats Esool 171
Youth to Youth 7

Z

Z plans 37, 146